"Twenty years ago when we started The Simple Way, we decided to worship on Sunday at the church closest to us. I'm glad we did. Kevin Yoho was the pastor. I remember hearing him challenge bad theology and the stigma of our neighborhood, known by many as 'the Badlands.' Kevin said this: 'Don't forget what they said about Nazareth . . . nothing good could come from there.' Kevin Yoho knew that God shows up in the margins. Yoho is a gifted theologian and urbanologist—helping people unpack the mystery of the incarnation . . . this idea that God put skin on and moved into the neighborhood, and invites us to follow. I remember hearing another pastor tell me that he initially thought we were missionaries here in 'the Badlands,' but then he realized that we were actually missionaries to the Church—inviting the church to come back to the neighborhood, and find Jesus on these broken streets. Pastors like Kevin Yoho are reminding the Church why she exists. And it is not just to have worship services on Sundays.

—SHANE CLAIBORNE, author, activist, founder of The Simple Way and Red Letter Christians

"Kevin Yoho gets it. *Crayons for the City* gets it. The book tells the story of one pastor's commitment to reconnect a struggling urban church with its struggling neighborhood in ways that transformed them both. It also invites readers to do something similar in their own way, in their own location. The book is filled with practical insights and wisdom, undergirded at every point by a profound theology of love and hope.

—DALE T. IRVIN, President and Professor of World Christianity, New York Theological Seminary

Crayons for the City

Crayons for the City

Reneighboring Communities of Faith
to Rebuild Neighborhoods of Hope

Kevin R. Yoho

Foreword by Raymond Bakke
Afterword by W. Wilson Goode

CASCADE Books • Eugene, Oregon

CRAYONS FOR THE CITY
Reneighboring Communities of Faith to Rebuild Neighborhoods of Hope

Copyright © 2017 Kevin R. Yoho. All rights reserved. Except for brief quotations in critical publications or reviews, no part of this book may be reproduced in any manner without prior written permission from the publisher. Write: Permissions, Wipf and Stock Publishers, 199 W. 8th Ave., Suite 3, Eugene, OR 97401.

Cascade Books
An Imprint of Wipf and Stock Publishers
199 W. 8th Ave., Suite 3
Eugene, OR 97401

www.wipfandstock.com

PAPERBACK ISBN: 978-1-4982-3087-2
HARDCOVER ISBN: 978-1-4982-3089-6
EBOOK ISBN: 978-1-4982-3088-9

Cataloguing-in-Publication data:

Names: Yoho, Kevin R., author. | Bakke, Raymond J., 1938–, foreword. | Goode, W. Wilson, afterword.
Title: Crayons for the city : reneighboring communities of faith to rebuild neighborhoods of hope / Kevin R. Yoho ; foreword by Raymond Bakke ; afterword by W. Wilson Goode.
Description: Eugene, OR : Cascade Books, 2017 | Includes bibliographical references and index.
Identifiers: ISBN 978-1-4982-3087-2 (paperback) | ISBN 978-1-4982-3089-6 (hardcover) | ISBN 978-1-4982-3088-9 (ebook)
Subjects: LCSH: Hope—Religious aspects. | Religion and justice. | Church work.
Classification: BV637.5 .Y64 2017 (print) | BV637.5 .Y64 (ebook)

Manufactured in the U.S.A. NOVEMBER 6, 2017

"Why a Stigma," by Sol Finkelman, used by permission.

To Melissa:

My best friend, wife, and partner on life's Moondance adventure

"Nazareth! Can anything good come from there?" Nathaniel asked.
"Come and see," said Philip.

—JOHN 1:46

Contents

List of Illustrations xi

Foreword by Raymond J. Bakke xv

Preface xxi

Acknowledgments xxv

1. Welcome to Our Neighborhood 1
2. Neighbors with Crayons 9
3. A Place Called Home 15
4. Words Have Power 30
5. Revolutionary Transformation 52
6. Connectional Design 71
7. Community of Learning 95
8. Engagement, Act 1: Reneighboring the Congregation 116
9. Engagement, Act 2: Reconnecting the Community 129
10. Engagement, Act 3: Restoring Hope 165
11. Community of Hope 178

Epilogue 189

Afterword by W. Wilson Goode 205

Appendix 208

Bibliography 211

Index 217

List of Illustrations

Table 1	Jesus' Descriptions Reveal Positive or Negative Responses 33
Table 2	Church Models Grid: Your church as a fortress in community 110
Table 3	Church Models Grid: Your church as a lifeguard station in community 110
Figure 1	Child's drawing of an angelic visitor to her neighborhood 1
Figure 2	Child's expression of family 9
Figure 3	Child's expression of faith 15
Figure 4	Ontario Presbyterian Church, circa 1925 21
Figure 5	Aerial photograph of Wilkey Church neighborhood 28
Figure 6	Child's drawing of the neighborhood 30
Figure 7	Transforming Stigma and Face Paradigm 39
Figure 8	Child's drawing of faith 52
Figure 9	Child's drawing of family 71
Figure 10	MissionWorks urban plunge logo 83
Figure 11	"I Can Do That" ministry logo 84
Figure 12	Church "Face" Models Chart 109
Figure 13	Church "Face" Models Chart (key) 110
Figure 14	Church Models Evaluation Chart 111

xii   *List of Illustrations*

Figure 15	Mission Leaders Prayer Breakfast promotion 112
Figure 16	Child's drawing of faith 116
Figure 17	Child's drawing of school 129
Figure 18	Arms of children shoot up during a Floor Talk session in the gym 135
Figure 19	Child's drawing of street violence that keeps parents and children in fear 149
Figure 20	Child's drawing of family conflict 150
Figure 21	Child's drawing of family conflict (exploded view) 150
Figure 22	Child obscures drawing of a gun originally depicted 151
Figure 23	Child draws overflowing trashcan the size of her house 152
Figure 24	Photo of Kensington row homes 153
Figure 25	Photo of Wilkey Church and row homes next door 153
Figure 26	Photo of Kensington street 154
Figure 27	Child's drawing of single family home with half-sized trashcan 154
Figure 28	Photo at corner of Rand St. across from Wilkey Church, showing burned-out vacant building where a child lived 155
Figure 29	Every block had multiple burned out homes, abandoned lots, and cars 156
Figure 30	Child's drawing of a row house fire that nearly took a child's life 157
Figure 31	Child's drawing of a row house fire showing child in the flames and mother safely outside 157
Figure 32	Children in the community expressed their feelings for Christopher's speedy recovery 158

List of Illustrations   xiii

Figure 33	The skill level was higher in the secondary intervention group. In this drawing of the neighborhood, row homes are more accurately rendered. 160
Figure 34	Child's drawing expressing hatred for what his neighborhood has become using only a black crayon 162
Figure 35	Child's drawing expressing affirmation of faith 162
Figure 36	Child's drawing expressing conflict between his real and idealized family 165
Figure 37	Photo of children with adults they learned to trust who invited them to go to an out-of-city camp experience 172
Figure 38	Photo of children at Lake Champion 174
Figure 39	Child's drawing of the home next to the church 178
Figure 40	Photo of the wall bearing the neighborhood stigma in graffiti 179
Figure 41	Photo of children reclaiming the graffiti wall after their return from the out-of-city camp experience 180
Figure 42	Photo of the transformed wall depicting the Ark and Doves of blessing arriving to their community 181
Figure 43	Photo of the free gifts of gratitude children offered their neighbors 184
Figure 44	Photo of Ontario Spirit's Cheer for God during a community worship service 184

Foreword by Raymond J. Bakke

Between 1994 and 1999, I had five marvelous years at Eastern (now Palmer) Seminary in Philadelphia, as professor of the global urban ministry doctoral program. Two of my amazing students, Kevin Yoho and Duke Dixon, both Presbyterian pastors, began inviting me into the Kensington neighborhood of Philadelphia.

To anyone outside Philadelphia with a serious wish to know what this city and this community was like, I recommend what I think is one of the most insightful books on city politics ever published in the United States: *A Prayer for the City*, by Buzz Bissinger. For a marvelously colorful (R-rated) account of Kensington history and social volatility when Mayor Rendell and Cardinal Anthony Bevilacqua and the police commissioner showed up before an angry community crowd, see the chapter titled "The Racial Trifecta."[1]

This was the social laboratory and community reality on the eve of the Philadelphia Presbytery's decision to send a young Reverend Kevin Yoho to be the pastor of Wilkey Memorial Presbyterian Church in the heart of Kensington, in hopes he might find a gracious way to close the church. Almost simultaneously, he joined our doctoral program, so that everything my colleagues and I would share in the academic program got tested, sifted, sorted, and sometimes rejected, no doubt, in the historic church that, in every external measure, shared the decline and fall of this old working-class neighborhood. Now, more than a decade later, after reflecting on his experiences for years, and from his office inside the executive ministries of the Presbyterian Church, Kevin brings us *Crayons for the City: Reneighboring Communities of Faith to Rebuild Communities of Hope*.

I was a strong Kevin Yoho supporter and advocate long before we both left the doctoral program in Philadelphia. Shortly after I ended

---

1. Bissinger, *Prayer for the City*, 65–77.

up with my international urban office at the historic First Presbyterian Church of Seattle, I strongly urged the senior pastor of a church that had lost its way in the heart of Seattle to call Kevin and install him as pastor to the powers of downtown Seattle. In truth, I think that after meeting Kevin, this pastor was too intimidated by his Kingdom spirit and love for all things urban to recommend that he come to Seattle.

For me, to read *Crayons for the City* was to revisit my own inner-city parish in Chicago. In truth, I needed this book back in 1969 when the community blew up in my face and, like all city pastors around the country, I was scrambling for resources and maps to hope. Like me, Kevin searched for resources in cities around the country. The fingerprints of our friend Bob Lupton of Atlanta and "reneighboring" fame are all over this book. For sure, Kevin honors all of us by taking our stuff, then translating, correcting, nuancing, and applying it in urban transformation, but his own effervescent creativity also takes him beyond what most of us imagined or achieved in other times and cities.

May I humbly suggest that there are at least four starting points from which readers of *Crayons for the City* can proceed—or four maps that will orient readers and enable them to learn from Pastor Yoho in his pastoral setting.

Map #1—The Children

Wilkey Church was begun with a vision that kids should not have to cross busy and dangerous streets to come to church, so we see that kids were part of the founding vision of the church. Intuitively and perceptively, Kevin figured out that urban neighborhood kids mirror rather than mask their true feelings. He learned how to use art and kids' drawings to reveal the depth of their despair, and so you will see how the arts and school fit into the story of renewal.

As an aside, Kevin might have reminded us of a hermeneutical clue for this nontraditional senior pastor response to a city neighborhood in crisis. He could have told the Exodus 31 story of Moses's struggle to lead that huge migration of former mudbrick makers from Egypt, who suffered forty years of unemployment in the bad neighborhood. As they survived on mere manna (the food stamp program of their day), God responded by giving them an art committee—two men, Oholiab and Bezalel, gifted by the Holy Spirit in crafts and beauty—to help them build a beautiful worship center in their awful neighborhood. Why? The biblical answer is pretty obvious. The poor need beauty as much as they need bread, because they live in ugliness.

So Kevin introduces the way hope is seen by the creative and reflective study of children's art. That is one map of this story that I found uniquely Kevin. Of course, he gives us insights into the best of modern psychology, but the proof of change and hope is seen in the kids and their art and the more than four hundred pieces of evidence he collected.

Map #2 — The City

Another map is to follow the history of Kensington itself in the larger Philadelphia context. Lincoln Steffens once called Philadelphia "the most American of our greater cities," and as Bissinger added, "No area embodied the tradition of industry and the white working class better than Kensington, with row house and church steeple and narrow street and the El and the spew of factory smokestacks all within its boundaries."[2]

So if you follow Kevin's map into this community, the struggle leading to the riots and tensions from New York and New Jersey to Watts will become clear to every reader. This micro story creates macro awareness for every other industrial city in America.

Map #3 — The Denomination and Regional Council Map

Pastor Kevin's third map is an introduction to how denominational regional councils, and most every other historic church judicatory, think about and respond to cities (and parenthetically, in my view, why all these historic denominations are in schism and decline in our day). Kevin is too kind to embellish the reality, but he was called to deliver euthanasia in ecclesia—to put a church out of its misery and to stem the drain of mission funds so that they could go to more worthy communities.

Not surprisingly, I note that American denominations were created in this country about the same time as department stores and labor unions, to package services for a country moving from fixed parishes on the East Coast to the hinterlands on the way to the Pacific coast and beyond. Now, all three of these venerable institutions are struggling to

2. Ibid., 70.

survive. Ward's dies, Sears closes stores, and most manufacturing occurs in nonunion states. Why? The world changed.

Remember Henry Ford and the creation of the Model T, which changed the world? After World War I, the world of autos changed, and Ford spent billions to push his fixed image of the Model T on a world that fled to other models. He literally shut down Detroit, finally, to retool and change, but Ford never made it back to first place.

Denominations and their seminaries evolved the perfect leadership model: the MDiv degree. It assumed a standardized church, which, like Sears, had cradle-to-grave brand name loyalty. The pastoral toolkit for effective preaching and ministry came, like Wilkey's first pastor, from Princeton, of course.

Now the world has changed, led by the engines of global economics, migrations, and city transformations everywhere. America has about 4.5 percent of the world's population, and whites make up just 13 percent of the people on God's earth. The nations are no longer across the oceans; they are across the streets in Philadelphia and Kensington. Presbyterians were served so well and so long by structures that used to fit. They and other denominations like them don't do well now.

Fortunately, Kevin is wired differently and has splendid emotional intelligence. He found ways to resist the prevailing denominational reward system by making downward mobility for himself and his family a veritable art form. He found that he needed to be incarnate, and not merely in car as a commuter in the city. He found the compass is not "needs assessment tools" but ABCD: asset-based community development. Contrary to outside expectations, he looked for signs of hope and strength, as islands in a sea of despair, and set out to connect the dots. He found the venerable Christian Community Development Association, which encourages all of us to seek out the least, last, and lost neighborhoods of American cities as the most fruitful places to be incarnate in the name of Jesus Christ. Kevin knows that incarnation is not simply our message; it is our model. The leaders are coming from places other than the white denominational maps and, for sure, other than the comfort zones of most of us. Like Nehemiah of old, we tithe warm, outgoing Christians into crisis neighborhoods to build relational bridges that link needs and resources. Slowly but surely, we seek to build on islands of hope we find in every place with the guidance and authentic power of the Holy Spirit.

Map #4—The Church Map

A fourth map into Kevin Yoho's world is to focus on the decline and then the seeds of renewal in Wilkey Church. Kevin found a little faithful core of old people with memories. Against all odds, they were holding on. Like the frightened disciples in the little boat (Mark 4), their fear was in their eyes, and Jesus was asleep and probably irrelevant to those fishermen. After all, what could the carpenter do about this? They were going down, probably soon.

What Kevin did was help them quietly recover their memory. While he put one arm tightly around this core group, he put his other arm around Kensington's other churches and institutions. He also got the mayor to come back and lead a meeting in his church. He was gently reintroducing resources that embellish hope slowly. He found that the way forward was a creative way backward into the history, going back to the founding mission statement of the church, and in the still visible images of their first pastor. He transformed himself from the young outsider with his own wildly exciting plans for renewal of church and community into the person who comes alongside to reaffirm what the people already knew. In some ways, he "outparented" them and engaged them to take the first steps to renewal.

Finally, I am delighted that Dr. Yoho is now teaching out of his reflection on his pastoral journey while he continues as a servant of the church. His first book radiates that infectious personality he brought to my classes fifteen years ago as we plunged into Philadelphia and New York together to learn by engaging ministry models in context.

And so I conclude: to God be the glory; to the earth be peace; to Kevin be courage; and to our cities be hope.

Preface

My first visit to Stetson Middle School was a memorable one. The school was located a few blocks away from the Philadelphia church I had recently begun serving as pastor in 1995. I was looking forward to better understanding the challenges the community faced and offering whatever resources I could that might be useful. An experienced community organizer named Teresa Dimitri had graciously offered to introduce me to the principal, Lucy Rodriguez. I had learned that students in an art class had created a mosaic mural on the school's second floor, and I wanted to see the students' creation.

We parked our cars and were walking up the city street when two gunshots rang out right in front of us. They were coming from someone hanging out the window of a slowly passing car. I heard the emptied shell casings hit the pavement. Another car then raced by as the perpetrator tried to settle their grievances right in front of dozens of children beginning their school day. The bang-bang scattered the children as they dropped to the sidewalk in an instant. When the immediate danger had passed, I walked up the school's stairs and, my heart still racing, said to a few students, "Wow. What about those gunshots?" Blank expressions met my startled look. "Yeah, heard them," they said, showing no evidence of concern. I called out to a student I recognized up ahead. "Did you hear the gunshots, Joe? It was just a few minutes ago!" "Hey, Pastor Kevin. Yeah, we heard 'em." "Aren't you concerned?" I asked him. "It happens all the time," he said simply. Nothing could have prepared me for that jolt. Shocking as it was, the jolt was not the gunfire but how unfazed the children were to the violence and imminent danger. I realized in that moment something had to change, and it would have to start with me.

A few months earlier Art Honoré, a leader for Philadelphia Presbytery, the regional council for the Presbyterian Church (U.S.A.), asked if I would be interested in serving a congregation that, in his estimation, might benefit from my leadership. Apparently, this church he had in mind was perilously close to closing its doors, and he thought I could help "with their future." Wilkey Memorial Presbyterian Church seemed to be like literally dozens of other Presbyterian city churches that had closed during the past twenty years. Art had worshipped at the South Philadelphia church where I served as interim and he remembered that I would be looking for a new challenge as soon as that work successfully concluded. "Before you get a new full-time position, why not help us out in Kensington for a few months?" I was not familiar with that part of North Philadelphia, but since I remained open to a new ministry opportunity, I decided to take him up on the invitation.

Kensington was similar to sections of any big city that your parents or thoughtful friends would surely caution you to avoid. I recall the first day I drove along Interstate 95 adjacent to the Delaware River and took the Allegheny Avenue exit heading toward Kensington, which I had passed by hundreds of times before without a thought. Densely populated neighborhoods of row homes were punctuated by pawnshops, liquor stores, check-cashing joints, delis and newspaper shops, laundromats, a few schools, and a gun store. And then there were the churches. Looking like fortresses without moats, church buildings occupied most every other block but looked just as abandoned as many of the shops. I would later learn why there were so many empty buildings, abandoned cars, and storefront Deliverance temples that served those who spent most, if not all, of their life on the streets. As I pulled up in from of Wilkey Memorial Presbyterian Church at the corner of East Ontario and 9th Streets, I had no idea what I had gotten myself into by accepting Art's invitation.

"It happens all the time." Joe's words haunted me as Teresa and I eventually made our way through the maze of kids leaving school for the day. As we studied the beautiful tile work on the wall in front of us, I saw the mural in a new light. On the left side of the mural were burned-out cars, drug paraphernalia, trash, and dark images. That was the neighborhood as they knew it to be. On the other side of a sharp divide grooved out of the tile diagonally from top to bottom was the street as the young artists envisioned it could be: bright, happy, and peaceful, with clean cars, colorful trees, flowers, and smiling, caring people. I knew immediately that the kids had a wonderful capacity to imagine something better. Why does it have to "happen all the time," I wondered? Could the violence stop? Can hope be restored? What is the role of the worshipping community in the community at large?

While Wilkey Church was looking for a dynamic preacher for Sunday worship, God sought leaders to embrace the possibilities of a new emerging future. Something as simple as crayons in the hands of children might help transform violence into hope. My life as a community pastor was about to change in profound ways, along with the worshipping congregation of less than *forty-five*. Together, we began a journey from stigma to hope as Kensington, home to *forty-five thousand* of our neighbors, became our home, too.

Acknowledgments

If any portion of this book could benefit from further improvement, none would be more deserving than this space for acknowledgments. I am indebted to many people who have courageously and sacrificially stood with me during its development and writing, especially the children and families of Kensington who have inspired new visions of hope. I am grateful to the congregation of Wilkey Church whose leadership dared to dream again. Words cannot express my thanks to the Ontario Spirit kids who are the leaders of a new millennium, including Joe, Christina, Hector, Albert, Qiydaar, Nicole, Heather, Margaret, Jessica, Leonardo, Sacoya, Virgen, Melissa, Shawn, Arnaldo, Angel, Antonio, Max, Samantha, Christian, Yalitza, Catherine, Delilah, Lynnette, Andrew, and many others, too—and of course, Christopher.

Reimagining a neighborhood to become a life-giving and vital community is one thing, but writing about the transformation and capturing its power in words and pictures is no less challenging. On many afternoons, when the kids were noisily bouncing basketballs and playing games in the gym one floor below, I resisted the pastoral urge to join in, instead dutifully sequestering myself in a classroom to think and write. I'll never forget how special it was when, occasionally, a few kids searched me out after noticing I had retreated to my writing room—they wondered why I wasn't in the gym with them. This book is why.

The many iterations of this manuscript benefited from the disciplined editing skills of the Reverend Henry Shaw, who likewise edited my articles for *The Living Pulpit*. Wipf and Stock's extraordinary publication team included editor Dr. Charlie Collier, with the excellent support of managing editor Jim Tedrick, assistant managing editor Matthew Wimer, and editorial assistant Brian Palmer. I am grateful for their confidence in my book's contribution to the church and community conversation and their high expectations and attention to the literary craft.

I will always be grateful to global urbanologist, the Reverend Dr. Ray Bakke, not only for writing the Foreword but also for modeling the importance of accountability and peer support in his own ministry. His example prompted our Kensington prayer breakfasts and monthly Mission Leaders' Prayer Gatherings. Dr. Bakke's many visits to Kensington and his personal involvement with worldwide congregational and community transformation keeps me centered and connected to what God is doing in cities around the world.

Few people know Philadelphia like its former mayor, the Reverend Dr. W. Wilson Goode Sr., who so graciously and ably wrote the Afterword. He was the city's first African American mayor and served for two terms. I came to know Dr. Goode when we were doctor of ministry classmates and he served as deputy assistant secretary of education under the Clinton administration. He left that position in 2000 to help organize Amachi, a national, faith-based mentoring program for children of incarcerated parents, which is now his ministry and life's work. I am grateful for his contribution to my own learning and the integration of ministry and deep community listening.

Inspiration for the extraordinary notion and strategy of reneighboring a city came forcefully and profoundly from the Reverend Dr. Robert Lupton of FCS Ministries in Atlanta, Georgia. Bob has done in Atlanta what I was only beginning to do in Philadelphia. He is to me a courageous Daniel Boone who served as a wise leader, offering me guidance and inspiration, especially in developing reneighboring strategies.

The Reverend Dr. Victoria Lee Erickson, formerly Chaplain at Drew University, served as a mentor. She was an incredible tour guide for my learning. I explored diverse disciplines well off my familiar map of experience as I designed a model of pastoral intervention at the intersection of the Bible, sociology, and neighborhood kids.

Uniquely gifted in the classroom and the boardroom, my street-savvy project supervisor was the Reverend Dr. Harold Dean Trulear, then of Public/Private Ventures, currently of Howard University Divinity School. Dr. Trulear knew the neighborhoods I was called to serve. He guided me to use the best pastor-practitioner tools that nurtured my own transformation.

No one person links to more city contacts than Ms. Teresa Dimitri, the "Queen Esther of Kensington," whose wonderful gifts included indefatigable neighborhood organizing, knowledge of Philadelphia, and experience. While on the staff of Kensington Action Now/Kensington

Area Revitalization Project (KAN/KARP), a community development corporation, she was also a Wilkey Church intern from Temple University, and on the staff of Philadelphia Safe and Sound, a partner in the Youth Violence Reduction Project (YVRP). She introduced me (even amid gunfire entering the school) to Mrs. Lucy Rodriguez, then principal of Stetson Middle School, who enthusiastically welcomed me and gave me access to a great group of kids in the fifth-grade class of Mr. Bowen, an innovative educator with a huge heart for his students. I also owe a debt of gratitude to Temple intern Ms. Pamela Stump and her entourage of helpers, who with her husband, Doug, kept our programs focused and organized.

My admiration for the people who call Kensington home includes the dedicated police officers of the 24th and 25th districts of the Philadelphia Police Department, area shop owners, schoolteachers, and residents. I am indebted to a talented group of colleagues, including my doctor of ministry classmate the Reverend Duke Dixon, then pastor of Union Tabernacle Church in Philadelphia, who now serves a congregation in New Castle Presbytery; Cornerstone Community Church's pastor, Joe Darrow; the Reverend Tom Wray; Charles Harris, Young Life's Philadelphia Urban Area Director; the Reverend Stanley Hearst Sr., A.M.E. pastor in Philadelphia; and the Reverend Anita Bell, without whose support our mission would have been unbearable. Shane Claiborne and The Simple Way community around the corner from Wilkey Church were awesome neighbors who were and remain a constant inspiration. Our after-school program would not have been possible without the able and energetic students of Eastern University. Their dedication and true capacity for caring was deeply appreciated by our community.

God's gracious gift of family and friends helped sustain me on my journey as an urban pastor. I owe a debt of gratitude to my then teenaged children, Kimberly, Jaime, and Jonathan. I know how much you sacrificed as I tried to listen to God's voice and recalibrate my life's mission and priorities.

Most of all, I affectionately dedicate whatever good may come of this book's publication to my best friend, partner, and wife, Melissa Arnott, EdD. Your amazing capacity to make the world a better place nurtures and inspires my life in countless ways. Your boundless spirit reminds me every day to pay attention to life's bottom line as God inextricably binds us and our family together in love.

1

Welcome to Our Neighborhood

Figure 1

A mother, noticing her five-year-old daughter drawing with crayons on some paper, asked, "What are you drawing?"

"A picture of God," the little girl said.

The mother remarked, "No one knows what God looks like."

The girl, busy with her crayons, assured, "They will when I get through."[1]

---

1. Associated Press, "Newsletter's Humor Spicing Up Faith."

Children fill the city streets of Kensington, a large neighborhood north of the city center of Philadelphia. Our children are in most respects like children living anywhere else. They play and go to school, laugh and cry, and come from various types of families. They can even show us what God looks like. As Dean Borgman rightly observes, "Ghettos, suburban towns, and rural areas share many of the same problems; drugs, crime, and violence are everywhere."[2] However, our children do have one unique characteristic: they live in Kensington, Philadelphia.

In Kensington, statistics paint a dark picture. Ninety percent of our kids come from low-income families. One out of every four students entering high school will not graduate.[3] Seventy percent live in rented homes. Twenty percent of the houses on their street are vacant.[4] Thirty percent of their parents are unemployed. The majority of Philadelphia's drug crime, including murder, prostitution, and drug arrests, occur on our streets.[5] "The Kensington neighborhood, once sustained by dense social networks that offered mutual support in modest economic circumstances, is now a source of problems, not solutions, for poor kids."[6] Those who move into Kensington do so because they can't afford to go anywhere else. To satisfy their budget or their addictions, people move onto our streets.

Neighbor Tom

While walking is good exercise, walking around the block to better understand the neighborhood is even better. The purpose is not to advertise programs or solicit support but to actively engage with residents and pay attention to what God is doing. "Walk with me" is a phrase that should be heard more often in our churches as leaders find ways to interact and learn outside the building. During one of my many walks through the neighborhood, I met Tom, a middle-aged man with a weary and worn appearance. I learned that he had intentionally moved to Kensington a few months before to satisfy his addiction. Though he works in the restaurant business in Bucks County, outside of Philadelphia, he chose to

---

2. Borgman, *When Kumbaya Is Not Enough*, 226.
3. Jones and McCoy, "District Gives Itself Failing Grade," A1.
4. Commission, *Philadelphia City Planning*, 10–15.
5. Private conversation with Philadelphia Police Commissioner John Timoney.
6. Putnam, *Our Kids*, 366.

relocate to Kensington and make the daily forty-five-minute commute to "be near the source" of his addiction, which I assumed to be drugs—only to learn, as the conversation continued, that his addiction was sexual in nature. Police Commissioner John Timoney has frequently stated that Kensington has the highest incidence of prostitution in Philadelphia. Many social capital and other assets are removed from the city and flee to the suburbs. For example, the locals purchase overpriced commodities at the corner store, but the typical store owner reinvests the earned income wherever he or she lives, outside the neighborhood—and most likely in a suburb. Tom represents a kind of social capital predator that the community has little power to resist. Tom works in the suburbs at a restaurant and reinvests earned income back into the urban neighborhood. Tragically, his behaviors are socially abusive because they negatively impact not only the victims of prostitution but also the neighborhood's quality of life and associated economies that promote injustice and racism. Historical and persistent injustice and abuse have fragmented our urban neighborhoods, presenting an enormous opportunity for faith-based organizations to directly engage and improve urban community ecologies.

Through a Child's Eyes

As soon as the opportunity presents itself to escape, the kids move out with their families to a better neighborhood, even if that "better neighborhood" is only a short distance away. In the local community newspaper, a desperate-sounding mother wrote an article titled "Through a Child's Eyes" in which she said, "We can't move because we don't have the money and we are not a minority. So me and my family are screwed."[7] They may get a job and save some money. A relative may provide a way of escape. Maybe the lottery will pay off for them. A financial settlement from an accident of some kind may provide the resources they seek. On the other hand, perhaps they really are "screwed."

The children learn early to abhor their neighborhood, their street, their school, their church, their family, their future. As Putnam rightly observes, "Kensington is today one of the most dangerous neighborhoods in one of America's most crime-ridden cities."[8] During Halloween some

---

7. V. Fran, "Through a Child's Eyes," *Star Newspaper*, June 24, 1998, Kensington ed., Letters to the Editor sec., 30.

8. Putnam, *Our Kids*, 231.

kids told me they were looking forward to getting lots of candy because their "mom was taking them to a better neighborhood for trick or treat." Imagine feeling compelled to go to another neighborhood to be treated.

In 1998, an ethic studies group, led by Ms. Hoa Tran, a Temple University PhD candidate, produced an ethnography/documentary video[9] that told the powerful story of Kensington through the eyes of five Kensington high school kids. The kids chose the topics and settled on drugs, prostitution, and violence. Their twenty-minute presentation expressed well the despair and anger they felt. It lacked hopefulness because they did not see any hope to report. Apart from the positive group dynamics enjoyed by the video crew, the tone was dark. This important work tells the story of what it is like to live in Kensington. The strategic value of the video, *Kensington Through Our Eyes*, is that it effectively demonstrates that too many faith-based ministries remain effectively silent, absent from public conversation, and have little impact on the community, leaving our kids essentially hopeless.

There are efforts underway to invite these same kids to continue their storytelling by discovering what is "good" in their neighborhood and perhaps even to progress to gathering solutions. Faith-based ministries are sadly and tragically silent on the street in areas like Kensington.

A different kind of youth video was produced by a Christian and Missionary Alliance team from the Eastern Pennsylvania district during one of their regional gatherings. Youth leaders had heard of our efforts to improve the quality of life in Kensington and sent their own crew to staff a mission project called Operation Liberty Bell. It told stories of hope in the midst of urban hopelessness and how transformation might be imagined. Caring people doing acts of kindness were a big part of the program as 150 high school kids from outside Kensington invested a weekend in the city. The eyes of those young people saw something different than did their counterparts living in the community. God was working in the hearts and minds of the kids and adults, who aligned with faith-based groups in Kensington that are out on the street, showing God's love to people in the name of Jesus Christ. The key to what the Alliance video documented was that street-connected local leaders can earn the right to be heard only after many months and years of in-the-neighborhood, relationship-building activities.

---

9. The William Penn Foundation funded the video as part of a five-year study of Philadelphia neighborhoods.

Why do popular religious-themed wall hangings, framed pictures, and photographs typically sold in religious and home goods stores feature biblical passages overlaying pristine mountain, meadow, or seashore scenes? Or why is it that a religious cable franchise provides only idyllic outdoor scenes for its meditative segments? What is it about our theology that precludes us from seeing God in urban environments, as if life-affirming Bible verses apply only to nonurban areas? Somehow we can more easily perceive God's connection and presence everywhere but in the city. This observation is descriptive, but it is not proscriptive. Since God is the Creator of all things, a proper theology of place must include every aspect of creation, including urban settings.

You will find no billboards along the interstate inviting people to move into under-resourced or distressed neighborhoods like Kensington. Nevertheless, it is home to more than sixty-five thousand people, most of whom express little hope for the future, unless they are lucky enough to escape. The emotional distancing of the church from the place where it operates is observed from the earliest examples of church history. As the Christian church spread from the Middle East to Asia to Europe, its expansion was so rapid that it barely had time to establish deep roots in the cities and towns it swept through. Certainly local communities of faith, often in house churches, connected directly to their context, but an overly individualistic emphasis of the church ensured that its roots in the culture remained shallow. An aversion to place required leaders in the early church to correct a distortion of otherworldism. For example, the Apostle Paul cautioned believers in the city of Thessaloniki to get back to their ordinary work when he wrote, "Make it your ambition to lead a quiet life, to mind your own business and to work with your hands, just as we told you" (1 Thess 4:11). The Christian church's important emphasis on spiritual things can be internalized as a distorted, inverted message of the unimportance of physical things. Over the centuries, the unchanging church was ill-prepared for the rapidly changing world around it. The church's place-aversion is well articulated by historical philosopher Edward S. Casey when he rhetorically asks, "Is it accidental that the obsession with space as something infinite and ubiquitous coincided with the spread of Christianity, a religion with universalist aspirations?"[10] Ecclesiology historically trumped missiology, or to put it differently, the inside institutional concerns took priority over the consideration of how

---

10. Casey, *Fate of Place*, xii.

the mission was impacting the world outside. Casey describes the Age of Exploration during the fourteenth and fifteenth centuries as "an era in which the domination of native peoples was accomplished by their deplacialization: the systematic destruction of regional landscapes that served as the concrete settings for local culture."[11] The theology of place, when correctly understood, provides an important and essential self-correction for the church's decisions, not unlike the maxim of the medical community drawn from the Hippocratic Corpus: "Do no harm."

This book is rooted in five years of community engagement as a pastoral leader in North Philadelphia. Its purpose is twofold: to document one community's story of transformation and to demonstrate how any faith community can experience its own story of transformation. The intervention described in these pages has empowered children subjected to the abuse of stigma to regain their clear and hopeful voice. Learning how to use the tools we developed in Kensington, the reader can embrace their history and neighborhood seriously and experience transformation, too. What we discovered in Philadelphia was that even closed and isolated fortresslike churches could become accessible, street-present, hope-bearing communities of faith blessing the entire community at large.

In "Neighbors with Crayons," you will become part of the story of the Kensington neighborhood of Philadelphia and how a congregation once wedded to its neighborhood became a stranger within a span of forty short years. Demographic tools help explain the shift in the community's narrative that the church fell victim to, rather than becoming a part of its telling.

Every organization and team of leaders has a story, and in "A Place Called Home" the reader is invited to explore the numerical, historical, narrative, and ethnographic data of our neighborhood.

In "Words Have Power," we will explore the behavioral and societal labeling and test the hypothesis of a stigma diagnosis for the Kensington neighborhood. The chapter demonstrates how intentional discovery can frame a process, design, and engagement towards a remedy. Various disciplines provide lenses for observing the power of words either to bestow a blessing or to cast the curse of stigma with its damaging consequences.

If living were a static experience, there would be no need for transformation or managing change. In "Revolutionary Transformation,"

---

11. Ibid.

we will explore the nature of transformation and be introduced to the domains of personal, missional, and corporate renewal and how they converge to fulfill the promise of comprehensive transformation.

The ancient inquiry "Who is my neighbor?" leads us to "Connectional Design" as we examine the concept of reneighboring. Most churches and other communities of faith were established as neighborhood gathering places led by local leaders who lived in proximity to the place of worship, witness, and mission. In many communities, as residents choose to relocate to other neighborhoods or to suburban areas, the once "neighbored" church becomes disengaged from the community. This chapter describes a process called "reneighboring" that reconnects the church once again so that it can become a strategic neighbor, which sets the stage for meaningful community impact.

Just as living things must grow and change, so faith communities must learn and grow if they are to fulfill their mission. In "Community of Learning," a compilation of mission affirmations was developed with leadership in the church. Thinking more deeply about the divine creation model led to an examination of how simple expressions of loving your neighborhood and making new connections can begin to reverse decades of disengagement in a matter of months. Complacency can be transformed into responsiveness as images of the church as a "fortress" give way to images of the church as "resource" for the entire community.

Like a three-act play, "Engagement in 3 Acts" tells the story of intervention in Kensington in three parts. "Engagement, Act 1: Reneighboring the Congregation" will examine congregational community-building and the strategic importance of establishing a learning team in your church. Ethnographic tools provide the learning stimulus that empowers the congregation to explore the sometimes stressful and even emotionally painful issues of neighborhood detachment and its effects. Because learning takes place in the context of a trusted community, the capacity of the entire team can rekindle an authentic strategic neighbor reconnection.

"Engagement, Act 2: Reconnecting the Community" describes the drawing intervention model designed to remove the effects of stigma by giving children an opportunity to express their true voice with crayons. Two groups of children, a primary intervention group at Wilkey Church and a secondary, control group at Stetson Middle School, were invited to do a series of crayon-drawing exercises. These expressive experiences powerfully transformed the childrens' own self-understanding and their spatial understanding of where they lived. Actual drawings by the children are examined.

The drawing experiences led to a merger of the two previously separate groups of children when they were invited to an out-of-city camping experience described in "Engagement, Act 3: Restoring Hope." Relationships of trust between caring adults and the children led to a transformation of the way we experience one another and God our Creator. Congregation, kids, families, and the broader community were all on stage for further engagement and growth when about three dozen young people returned home after a life-changing camp experience.

In "Community of Hope," the evidence of a transformed commufnity, congregation, and the children themselves is evaluated. An Institutional Review Board (IRB) provides necessary oversight, monitoring, and review of behavioral research that involves human intervention because evaluations and observations of transformation are profoundly experienced by participants. Photos depict the transformation in the community though wall murals.

The Epilogue invites the reader to apply lessons learned as a community pastor and leader. We will start with a balcony-view analysis and reflection on mission outcomes and sustainability. Progressively zooming out from the streets of Kensington, we will apply our reneighboring principles to other cities across the United States as we examine mission connectivity in Wisconsin and New Jersey. Zooming further out, we will consider 1849 Kensington and the mountains of modern-day West Virginia to learn a lesson about the difference between mining and farming as it applies to designing sustainable ministry models.

The Appendix includes supporting material. The community intervention project produced hundreds of crayon drawings by more than 150 children. The neighborhood children were also photographed by renowned photographer Judith Joy Ross. Her works are in public and private galleries from San Francisco to New York. We were delighted that our neighborhood transformation caught Ross's attention as a professional photographer. She presented dozens of prints for us to use as a way of telling our story since the children and their parents participated so enthusiastically in the portrait project.

Drawings, photographs, and additional resources are gathered as a freely available online companion to the book at the author's website, www.crayonsforthecity.com.

2

Neighbors with Crayons

Figure 2

> For if you remain silent at this time, relief and deliverance for the Jews will arise from another place, but you and your father's family will perish. And who knows but that you have come to royal position for such a time as this? (Esth 4:14)

When a row home at the end of the street burned down, Christopher, a small boy, was seriously injured and his family was displaced. The incident also left profound scars on the entire neighborhood. While the loss was devastating to Christopher's unemployed single mom, who was desperately trying to get a job, his was only one home among the many other inadequate public housing units. Children attended underfunded schools with under-resourced teachers and played on unsafe streets, between abandoned cars and in the shadow of closed churches. Too many closed churches. The neighborhood needed something more powerful than deficits. Christopher's neighborhood deserved a different story built on assets, not deficiencies.

As the pastor of a church in the city, I was determined to learn how ours could be an authentically urban church, a community of faith that was deeply connected with the city, not just located in a city. Even with all the education and training I had received as someone from a middle-class family—my dad was an attorney, my mom a government worker—including four years of college, three years of seminary, and three successful pastorates, I knew just enough to realize I was ill-equipped to make the differences that were needed in the community I found myself called to serve.

One afternoon a few dozen children in the North Philadelphia neighborhood of Kensington were each given a bag of beautiful sea glass from the Jersey shore. Years of relentless polishing by sand and surf turned the dark broken glass into shiny lenses of color. Glass was transformed from bleak to bright. What kind of future could emerge if children and their families experienced God in a new, more authentic way? Like putting the shards of their dying neighborhood through divine sand and surf to fashion a new vision of hope and beauty, smoothed and reshaped, to light up their neighborhood and a new future.

Can you imagine your city or neighborhood as a place of possibilities? H and Ontario Streets in Kensington was our intersection where a congregation and a neighborhood could imagine possibilities for a better future. We lingered together long enough to become partners, transformed from stained, broken spirits into renewed, brilliant reflections of Jesus Christ.

In the wake of the fire that destroyed his home, Christopher had been rushed to the burn unit of St. Christopher's Hospital, where he was now recovering. His eyes sparkled as his fingers rubbed the smooth red, blue, and green glass brought to his bedside. He imagined the tales told by the sea glass, how it was transformed from darkness to light. He would later enjoy crayon drawings from his neighborhood pals and all these connections helped him realize that God loved each of them and was present with them always, even in in the flames.

God with us is the core motivation for the church's mission. The motives of nonprofit and charitable organizations are fundamentally different from their for-profit counterparts. Charities, foundations, and worshipping communities such as churches, synagogues, temples, and mosques are driven by their motivations to achieve their mission. Nonprofits are established to serve a socially valuable purpose for the public good. Though the interests of the public change over time based on shifting contexts and community needs, the motives of a worshipping and witnessing community should be clear even during tumultuous and disruptive change. But this has not always been the case.

Disruption

For example, the highly anticipated and dreaded technology reset that occurred on the eve of the new millennium in the year 2000 pointed to the inability of many computer systems to address, accommodate, and adapt to a disruptive technical change. Technology companies deployed teams of software engineers equipped with abundant resources to rethink the programming, rewrite the underlying code, and relaunch entirely new versions of their operating systems. The technical disruption was eventually met with effective innovation, but what of the church's engagement with social and community change?

The millennial *technical* disruption can be understood as analogous to a millennial *ecclesiastical* disruption that still affects the lives of individuals and families in congregations and communities. This ecclesiastical disruption is evidenced by the decades-long and persistent inability of faith-based[1] systems to address, accommodate, and adapt to the urbanization of American life. At the dawn of the new millennium, more than 50 percent of the world's population lived in cities for the first

---

1. Faith-based organizations (FBOs) are communities of faith, which of course include churches and other Christian ministries that invite people to worship, bear witness, and serve others. FBOs are not just localized in churches in the Christian tradition, however, but also include those communities of faith that may gather in mosques (Muslim), synagogues (Jewish), or temples (Hindu), for example. While my own point of reference is the church as a Christian community of faith, I acknowledge that the principles of community engagement can likewise be applied to other traditions and faith-based organizations.

time in history. Many congregations and faith-based service providers have ignored this shift. Though deriving the benefits of tax-exempt and charitable status in state and federal tax codes, churches struggled, and often failed, to effectively serve the public good, exchanging their original motivation for self-preservation. As community citizens as well as communities of faith, churches have become increasingly detached from the communities that they were chartered to serve—especially inner cities.

Faith-based organizations, denominational systems, regional councils, individual congregations, and worshipping communities face new challenges and must aggressively embrace opportunities if they are to fulfill their mission in an urban or any other context.

What we need are ecclesiastical engineers and social entrepreneurs equipped with the right resources to rethink the programming and rewrite the underlying code. Then we can relaunch new versions of operating systems to build new spiritual networks and innovative ministry and mission models. Leading disruptive innovation will necessarily invite conflict, especially from those who seek to maintain the status quo as incumbents. New spiritual networks must be constructed regardless of the terrain encountered.

This book is about the leader's role as an ecclesiastical engineer and social entrepreneur introducing needed disruption by trying to pay attention and reinvent the way ministry engages the greater community. Our neighborhood's mental map became distorted as a result of stigma and its associated consequences, including impaired family, educational, economic, and political systems. This is a story about a journey to shift the mental map from stigma to hope by realigning the motivations of a church to serve the public good with the good news.

This is also a story about how a community of faith in the inner city of Philadelphia chose to embrace God's preferred and emerging future by employing its capacities and assets, transforming strangers into strategic neighbors.

How do individuals in a worshipping community go from being a stranger in the neighborhood to a strategic neighbor? "Strategic neighbors" are "the best thing we can offer an urban neighborhood."[2] Robert Lupton argues that they are different from "urban workers" and volunteers who enter a neighborhood to "help" and drive back home after their shift. He describes strategic neighbors as "people who have a

---

2. Lupton, *Renewing the City*, 173.

deep commitment to loving God and loving their neighbor . . . They are the frontline troops who go into neighborhoods where good neighbors are in short supply. They buy houses, join the neighborhood association, help organize crime watches, build relationships with neighbor kids, offer support to single moms, take seniors to the grocery store. In short, they are the embodiment of good news . . . There is nothing so important—so essential to the return of wholeness to an urban community—as a handful of committed neighbors who will make the neighborhood their own."[3]

The journey to reneighboring is not an easy one for most congregations to undertake. Can a congregation fall in love with its neighborhood? Can it internalize a new motivation like Queen Esther's when her uncle Mordecai warned, "If you remain silent at this time, relief will arise from another place and you will perish"? Of the message of Esther, Ray Bakke says, "When sin gets written into the law code, you can't just repudiate it. You've got to access power and change it . . . Some people have to go inside the black holes of politics and practice power and change law. This is absolutely true. You can't just change the streets on the streets. People have to go up to the power and down to the powerless."[4]

Esther's uncle Mordecai reasoned, "Nevertheless, maybe, just maybe, you have come to a special position for such a time as this." Worshipping and witnessing communities, especially in our cities, have a responsibility to change the structures—and not just the structures of city government, but also the even more impaired and unjust structures of our congregations, councils, associations, and denominations.

What you will discover in these pages is an invitation to individuals, churches, and community organizations to step outside their organizational silos and become strategic neighbors. It is time for practitioners to deliver authentic, successful, sustainable urban ministry. Reneighboring is the intentional practice of becoming a neighbor once again instead of remaining a stranger in the neighborhood. This book is about developing a new set of competencies that will enable a community pastor as an ecclesiastical and community network engineer to realign a church's mission motivations to serve the public good. It is also a story about how a community of faith in Philadelphia chose to embrace God's preferred and emerging future with successful, sustainable, fresh expressions of the Gospel.

3. Ibid.
4. Lee, "Uncomfortable Takeaways," paras. 5–6.

How do pastors and other congregational leaders grow and change from being a stranger in the neighborhood to a strategic neighbor? The journey is not an easy one for most congregations to undertake, but I believe that every church can fall in love with its neighborhood and build a new community of hope.

Crayons for the City starts with the reader's place in the world and offers a new methodology of mission engagement. Practical, actionable steps can be adapted to the reader's unique context. As I hope you will discover in these pages, your worshipping, witnessing, mission community can increase its vitality, energy, and satisfaction, and that can impact your entire community's spiritual and social wellness. *Crayons for the City* will provide the reader with possibilities not only for imagining a better future but also, with God's help, embracing a better future, even if all you have is a few boxes of crayons.

3

A Place Called Home

Figure 3

The drug walk around McPherson Library, at E and East Indiana Streets in Kensington, was a revelation. About one hundred residents, half a dozen police squad cars, and two TV crews with their glaringly bright spotlights crowded the corner while we waited for the Street Leader to get things started. The targeted homes were not alerted to the offensive by broad-based public announcements. Earlier that morning, I received a telephone call from the associate editor of the local paper informing me of the drug walk that was to occur only four blocks from the church I served as pastor. Not wanting to put an announcement in the paper to forewarn the occupants, the word went out on the street. This particular corner had not always been the drug war zone it had come to be. I wondered, as I had numerous times before, how had the neighborhood come to this? More importantly, I marveled at the energy level of the organically forming crowd as the sun set over the row homes. Here was evidence of a social power I had not previously seen, a collaborative effort to get rid of a problem. I was humbled by their love for the street they called home.

I introduced myself to a neighbor I'll call Louis. He offered me coffee from a little table set up on the sidewalk for the occasion. I asked him which house was being targeted first. "Oh, right there," Louis answered quickly, pointing to a house a couple of doors away. The bright TV lights were now pointing right at the closed windows of the house. "Wow. I wonder what its like living next to a drug house," I asked. "Well, I can answer that," he offered. He was about sixty-five years of age, wearing a town watch jacket with a flashlight attached to his belt. "This is my table, and my coffee, and we're standing in front of my house." Louis looked intently at the targeted house. Shaking his head, looking around at the growing crowd, he sighed, "These drug dealers have made this street a living hell. Hookers bring their johns from the Avenue all times of day and night, right past kids playing, across from the library. Selling drugs, it's gotta stop."

Finally, the organizing leader arrived from his West Philadelphia home. They call him "CB," and he is renowned for outrageous and passionate chanting and public ridicule of drug dealers. After the requisite and thankfully brief introductions of local politicians and the new assistant district attorney, the entire crowd stood in front of that drug house, TV lights glaring. "Up with hope—down with dope!" CB started. The voices of the crowd joined in and wailed against these "invaders" of the neighborhood: "Up with hope—down with dope! Up with hope—down with dope!" "We want you to leave our street, taking your drugs and hookers with you," CB demanded. Louis stood there, smiling. "Maybe there's hope after all," he said. Maybe, indeed.

Operation Sunrise

Philadelphia Police Commissioner Timoney publicly announced a multi-department effort named Operation Sunrise from Wilkey Church's pulpit on June 14, 1998. This Kensington community meeting was called jointly by the mayor's office, police districts 24, 25, and 26, and representatives of city agencies and the federal government. The objectives of Operation Sunrise included (1) reduction of drug trafficking, (2) reduction of youth violence, and (3) reduction of vacant and dangerous housing and lots. More than three hundred people and media representatives attended the meeting, the intention of which was to inform and establish connections with neighbors and faith-based organizations, although none of these groups were consulted in the operation's design or execution. During a private conversation in my office with Commissioner Timoney, I asked about this exclusion. Commissioner Timoney pointed to the need for security, for preventing the targeted drug community from preparing for this kind of offensive. He did admit his desire to include faith- and community-based participation in the future, however. Strategic partnerships between faith-based organizations and the city and federal government can be effective in getting a neighborhood back to work again, but Operation Sunrise was not such a partnership and did not live up to its promise. According to Public/Private Ventures, which documented initiatives in Kensington, "This effort, which was operational in June 1998, could have impacted the homicide rate but faded away in early 2001."[1] I personally witnessed the offensive literally roll down the streets of Kensington on Monday morning, June 15th, and as its name promised, it was launched at sunrise.

Kensington, Philadelphia

Situated along the shores of the Delaware River, about two miles northeast of Philadelphia's City Hall, the area of Kensington was settled in 1630 when Dutch trappers and explorers "discovered" the Lenni Lenape Indians' summer camping grounds with its abundant fish and game. Later, in 1680, the Dutch sold the land grants they acquired to Swedish colonists, who were subsequently conquered by the English. The English Quakers came in great numbers, purchasing more and more land from the Indians and setting up homes and neighborhoods to the north of the future Penn Treaty Park, where in 1682 William Penn purchased land establishing the city of Philadelphia. Quaker and other Protestant religious worship was commonplace in Pennsylvania, "with the first Quaker meeting in the

1. McClanahan, *Alive at 25*, 22.

province."[2] The future city of Philadelphia, which would be established to the south, was still a dream. Almost two hundred years later, in 1854, its younger neighbor swallowed up the city of Kensington, and a premier fishing and shipping town became part of the City of Brotherly Love.

Street conflict was commonplace throughout the entire history of the area. Groups of families fought hard for their economic well-being. Individual effort existed to support the community. With the coming of the English colonists, the Swedes moved to the south. The Indians were always displaced, forced to go somewhere else. When the Revolutionary War broke out, Kensington provided motivated volunteers, called the "Kensington Artillery," who fought the British in the streets when the enemy captured Philadelphia in 1777. Kensington residents defended the site of Penn's Indian treaty, an important local landmark.

The Protestant Christian faith was the predominant religion of Kensington families in the late eighteenth century. In 1780, local congregations organized the first soup kitchens, which were, of necessity, commonplace. When the war finally ended in 1783, shipping and textile industries came back to life. Mills replaced farms, and factories heralding the coming industrial revolution replaced homes as families built new ones further up the river. Community services became increasingly important to the laborer and blue-collar majority. The numbers of unemployed and underemployed grew. Kensington citizens marched to City Hall to protest the Jay Treaty, but Kensington would move from political protest to ethnic fighting in the early 1800s with the increase of immigration. Racial groupings continued to preoccupy people as every group attempted to use resources for their benefit.

Factory doors had signs that read, "Irish need not apply." "Issues surrounding work, religious affiliations, and lack of police"[3] were constant sources of conflict. Railroad riots pitted class and ethnic groups against each other, the conflict even affecting the placement of the railroad itself. Irish immigrants, who brought Roman Catholicism to Kensington, were not at all welcome in most neighborhoods. The year 1844 saw the Kensington Riots between nativist groups, who were Protestant, and Catholic immigrants from Ireland and Germany; the riots were the worst social upheaval in Philadelphia's history to that point. The public schools prohibited the reading of the Roman Catholic Douay Bible. The

---

2. Catrambone and Silcox, *Kensington History*, 7.

3. Ibid., 15.

Presbyterians, Baptists, Lutherans, and other Protestant denominations considered the Catholics as outsiders, the pope against the American way of life. The Catholic children, they argued, needed to read the King James Bible in school as a means of becoming "Americanized." The children endured many conflicts and policy debates in the Philadelphia schools, which finally resulted in "no Bible reading at all," while the bickering "Christians" searched for a more permanent solution that never materialized.

Kensington historian Peter Binzen has identified Kensington as a "Whitetown," a label it shares with other communities with predominantly white, ethnic European residents. In the realm of education, "the Irish, who once considered themselves a mythical breed apart, held 'race conventions' of their own,"[4] wanting to have their own Irish curriculum, which demonstrates the intense energy all racial groups bring to the table. Even the early church's establishment of deacons in Acts 7 was a result of the perceived unequal treatment of Hellenist and Jewish widows in the church. Race issues (including racism, ageism, sexism, and classism), which were essentially unresolved in the 1800s, continued to influence public, private, religious, and industrial life in Kensington throughout the twentieth century.

The early 1900s brought industrial dollars to Kensington. With industries such as glassmaking and shipbuilding, and with the manufacture of saws and Stetson hats, Kensington became the original working-class neighborhood. Its boundaries grew as more and more factories were built and more and more immigrants arrived: Scottish, Irish, Polish, German, and Italian. African Americans, as well as immigrants from Puerto Rico, also moved into Kensington. There was room. There was room because the streets and neighborhoods kept moving up the river and further west. The maps of the time show that an incredible expansion occurred during the early years, but there was no discernible city plan except to segregate the ethnic groups into convenient neighborhoods. It was hoped segregation would minimize racial tension. As Peter Binzen describes the inability to pinpoint Kensington on a map, "Kensington is more a state of mind than a geographic entity; its boundaries shift as housing patterns shift."[5]

Groups of families organized their neighborhoods around trade skills, forming trade unions and guilds. Fraternal lodges and orders were

---

4. Binzen, *Whitetown*, 52.
5. Ibid., 86.

typically designed to bar certain ethnic groups. These volunteer associations were attractive to residents because they offered a way to provide protection from crime, layoffs, firings, and the consequences of business failures. It was a Kensington expectation that everyone belonged to a group that provided advantage and insurance to protect the member's family from an uncertain future. People developed a disproportionate trust for their particular group and a patent distrust for other groups and the society at large. Community efforts were secondary to fraternal ones. The Lutheran Settlement House, for example, expressed a clear faith statement and social commitment that was unique in its effectiveness to organize neighborhoods in southern Kensington. Northern Kensington lacked a capacity for religious tolerance. While Protestants defended and enjoyed their denominations' distinct forms of governance and theological beliefs, they rallied around a common dislike of the Romanists, whom they considered a threat to their way of life.

The Salvation Army began its work in America at a site in Kensington in 1880, underscoring the necessity to address the social and economic woes experienced by the people there. Resources in Kensington were ill-equipped to meet the challenges of a new millennium. As Kensington approached the twentieth century, its story was that of a city still in turmoil internally while externally it had all the staid solidarity of a hard-working neighborhood.

Pre-1940: Ontario Presbyterian Church

In 1907, a group of pastors and laypersons visited the northern neighborhoods of Kensington from the Presbytery of Philadelphia, the regional governing body for the Presbyterian Church. The motivated and organized group of leaders resulted from prayer meetings introduced years earlier by Dwight L. Moody, the famous evangelist from Chicago, and local department store founder and developer John Wanamaker, a Presbyterian layperson. Though other denominations increasingly offered social and spiritual services, the Presbyterians organized their outreach efforts as the Summer Evangelistic Committee (SEC). Energized volunteers and pastors visited neighborhoods beyond the reach of existing Presbyterian churches. The SEC operated Bible school programs for children and adults. Neighbors attended church services set up under the tent on transformed vacant lots.

The intersection of Kensington and Allegheny Avenues had become the center of commerce for greater Kensington, with the trolley line offering economic support. Families kept moving farther north of Allegheny Avenue and between Kensington Avenue and Front Street. Church leaders reported that "being further removed from their church homes created the problem of children reaching Sunday schools and churches without being exposed to the dangers of crossing main city highways."[6] By original design, the congregation was charged to serve its neighborhood.

The SEC, finding no Presbyterian witness at Kensington and Allegheny, set up a tent at E and Westmoreland Streets, just a block or two away. The ministry was a great success, with many children involved in that first summer's program. Between 1907 and 1909, several other locations were utilized for Christian witness, the tent being used during the summer months while a building at or near Kensington Avenue provided a place of worship during the winter. A Princeton seminarian, Jesse Lonsinger, served the small group. Upon his graduation he moved to Westmoreland Street, and arrangements were made to purchase a location for a future church at the southeast corner of H and Ontario Streets for $6,000, the funds being raised by a membership of forty-one and a Sabbath-school enrollment of ninety. (See photo of Ontario Presbyterian Church from 1925.)

Figure 4

6. Ontario Presbyterian Church Anniversary Committee, *Silver Anniversary Review*, 3.

The ministry of Pastor Lonsinger was deeply appreciated by the congregation. His Princeton diploma still hangs on the wall in the church hall named in his honor.

The outreach to the neighborhood was effective, involving many leaders in teaching and planning. When the large SEC tent became unavailable, a portable chapel was purchased from the Methodist Episcopal congregation located at 7th and Erie and moved to the new location. In 1910, the Presbytery of Philadelphia formally constituted the congregation as the Ontario Presbyterian Church, the name "being selected as being significant of its location on Ontario Street."[7] In 1911, the congregation installed its organizing pastor as the first pastor of the church. The motto the congregation adopted after its first full year of ministry was from Psalm 126:3, "The Lord hath done great things for us; whereof we are glad." You can still see the faint image of these words painted long ago along the inner sanctuary wall.

Several church building projects were completed, providing needed space for expanded ministry programs. Many volunteer leaders from the congregation became employed full-time in church ministry. The neighborhood considered Ontario Presbyterian welcoming and responsive to their needs.

The Great Depression hit Kensington hard—mills and shipyards closed. Those who lost their jobs in the neighborhood began to seek work outside the city. Suburbs were just beginning to form around Philadelphia, and they offered not only jobs but housing. Financial and economic resources were scarce in Kensington, and as families relocated, their collective social and community resources went with them, making an already desperate situation even worse for those who remained.

1940 to 1998: Wilkey Memorial Presbyterian Church

After more than thirty-three years of ministry on the corner of H and Ontario Streets, the name of the church was changed to Wilkey Memorial United Presbyterian Church in 1941. While changing the church's name might at first appear to be only a technicality, it represented a fundamental disconnect from its community context.

The pastor, the Reverend Jesse Lonsinger, was adamantly opposed to the name change under any circumstances, as I learned during personal

7. Ibid., 11.

conversations with current church members. "They're just words," recounted a senior member of the congregation when speaking of the name change. The prevailing attitude of the congregation was centered on the financial benefits that they would enjoy. The Wilkey sisters, who had no previous connection with Ontario Presbyterian, offered their property and approximately $50,000 to the Presbytery of Philadelphia. They insisted that upon their death a church be established with their money, on their property, and that the name of the church bear their own. As it turned out, the Philadelphia Board of Education acquired the property from the Presbytery of Philadelphia, which had accepted the funds in trust. Then word was on the street that the Wilkey estate money was available for use by an existing congregation as long as the name change met the conditions of the will. The leaders of three Presbyterian churches—Palethorpe, Bethany, and Ontario—sent letters to the Presbytery requesting that their congregation receive the funds; all three would be willing to become "Wilkey Church." Some insiders at the presbytery thought Ontario's proximity to the Wilkey sisters' estate placed it at the top of the list, and ultimately it received the bequest.

However, the heirs of the estate took the presbytery and Ontario Presbyterian Church to court, and though the church prevailed in the end, court costs and fees reduced the amount of the estate to less than $25,000. Because of poor health, Pastor Lonsinger, who had already curtailed his pastoral duties for some months due to illness, resigned in April 1941. The congregation formally adopted its new name one month later. The name change was a death knell to neighborhood ministry on that corner.

The congregation should have resisted its preoccupation with itself. This preoccupation was beginning to take its toll. During those years, the congregation started to grow distant from the neighborhood. More and more families began moving farther away from the encroaching city of Philadelphia, with its diverse economic and racial mix, as the city moved farther and farther up Kensington Avenue. Lloyd Hartley, in his retrospect on urban literature, reports that Philadelphia was typical of northern and northeastern U.S. cities in its "expanding population of migrating African Americans and Puerto Ricans during and following the war, and its rapid suburban expansion."[8] The urbanization of inner-city neighborhoods was scratching at yet more streets and the majority of

8. Quoted in Green, *Churches, Cities, and Human Community*, 315.

residents living near the church were not tolerating these racial, social, and economic changes.

The roots of the Ontario congregation, now informally referred to as Wilkey Church, were in evangelistic mission and neighborhood ministry, which grew out of the Summer Evangelistic Committee's community analysis and assessment. They determined that the plight of the Sunday school children and the risk they faced crossing busy streets warranted a Christian presence. Getting children safely to church activities was mission-critical to those early church leaders. Recapturing this historical capacity is incredibly powerful.

Out of that loving commitment, the tent invited more and more families to organize themselves there. "These people really care about our kids," a resident of Kensington might have concluded in 1907. "We don't have to worry anymore about crossing Kensington Avenue for church on the Lord's Day, dear. We can worship at Ontario Presbyterian, at the tent right around the corner. And they offer special Sunday school classes for the kids." The neighborhood was then considered suburbia; urban ministry did not underlie the initial mandate, but neighborhood outreach did. The neighborhood capacity must determine the nature of transformational ministry.

The point of naming a church is to identify the unique message of the congregation in a certain neighborhood. Congregation names are vehicles for mission. When a name no longer represents a congregation's unique message, or when a congregation wants to promote a different message in the neighborhood, the name may need to be changed.

When its name changed from a neighborhood-based name to a personality-based name, Ontario Presbyterian's effective neighborhood mission diminished. As the marketing world observed when Michael Jordan switched his athletic shoe endorsement from Reebok to arch-rival Nike, the sales changed overnight. Instantly, Reebok was out and Nike was in, because the kids bought the personality, not the shoe manufacturer. In 1908, 100 percent of the congregation of forty-one lived in the immediate neighborhood. In 1925, the church reported its highest membership of 775 people to Presbytery. More than 75 percent of these people lived in the immediate neighborhood.

With the community based on industry and mills, the 1920s saw the attendance and neighborhood involvement of the church at its peak. When the Depression of the late 1920s and early 1930s impacted the neighborhood, the church established a deacons' board to help meet the financial needs of struggling families. The realities of an unstable neighborhood economy took a toll. As the economy of a neighborhood goes, so goes the economic base of the church. A neighborhood without a strong, viable economy will deteriorate, unless the church takes a stand and begins to work on systemic and economic solutions.[9]

According to church records and personal interviews, it seems that elders, trustees, and members began moving out of the immediate neighborhood in the 1950s, after the initial exodus of about thirty families in 1941 (which occurred after the church's name change). The attendance from 1908 to 1930 steadily increased. Then, after the downward bump of the Depression and the upward bump following World War II, there was a kind of stasis in membership. In 1960, according to church records, 30 percent of the membership lived outside the neighborhood. In 1980, only 30 percent remained in the neighborhood. By the year 1990, less than 10 percent of the membership was made up of neighborhood folks. With no parking facilities, no suburban or regional mandate, and without a clear mission to the city, Wilkey Church was effectively cut off from its own neighborhood—it became a stranger.

Sociologist Georg Simmel might have been describing Wilkey's relationship to its community when he wrote, "The stranger is by his very nature no owner of land—land not only in the physical sense but also metaphorically as a vital substance which is fixed, if not in space, then at least in an ideal position within the social environment."[10] Michael J. Christensen, in his handbook for urban ministry, rhetorically asks, "Why is old First Church invisible to the community while Pilgrim's Rest Ebenezer Baptist Church is well known and respected? Because old First Church, somewhere along the way, stopped serving the community, became a commuter church, and lost touch with the neighborhood. Pilgrim's Rest, on the other hand, stayed involved in the community and was available to serve, and this is reflected in its name."[11] The bad news is that though there are many churches in urban areas, there are very few churches doing urban ministry, because they have become strangers. The good news is that a congregation is not victim to its past or slave to its present and need not remain a stranger. We don't need more churches

---

9. Lupton, *Return Flight*, 19.
10. Simmel, "The Stranger," in Lemert, *Social Theory*, 201.
11. Christensen, *Call for Compassion*, 87.

simply located in the neighborhood; we need more congregations connecting with the neighborhood.[12]

When the neighborhood has become a stranger to the congregation, the leader's priority task is to reneighbor the church back to the neighborhood so that the church becomes a good neighbor once again. Every congregation must connect to its own neighborhood. While a church can do more and have influence beyond the local community context, it dare not do less.

The name change was at least symbolic of an important lack of congregational interest in the neighborhood—in effect, it gave the congregation "permission" to divest itself from the problems its members sought to flee by relocating their homes to the suburbs. Churches especially must develop a theology of location inextricably bound up with their theology of mission. I am hoping that someday our congregation will again have its location in its name—and maybe, instead of the limited word *Presbyterian*, include a word such as *Community* or *Neighborhood*. For me, that would describe where we are and who we are.

Our church was named Ontario Community Church precisely because it was chartered to be a transformational presence in that community. Earning the right to be that kind of presence requires a ministry reboot that begins with a respectful, deeper understanding of the community's context.

Capacity for Ministry: Wilkey Church

The half-mile radius around Wilkey Church is a mostly residential area, row homes built in the 1920s, with the remnants and decaying shells of large mills and factories peppering the landscape. Eighty percent of the large buildings are vacant, run-down, often sites for homeless squatting, drug dealing, and vandalism. Some of these large structures are being utilized by businesses, but many are mere shadows of what they once were.

To better understand the historical and current capacity of the congregation for ministry, our leadership collected and analyzed relevant and reliable information about the church itself. My intervention in Kensington as part of a doctor of ministry program benefited from the

---

12. Linthicum, *City of God*.

formation of an Institutional Review Board, including leaders from the church and community.

Avery Dulles' six congregational identities in his *Models of the Church*[13] is a useful lens for understanding the church's core values and exploring its spiritual DNA. The models include (1) Church as Institution—an ordered community for governance, ecclesiastical practice, and sacraments; (2) Church as Mystical Communion—a worshiping community of believers; (3) Church as Sacrament—the visible sign of God's presence through its buildings and in the lives of its adherents; (4) Church as Herald—a witnessing community inviting others to faith; (5) Church as Servant—a mission community that promotes justice, peace, reconciliation, and compassion; and (6) Church as School of Discipleship—a community for spiritual formation, learning, and growth.

When Ontario Church began, the congregation was best described as a Herald church. The mission challenged the status quo. The congregation was proactive and it addressed neighborhood problems in the name of Jesus Christ. As time went by, the engagement seemed to be localized within the church itself, and not externally in the community, and so it could be described as more of an Institution church. Between the years 1925 and 1965, the church offered many programs that appeared to meet congregational needs, but the racist and neighborhood-abandonment issues skewed the understanding of these needs. As an Institution, it focused primarily on self-preservation and conserving its own resources to maintain its governance and internal order. The church failed to address important community issues, including root causes of poverty, systemic racism, and neighborhood abandonment. While the congregation would have self-described as a Servant, in fact it was an Institution. Over the years, the church diminished its capacity to be the Herald and Servant every church is called to be.

Demographic Realities: Usable Present

Wilkey Memorial Presbyterian Church is located at the corner of H and Ontario Streets in the Kensington neighborhood of Philadelphia. We won a grant that paid a photographer to provide an aerial photograph of our neighborhood. We had it printed and mounted on a large, three-foot by four-foot foamcore board that we took everywhere to help

---

13. Dulles, *Models of the Church*, 1–7.

us tell the neighborhood's story. As a leader, it is essential to acquire and study relevant demographic data such as that provided by MissionInsite.[14] For example, the number of widowed or divorced persons in Kensington is 1.5 times the national average, and the percentage of single heads of household with children is more than 50 percent greater than the national average. This suggests an opportunity to implement educational and community-building services that can stem not only family fragmentation but also the attendant incarceration and economic and social fragmentation in the community. "This fragmentation

Figure 5

or breakdown creates a context where trying to solve the symptoms only sustains them," writes Peter Block.[15] Even more of our families would have moved out long ago were it not for the sharp decline in real estate prices. In North America, the presumption still exists that during the course of a working person's lifetime, personal income and home real estate market value will rise. But during the past twenty years, both have experienced sharp decline, shattering family expectations.

Housing statistics indicate that in our North Philadelphia neighborhood, the number of families living in shelters or on the street is four times the national average. In 1993, homeowners outnumbered renters within a three-mile radius, but updates from local congressional staff indicate that only 65 percent of the families within a half-mile radius

14. See www.missioninsite.com
15. Block, *Community*, 53.

of Wilkey Church currently own their homes—at least a 10 percent decrease from five years ago.

Though still predominately a European-American neighborhood, trend figures and local sources indicate a decline of this group. Hispanic, African-American, and Asian groups now show about 30 percent Hispanic, 35 percent African-American, and 2 percent Asian within a 0.3-mile radius. The realities of this mix indicate a capacity for intentional non-European-American ministry. Identifying and cultivating Hispanic and African-American leadership has lagged behind the direct service to this demographic in the community. North Philadelphia neighborhoods have been predominately non-European ethnic for a longer period than Kensington and thus have a mature base of leadership. Building relationships with the adjacent neighborhoods enables partnerships to meet this challenge. Growing out of our monthly pastors' prayer breakfast, a bilingual community worship service intentionally connected our northern Kensington churches with Hispanic and African-American churches from west Kensington and North Philadelphia. In all, seven churches and more than 150 people celebrated a common commitment to their faith and a love for the neighborhoods we live in.

Fifty percent of those living within a half-mile radius of Wilkey are Surviving Multi-Ethnic Urbanites (3,000 households), while 33 percent are Working Urban Singles (1,900 households). Our congregation is in fact reaching a minority of the population—we are representing only five of the neighborhood's eighty-eight households in the demographic category Aging Cautious Retirees (those who are ready to move to retirement homes outside the neighborhood or who will die within twenty years) and eight hundred Empty Nesters. This neighborhood diversity presents an enormous challenge—and opportunity.

"Youth are a unifying force in community," Block observes. "An alternative future opens when we shift our view of youth (say 14 to 24 years old) from problem to possibility, from deficiency to gift."[16] Shifting from problems to asset-based possibilities became the next point of engagement.

---

16. Ibid., 216.

4

Words Have Power

Figure 6

Jesus reached out and touched him, saying, "Be clean." Then and there, all signs of the leprosy were gone. Jesus said, "Don't talk about this all over town. Just quietly present your healed body to the priest, along with the appropriate expressions of thanks to God. Your cleansed and grateful life, not your words, will bear witness to what I have done." (Matt 8:3–4 MSG)

Stigma through the Lens of History

Recall the old children's adage "sticks and stones will break my bones, but words will never harm me"? Of course, words can hurt and our words matter. The Bible's Levitical Code is derived from the book of Leviticus. It describes the effects of stigma and the social isolation imposed on those deemed to have an infectious disease such as leprosy. Upon discovering her infectious disease, the priests removed Miriam from the general population for seven days (Num 12:15). Most others with an infectious skin disease were kept in isolation indefinitely, as described in Leviticus 13:45–46: "The person with such an infectious disease must wear torn clothes, let his hair be unkempt, cover the lower part of his face and cry out, 'Unclean! Unclean!' As long as he has the infection he remains unclean. He must live alone; he must live outside the camp." The Levitical priest had the responsibility to diagnose skin diseases. If leprosy was confirmed, the priest had the authority to mark the person as "unclean," putting them out of the camp indefinitely. Once removed, there was no recourse to a physical cure and therefore no hope of returning to the community.[1]

There was no intervention afforded those diagnosed with this illness. There was a precise Levitical cleansing protocol that determined if the stigma could be removed from those whose symptoms diminished or who were cured of a less serious disease. Unfortunately, the priest rarely had reason to pronounce anyone cured of leprosy. Jesus reminded his hearers that in Elijah's time, only Naaman was cured of leprosy (2 Kgs 5:1ff.), and many had to endure the severe social consequences, which were as painful in many respects as the physical ailments themselves.

The stigmatic nature of leprosy even regulated the disposition of the body after death. Typical burial narratives reported that the deceased "rested with their fathers and were buried with them," as was the case with Jotham (2 Kgs 15:38) and Ahaz (2 Kgs 16:20), who did not have leprosy. Honor and respect for the deceased were conveyed through the close proximity of the bodies in burial. If the deceased had leprosy, honor and respect were nowhere to be found. We read in another burial narrative, "Uzziah rested with his fathers and was buried near them in a field for burial that belonged to the kings, for people said, 'He had leprosy'" (2 Chron 26:23), and of Azariah's burial we read, "Azariah rested with

---

1. Unlike noninfectious "unclean" designations that had a corresponding and specific period of outcast status, i.e., seven days; see Leviticus 11 and 12.

his fathers and was buried near them in the City of David" (2 Kgs 15:7). Uzziah and Azariah were victims of leprosy. The stigma endured even after death.

Stigma can be redemptive, as seen in the unique case of Cain as told in Genesis. After he killed his brother, Abel, God set a curse on Cain to live in exile. He feared for his life and believed that anyone catching him would kill him. God offered a remedy, which we read of in Genesis 4:15, where God assures Cain that no one will harm him: "The LORD said to him, 'Not so; if anyone kills Cain, he will suffer vengeance seven times over.' Then the LORD put a mark on Cain so that no one who found him would kill him." This stigma was a sign that sent a clear message, which Cain could not remove until he found a remedy to lift it. He never did.

The Apostle Paul attested to his apostolic authority using the image of a stigma when he warned, "Finally, let no one cause me trouble, for I bear on my body the marks of Jesus" (Gal 6:17). Unlike every other occurrence of the word "mark" translated from the Greek root for "write," this verse uses the classical root word for an animal branding, στιγματα, the only mention of stigmata in the Greek New Testament.

It was the Greeks, ever preoccupied with the human form, who originated the term *stigma* to refer to bodily signs "designed to expose something unusual and bad about the moral status of the signifier."[2] The unmistakable mark bore witness to what was missing on the inside based on the appearance of the outside.

Those who have been stigmatized, labeled like material judged to be deficient, are not without hope. As Origen wrote in the third century, the poor are said to be "the rag, tag and bobtail of humanity. But Jesus does not leave them that way. Out of material you would have thrown away as useless, he fashions [people of strength], giving them back their self-respect, enabling them to stand on their feet and look God in the eye. They were cowed, cringing, broken things. But the Son has set them free!"[3]

---

2. Goffman, *Stigma*, 1.

3. Origen (third-century AD), quoted in Linthicum, *City of God*, i.

Jesus and Stigma

In the first chapter of the Gospel of John, we observe a striking difference between Andrew's description of Jesus to Simon and Philip's description of Jesus to Nathanael (see Table 1).

Table 1: Jesus' Descriptions Reveal Positive or Negative Responses			
Speaker	*Listener*	*Descriptor*	*Response*
Andrew	Simon	Jesus the Messiah	Positive
Philip	Nathanael	Jesus of Nazareth	Negative

John 1:35 illustrates the reality of stigma. Meeting the Messiah was a wonderfully attractive idea to Simon. John the Baptist had been preparing his disciple Andrew to meet Jesus, the Messiah. It would fulfill the desire of his heart. By contrast, notice how Philip introduced Jesus to Nathanael. Philip described Jesus not by his title but by his hometown. Nathanael held a preconceived bias (though popularly understood to be a deserved attribute), namely, that Nazareth was a bad place to come from.

When Philip invited Nathanael to meet Jesus he said, "We have found the one Moses wrote about in the Law, and about whom the prophets also wrote—Jesus of Nazareth, the son of Joseph" (1:45). He appealed to Nathanael's knowledge of the Scriptures. But for Nathanael something did not quite fit. "'Nazareth! Can anything good come from there?' Nathanael asked" (1:46). Only by Philip's challenge did Nathanael make his way towards Jesus. The solution for Nathanael was to encounter Jesus who "saw him under the fig tree." Incredibly, he knew Jesus saw him for who he really was. This awakened his interest and overcame his repulsion of the Nazareth stigma that Jesus bore. He saw Jesus differently after realizing that Jesus saw him completely.

Jesus grew up in Nazareth. He knows what it is like to live in a stigmatized community like Kensington. Nazareth, "which rests in a hilltop basin that today seems to shut out the outside world," was regarded as an isolated village.[4] The stigma attributed to Jesus took on a deeper significance when "nail-pierced hands" became a sign of the resurrection.[5]

---

4. Teringo, *Land and People Jesus Knew*, 20.

5. Compare John 20:27, "Then he said to Thomas, 'Put your finger here; see my hands. Reach out your hand and put it into my side. Stop doubting and believe,'" and John 20:25, "So the other disciples told him, 'We have seen the Lord!' But he said to them, 'Unless I see the nail marks in his hands and put my finger where the nails were,

Church history chronicles several people who experienced the marks of Jesus. Stigma in this context refers to a singular mark, while stigmata refers to multiple marks, which were externally observed, rather than to a societal stain or association. The most well-known stigmata were experienced by Saint Francis of Assisi, who in 1224 was believed to so identify with his Savior's death that on his hands appeared the nail-pierced marks. As of 1894, 321 cases had been recorded, and there have been many more. The Italian stigmatic Padre Pio died in 1968; in 1997 he was declared "venerable," a step on the road to sainthood.

In 1992, a stigmatic Catholic, Father James Bruse, displayed similar wounds. The Bruse account was more than just a reporting of the stigmata—religious statues wept and changed colors in his presence, and several people experienced healing. Some church authorities and many skeptics questioned the report's veracity. To be sure, many stigmatic reports are hoaxes, or they may be psychosomatic, that is, a physical manifestation of the stigmatic's mental condition rather than a religious or authentic divine source as in the case of the Apostle Paul.

Stigmata are not a variant on "getting your ears pierced." The stigmatic wounds reportedly just appear and sometimes keep on appearing. A classic nineteenth-century case was Louise Lateau, who reportedly got them every Friday for fifteen years. These historical examples amply demonstrate the profound power of stigma. Yet, it must be remembered that Jesus was not only "from Nazareth" but in fact referred to himself with the transforming and powerful words "I am Jesus of Nazareth" when addressing Saul on the road to Damascus (Acts 22:8).

Stigma through the Lens of Media

Today some businesses can leverage the negative connotation of a word and redirect it to their advantage. Such is the case with an Italian marketing company named Stigma. When I inquired about their brand, they offered the following explanation of how they chose such a name for their business:

> The name Stigma was chosen for several reasons. One was that it was short and monosyllabic. The second was that it was synonymous with "branding," the type of advertising challenge that we face. Third is that the word traditionally does portray a negative

and put my hand into his side, I will not believe it.'"

connotation, and we felt that we could put a positive spin on it, making it stand out in clients' minds.[6]

The nature of stigma is clearly negative even when a company seeks to use it as a compelling reverse attribute or challenge. More often than not, we reserve stigma for appalling behaviors, conditions,[7] or areas, and severely debilitating diseases such as leprosy and mental illness. Welfare stigma analyzes the effects of stigma within an economic program evaluation.[8] The Presbyterian Church (U.S.A.) produced and distributed a media campaign with full-color posters and fact sheets to its churches entitled "Lifting the Stigma of Mental Illness." It featured the image of a butterfly, implying that the power to lift the mental illness stigma could come from within. However, as I have learned, the nature of stigma is such that it cannot be lifted alone. If it can be lifted through one's own ability alone, it is not a stigma. Mental illness professionals, in particular, have even sought to disassociate the illness from stigma, with one doctor arguing that "the stigma surrounding the mentally ill constitutes a serious problem" and that "we need to pay more attention to how the names we use to label disorders such as depression promote stigmas."[9] Promoting stigma by using the label of "stigma" underscores its devastating impact. Dr. Bernard Arons, director of the Center for Mental Health Services in Washington DC, observes that stigma is both real and painful.

Some communities promote themselves as good places to live by displaying advertisements and billboards in neighborhoods generally regarded as deficient. A billboard along a highway that bisects Kensington advertised the desirability of the Pennsauken community, located across the Delaware River in New Jersey. It might as well have read, "Move to a Safer Neighborhood—Come to Pennsauken." Our messaging can send subtle messages of unacceptability. Media can reinforce stigma and undermine hope.

Stigma has a profound effect on people who endure it. Sol Finkelman described his own understanding of stigma in his moving poem titled "Why a Stigma."[10]

---

6. Victor Chan, principal of Stigma, personal message to author.

7. "Welfare stigma" is another association for the stigma label as well as the title of a volume on that subject. See Wüstenbecker, *Welfare Stigma*.

8. Wüstenbecker, *Welfare Stigma*.

9. Kimel, *Slackers, Stigma, and Depression*.

10. Finkelman, "Why a Stigma."

With mental illness people live,
By many it's not understood,
Not much relief can doctors give,
A stigma covers like a hood.

All heart conditions we accept,
And diabetes is no shame;
But mental illness is unwept,
As though somehow they are to blame.

In ancient times 'twas thought a curse,
By God or witch had been induced;
To date we can't this myth reverse,
From ancient lore we can't be loosed.

As illness treated by doctors all,
So many stages have they named;
To anyone this may befall,
For disrespect we should be shamed.

Stigma through the Lens of Sociology

Understanding Community through Social Encounters: Erving Goffman

Using the lens of sociology, pastoral leaders can more completely understand the interactions that can either improve or, in many circumstances, impair effective transformational engagement. To noted sociologist Dr. Erving Goffman (1922–82), social encounters define our world, "involving [us] either in face-to-face or mediated contact with other participants."[11] Goffman refers to the deeper self that can be shown and known as our face. The face we have is defined in terms of approved social attributes, and our feelings "become attached to it."[12] If events establish a face for me that is better than I expected, I feel good. If not, I feel bad. I put forth a line, as Goffman puts it, that is either affirmed or denied. Sometimes it may be a draw, so that our feelings are not changed one

---

11. Goffman, "On Face-Work," in Lemert, *Social Theory*, 358.
12. Ibid., 359.

way or the other. We may be said to save face when our response to an encounter is consistent with what others expected, or we may be said to lose face when our response is not consistent, thus feeling humiliated. For Goffman, the neighborhood of Kensington (or one of its sixty-five thousand residents) may be said to put forth a line, a face, to the general society around it, and the response from the society to it. Both together form its self-understanding. Kensington has accumulated social interaction data points for more than 250 years. Individuals and systems, like neighborhoods, can be affected by stigma, often correlated to abusive or inappropriate use of power.

To help us visualize community stigma, let's substitute the word "Kensington" each time Goffman uses the word "he" in his original text, as follows: "If *Kensington* is in wrong face or out of face, *Kensington* is likely to feel ashamed and inferior because of what has happened to the activity on *Kensington's* account and because of what may happen to *Kensington's* reputation as a participant."[13] Goffman gives us insight into how a neighborhood can become stigmatized through encounters that repeatedly and continuously reinforce that the community is in wrong face. Stigma that is imposed by social processes "can be firmly entrenched in the particular locale and social groups that make the context meaningful."[14] Stigma is experienced personally but can be localized contextually.

Goffman's "face" concept also speaks to the encounters of a church member who travels a distance to the location of the church. Such a person may "sense" she is in wrong face or out of face. She is likely to feel ashamed and inferior because of what has happened to the neighborhood on her account and because of what may happen to her reputation as a participant.[15]

Goffman described stigma as having two characteristics: that of being discredited and that of being discreditable.[16] Face-to-face interactions will necessitate a way of managing the stigma, but Goffman does not offer any solutions for its elimination. For those who interact with the

---

13. Ibid., 360.
14. Howarth, Nicholson, and Whitney, "Stigma," 4.
15. Goffman, "On Face-Work," in Lemert, *Social Theory*, 360.
16. Goffman, *Stigma*, 4.

discredited, tension management is suggested, and information control is prescribed.[17] The three domains of stigma include

- physical stigma (deformities, dwarfism, disabilities);
- character stigma (alcoholism, addiction, attempted suicide, unemployment, mental illness); and
- tribal stigma (race, ethnicity, religion).

Those living without stigma are a baseline that is considered normal. The person who possesses an undesirable differentness has a stigma, and when it becomes known to him, the response can include hopelessness, humiliation, anger, or aggression.[18] Goffman sees the attribution of stigma as a root of discrimination, and thus racism, classism, nationalism, sexism, ageism, and genderism can be understood as universally applied stigmas due to differences. The tribal stigma is particularly onerous since there is no rite of passage by which a person in one discredited group can enter into a so-called normal group.

Goffman correctly observed that even if a person successfully attempts a remedy for his stigma, the person moves to another discredited group, namely, that of the previously stigmatized,[19] and the cycle of victimization ensues. A remedy may be possible with physical and character stigma types, such as when an individual seeks an operation or treatment to diminish the undesirable differentness. A remedy for tribal stigma such as race is decidedly more problematic.[20] Relief may be found in "purposeful social action."[21] Although Goffman helps put a face on stigma, he has no resource to offer a stigmatized neighborhood like Kensington that would remedy its virtual stigmatized image. Kensington suffers from a tribal stigma rooted in its political, geographic context, passed on to each successive generation. There exists the possibility that Kensington can discover its true identity. Kensington's virtual identity is in the eyes of society that imputes the stigma. As with individuals who are victimized by physical, character, or tribal stigmas, Kensington's authentic identity

---

17. Ibid., 138.
18. Ibid., 128.
19. Ibid., 9.
20. See Wailoo, "Stigma, Race, and Disease," 531–33.
21. Goffman, *Stigma*, 138.

must be imputed by someone or something that is an authentic, reliable, and superior source, namely, God the Creator.

Using Goffman's understanding of "face" as a lens, we can construct a paradigm of transformation to track renewal in Kensington, as depicted in the Transformation Paradigm for Intervention (see fig. 7).

Figure 7

G%%od%%, *face established*

I%%mage-bearer%%, *face born*

S%%in%%, *facelessness*

S%%tigma%%, *face stained*

I%%ncarnation%%, *face loved*

B%%roken body%%, *face died*

R%%esurrection%%, *face restored*

R%%estored body%%, *face lives*

A%%scension%%, *face lifts*

S%%tigmata%%, *face sees*

F%%orgiveness%%, *face free*

I%%mage-bearer%%, *face reborn*

G%%od%%, *face enjoyed*

We can see as we move clockwise through the paradigm that it begins and ends with God, a framework for the story of the good news. David J. Bosch, the influential missiologist and theologian, recognized the larger Creator Context when he wrote, "The life and work of the Christian community are intimately bound up with God's cosmic-historical plan for the redemption of the universe."[22] The paradigm attempts to identify discrete, sequential transformational phases along a continuum of God's interaction with the whole created order. It begins with God. We understand *face established*. Humanity created in God's image becomes the image-bearer (Gen 1:26–27) with a *face born*, male and female. As described in the creation narratives (Gen 1–3), we understand sin's consequence (*facelessness*), when humankind moved out from the face of God (Gen 3:8). Sin, like a mark, a stigma, left the *face stained* (Gen 3:23). When God

---

22. Bosch, *Transforming Mission*, 150.

became flesh and blood in the incarnation (John 1:14), Jesus—the perfect man, Son of God—displayed a *face loved* (Luke 3:22). With the sacrificial death, *face died* with Jesus' broken body (1 Cor 11:24). But the paradigm then takes a redemptive turn with the good news of Jesus' resurrection, with *face restored* (1 Cor 15:21). Jesus' resurrection body bears witness as *face lives* (John 20:26–27), and with the ascension *face lifts* up again (Acts 1:9). Goffman's lens helps us understand Kensington's stigma diagnosis, which is represented as *face sees* along the continuum. That is, the entire community that is marked with a stigma can be engaged in a process of self-understanding and discovery to see the stigma themselves. (Consider similar moments of transformational self-understanding: the women at Jesus' empty tomb "remembered his words" [Luke 24:8]; the men who left Jerusalem along the road to Emmaus did not know that it was the risen Jesus speaking with them until "their eyes were opened and they recognized him" during a sacred meal [Luke 24:31].) We recognize the marks on ourselves and can also identify with the marks on Christ's body so that when *face lifts*, we understand that the mark can be removed from the community, too. Forgiveness sets the (once stained) *face free*. In this redemptive experience of transformation, the entire community becomes an image-bearer with *face reborn*. God is experienced in the community as *face enjoyed* when the transformation process is accomplished.

Building Community through Social Encounters: George Mead

George H. Mead (1862–1931) is one of the social interactionists who add an inner dialogue to Goffman's helpful analysis of external face-to-face encounters. If Goffman is correct, the historical stigmatizing has substituted the virtual for the actual identity of Kensington. Where Goffman concludes with a vague solution for purposeful social action, Mead steps in and provides a paradigm for the stigma's removal through self reimagining.

Mead suggests that "the self cannot appear in consciousness as an I, since it is always an object, that is, a Me."[23] The I and Me are produced through engagement, and for Mead, everything is based on community and relationship. The self cannot perceive of itself except as an object. We talk to ourselves; we do not see our selves. I talk to myself, and I remember what I said. When I remember what I said I relate to this memory as

---

23. Mead, "Social Self," 374.

a Me.²⁴ The I reacts to the self through the attitudes of others. Through the attitudes of others, we come to know the Me. We react to the Me as an I. "The I of this moment is present in the Me of the next moment."²⁵ Who I am (Mead's Self) is defined by the parts of me that others engage (Mead's Me). My evaluation of that interaction—good or bad attributes of stigma, for example—tell me who I am. For Mead, the self is that part of us that is not the organism of the body. Rather, it is both object and subject. Self needs objectivity, so that I can talk to my self. The self cannot comprehend the whole thing.²⁶

The Me is that part of the self that is created by others, maintained in community, viewed by the self as the outside, external person would, through the I. It is my self package that can be offered in the context of social experience. It is the attitude others give to my Me. I have lots of selves expressed through Me's—one for each distinctive social setting.²⁷

To continue the Mead paradigm, keep in mind that stigma is closely correlated to behaviors of discrimination. An I without Me equals slavery. "Assumptions about stigmatized identity often informed broader discriminatory social policies,"²⁸ writes Dr. Keith Wailoo of the department of history at Rutgers University. (He compellingly underscores this point with a cartoon illustrating the American Red Cross's practice of racial segregation of blood plasma during World War II.) An individual cannot possess an I if there is no Me. Without a Me, it is understood that I have no memory, no organized sets of attitudes about others, and thus have no self to be observed by others in the first place. Without a Me, I am I-less, and remain without political power and social legitimacy. The I is that part of Me I respond to directly. The attitude of the community to Me is their response to my Me, while my response to my Me is my I. A Me can be stigmatized, despised, counted worthless in its interaction with the outside. The Me wears the stigma, as does the I. It is the Me of the stigmatized individual or neighborhood that must be altered. This understanding of identity formation and deformation will help us develop an intervention of transformation for the Kensington community, especially the children suffering stigma rooted in their location.

---

24. Morris, *Mind, Self, Society*, 174.
25. Ibid.
26. Ibid., 142.
27. Ibid.
28. Wailoo, "Stigma, Race, and Disease," para. 15.

Kensington's Children

The children in Kensington live in a community that has been unfairly tarnished with the stigma of worthlessness, which has substituted a false identity for the authentic identity. However, stigma can affect many different Me's, since we have multiple Me's. The I interacts with each of them. Individuals can choose not to interact with the attitude description others have given, believing themselves to be invincible compared to others. But in that case, there is no dialogue in seeing the Me as an object; the I is voiceless and disconnected. The person is enslaved, not involved in the community wholly or authentically. Removing the stigma requires an alternative observation, a new Me that is affirmed and honored, not detached.

Mead and Goffman provide tools to reimagine and rebuild the children's self that is created in God's image. To remove the stigma, an intervention can be designed to resource a new I for the children. The intervention can help them reconnect, reimagining their deeper, truer self. Then a new, accurate I can insist that others "take a different attitude" which shapes or recreates a new Me.[29] A drawing intervention will enable the children to express themselves through trusting relationships with the church's leaders. Through responsible pastoral care, the church's leaders can help them create a new self by introducing them to the God who loves them.

According to George Mead, "Thinking becomes preparatory to social action."[30] From this inner conversation of thinking the church can become effective agents of transformation in the neighborhood. "Then you will know the truth, and the truth will set you free" (John 8:32).

Kensington as a Type of Nazareth

In 1909, Kensington residents found work in 211 different job classifications, according to the United States Department of Commerce. Ninety-plus years later, in 2000, only seventy job classifications made the list. In the most recent census data, more than 25 percent of our families lived below the poverty line and 15.9 percent were unemployed.[31] As

---

29. Mead, *Mind, Self, and Society*, quoted in Lemert, *Social Theory*, 248.
30. Ibid., 246.
31. See *Socio-Economic Characteristics for Philadelphia Census Tracts: General Characteristics of Persons: 1990.*

Dr. Robert Lupton discovered in neighborhoods similar to Kensington in Atlanta, Georgia, "A community will not remain healthy if it is not economically viable."[32] In Kensington, organizing against the dangers of drugs became an economic issue not just a moral one. Some organizations have "defined the police as bad and argued that drug sales were a rational economic choice for the poor teenagers who were the breadwinners in many households."[33]

Vacant houses and abandoned lots pepper the run-down blocks of Kensington, which suffers one of the highest vacancy and abandoned lot ratios in all of Philadelphia, lending credence to a persistent neighborhood repulsion in the minds of area residents, whether they live in Kensington, have left Kensington, or merely have heard disparaging news about the community. High incidences of arrests for violence, prostitution, and drugs earned Kensington the "Badlands" designation frequently used by the city's own police commissioner in 1998, and for more than a decade the name persisted as a potent, unforgiving judgment.[34]

From Wilkey Church's pulpit, on June 14, 1998, Police Commissioner John Timoney announced the beginning of Operation Sunrise, the City of Philadelphia's multi-department effort to curtail lawlessness and blight. The Kensington community meeting was jointly sponsored by the mayor's office, Police Districts 24, 25, and 26, and representatives of city agencies and the federal government. The objectives of Operation Sunrise included reduction of drug trafficking, reduction of youth violence, and reduction of vacant and dangerous housing and lots.

More than three hundred people and media representatives attended the meeting, which was intended to inform and connect with neighbors and faith-based organizations, although no organizations were consulted in the operation's design or execution. When I asked about this exclusion, Commissioner Timoney pointed to the need for security, not wanting the targeted drug community to be able to prepare for this kind of offensive. He admitted his desire to include faith- and community-based participation in the future, however. Strategic partnerships between faith-based organizations and the city and federal government rarely happen without intentional leadership. We were just beginning to demonstrate that faith-based organizations were committed to being a strategic neighbor and

---

32. Lupton, *Return Flight*, 19.
33. Goode and Schneider, *Reshaping Ethnic and Racial Relations*, 258.
34. Kissane, "We Call It the Badlands."

eager to get a neighborhood back to wellness and work again. Operation Sunrise was no such partnership and did not live up to its promise. I witnessed the operation literally roll down the streets of Kensington on Monday morning, June 15th, at sunrise, as expected. Though laws can be enforced, hope cannot be. Neither could laws lift Kensington's stigma, which sapped the spirit out of the neighborhood.

Kensington was a forgotten place. Those who live there now want to leave. Those who moved away deny having lived there at all. Those who hear about it intend to stay away. According to Philadelphia journalist Buzz Bissinger, Kensington was "a neighborhood in the city that was no longer a place to live in, but a place to escape from if you were somehow lucky enough to have the means of escape."[35] For more than a century, Kensington has been a stigmatized neighborhood. But it does not need to remain that way. The residents, especially the children, deserve better. Every community deserves safety and justice, and to experience community wellness—to live in hope for God's preferred future.

A billboard at Castor and McGee Streets shows a monoethnic police officer helping two kids cross a street in a pristinely clean community, and the caption reads, "Pennsauken, New Jersey: A Nice Place to Grow." I agreed with a community leader who wrote a letter to Mayor Rendell saying it should come down because it was racist, elitist, and derogatory. The mayor called the leader and told her that if the billboard company had a city contract, he would pressure them to take it down; if not, there was not much that could be done, but he applauded her city pride. These kinds of messages reinforce a community's stigma and perpetuate negative self-esteem.

In the main corridor of Kensington High School hangs a drawing bearing the inscription, "Coat of Arms of the Baron of Kensington." Most people name their towns and cities after what they want to be, or after what they treasured in the past, or to mark a historical event or location. The Baron of Kensington was an affluent leader of a long family dynasty that flourished until the industrial demise of the nineteenth century that devastated communities in America and Great Britain. Kensington had been a favored neighborhood in London. It was close to the Houses of Parliament; many well-known shops and businesses thrived there. What did the London immigrants settling Kensington in the late seventeenth century want to reimagine on this side of the ocean? Whatever happened

---

35. Bissinger, *Prayer for the City*, 71.

to Kensington of Philadelphia's aspirational memory that threaded back to the Kensington of London?

The Kensington neighborhood in Philadelphia was in steep decline during two important periods: the mid-nineteenth and mid-twentieth centuries. This was paralleled by its archetype in London. Though today Kensington of Philadelphia has yet to recover from its desperation, Kensington of London is a thriving neighborhood again.

Atlanta—Another "Kensington"

There are other places like Kensington, such as East Lake, a neighborhood near Atlanta. In the 1960s, East Lake, like many other urban areas in the United States, was home to federal government building projects. The construction of housing was below even minimally acceptable standards for similar projects. After residents moved in, the plumbing did not work, and a bad smell permeated the area—it was a disgusting mess. The project contractor received his money and shortly thereafter moved to Mexico, leaving the needed repairs undone. East Lake suffered from a stigma, one that exists to this day. People reflect the environment they are in, and violence was rampant. It was known as Little Vietnam because the street violence and carnage mirrored the war-torn Asian country.[36] Fear and suspicion persisted until other housing projects were constructed nearby. Eventually the original East Lake project was abandoned and torn down.

The East Lake residents who lived in adequate housing in that lower-income part of town began to subdivide their area into communities with distinctive names such as East Lake Meadows, to distance themselves from East Lake's reputation.

For many years a private golf course was located adjacent to the East Lake community. The white, affluent members drove through the devastated African-American housing projects to play golf until the condition of the course deteriorated. The golf course closed sometime after the East Lake project was torn down. Tom Cousins, a well-known developer and businessperson active in his church leadership, bought the East Lake Golf Course and Country Club and subsequently renovated the entire facility, creating one of the nation's ten best courses.[37]

36. Lupton, *Return Flight*, 35.
37. Lupton, *Toxic Charity*, 98.

This spark of redevelopment lifted the spirits of the entire neighborhood. Though most of the country club members are affluent, white males, some have used the resources of the rebranded club to benefit local residents and nonmembers. Kids from the refurbished housing community organized to take golf lessons through the local school and have been invited to join the club. They have opportunities not only to learn and play but also to participate in mentoring relationships with community and business leaders. The economic vitality of the entire community has helped diminish the stigma associated with East Lake. The inadequate housing projects were replaced by safer and more attractive units. Ownership of the units alternated between the housing authority and units owned by Christian Community Development Corporation (CCDC) and became homes for church and community leaders' families. The goal is to house residents of mixed income who pay between $820 and $1,020 per month for CCDC units, while public assistance is offered for the other units.

In spring 1998, the apartment management hired a chaplain for the housing complex, but not to start a new church. Rather, the chaplain's purpose was to encourage residents to become connected to neighborhood churches in order to foster community building. The ministry of real estate as illustrated by the East Lake Country Club model takes the theology of location seriously. The neighborhood affirms the value of every resident. This kind of community renewal builds trust and reduces violence.

If you have discovered that your community suffers from persistent neglect, abuse, or even stigma, an external force must be introduced into the community system to resource a remedy. While healthy systems may self-correct, an unhealthy system lacks the capacity to remediate its deficiencies. Since stigma by its very nature is internalized, only an external force can provide what is needed to release the stigma's debilitating grasp. The discipline of asset-based community development[38] provides an important framework that makes external collaboration essential to success. The power of broad-based community connections was well expressed by the United Nations in 1972:

> Community development is the process by which the efforts of
> the people themselves are united with those of governmental

---

38. See Kretzmann and McKnight, *Building Communities from the Inside Out*, 1993.

authorities to improve the economic, social, and cultural conditions of communities; to integrate these communities into the life of the nation; and to enable them to contribute fully to national progress. This complex of processes is made up of two essential elements: the participation by the people themselves in efforts to improve their level of living, with as much reliance as possible on their own initiative; and the provision of technical and other services in ways that encourage initiative, self-help, and mutual help to make these more effective.

Conversation with Police Commissioner Timoney

Both asset-based community development and asset-based spiritual development depend on making access available to achieve vitality. One of the key community assets I discovered was the police force. Most of the officers I met and worked with from the 24th, 25th, and 26th police districts were community servants and able defenders of all that was good in Kensington. I also discovered that they were not able to deploy resources other than crime prevention. They had the tools of law enforcement at their disposal. I welcomed an opportunity to meet with the Philadelphia Police Commissioner, John F. Timoney, who visited with me in my office. He and other law enforcement and city officials were attending a community meeting at Wilkey Church to address concerns about the recently begun Operation Sunrise.

One thing became obvious to me in my open conversation with Commissioner Timoney: the objective of Operation Sunrise was to remove the drug dealers from Kensington, and nothing else. He framed it this way: when the drugs are gone, the problems are gone. I told him that having safer streets was a great idea. Our neighbors deserved streets safe enough for kids to play and adults to walk to work. But Commissioner Timoney and I were in agreement that the persistent, pervasive feelings of hopelessness many in our community expressed would remain unaddressed if there was no intervention that addressed them directly. The problem-solving, deficit model of policing was simple, but it simply would not work to build the capacity of the community at large. It might shift the problems to another part of town, but it would not affirm the worth and value of the residents or provide the infrastructure of hope.

The infrastructure of hope is contextual, and for us it included mentoring, GED programs, job skills training, job readiness training, affordable housing, access to health care, and neighborhood safety issues, among other things. Capacity building in our community would require a rebuilding of the economic structures, educational structures, and the nonprofit structures, too. The church had a part to play in the community, as well.

And what about the drug dealers and the prostitutes in the Operation Sunrise area? Commissioner Timoney and other well-meaning residents would have been pleased if the prostitutes and dealers had left Kensington and simply moved somewhere else. Since Operation Sunrise was a deficit model, the indicators for success were determined to be the elimination of drug dealing and instances of prostitution. By removing from the streets what to many were bad actors, the problem would be solved. Or so they thought.

I had already observed the ineffectiveness of Op Sunrise during the five months since the police crackdown on drugs at the corner of Lehigh and Kensington Avenues. This corresponded to a dramatic increase in illicit activity closer to Wilkey Church at Kensington and Allegheny Avenues. Commissioner Timoney and others in law enforcement ignored several economic and sociological realities in our community.

Street Economics

The street economy in Kensington was based on the incoming dollars from many illicit activities, but not all the cash that came in went out. Economic vitality requires that there be a flow of money to benefit the neighborhood, to provide kids with clothes and families with food and housing. Using the metrics of law enforcement, success would be achieved by eliminating the drug dealing—but without the income from that activity, even if Op Sunrise was successful, how would families get what they needed? How would the rent get paid? In any urban neighborhood, there are complex and interconnected systems at work, and if the tactical law enforcement solution does not have a strategic and collaborative component, the human cost of pain and suffering will remain.

What would happen to houses vacated by the drug dealers? Though it may have seemed ironic to some outsiders, the drug dealers were considered to be model tenants by the absentee landlords collecting their rent in full, on time, often in cash and in advance. The vacancy rate was already incredibly high.

A shooting incident a few blocks away resulted in the death of a young person. He had dropped out of school. For his family, he was the sole breadwinner. The youth, whose name was not made known to me, was involved with a gang and earned an income that supported not only him but also his grandmom and younger siblings. When he died, the family was grief-stricken, of course, but also financially destitute. As it turned out, neither social services nor the faith community responded to this tragic loss. I learned that it was the gang members and drug dealers who provided for his family. The illicit economies, though deplorable, unjust, and cruel, are the sustaining economies of many inner-city neighborhoods. Until the community at large addresses the systemic economy with viable alternatives, the infrastructure of hope will never supplant the illicit ones.

Healthy Church, Healthy Community

I asked Commissioner Timoney in what ways the faith-based community could cooperate with the Op, and he said that churches were important but that he didn't know specifically what they could do. To him, it was a matter of relocating illicit activity. I told him we cared about the neighbors *and* the drug dealers, the people factors, the systems, and offered our support in working to build a better community.

What appeared to be a new idea to Commissioner Timoney was my assertion that churches cannot be healthy if the neighborhood is not also healthy. Churches should have been in the loop from the beginning of Operation Sunrise so that they could intentionally provide support services and work on an alternative to the illicit economic base, together with the government, the business sector, and the educational system.

We wondered together what would fill the vacuum if we got rid of the drugs. He said he was interested in exploring this in the future. He also spoke of the "perpetually poor" and the recent political push concerning back-to-work initiatives. Essentially, he was a lawman. His very Irish Catholic background helped him understand the old Kensington ethnic fighting and religious conflicts, but his law enforcement models would likely require additional reflection. There is no sacred and profane, no winners and losers, no good and bad in any community. There is simply community, and the health of the whole is dependent on the health of the parts. The faith-based community of churches, synagogues, and mosques needed to do a better job of engagement if the whole community was to benefit. We cannot pretend that all is light in the sanctuary when the streets remain dark.

Causes or Symptoms: Know the Difference

Many law enforcement officers like Commissioner Timoney are coming to understand that drugs, prostitution, and other illicit activities, including graffiti and youth violence, are symptoms of bigger and far more serious problems. They are symptoms of hopelessness, and faith-based partners must address it along with the underlying causes. The solution is fundamentally about people and about the future. My interventions with the kids have given me four hundred drawings by youth on the street, both in my Ontario Spirit program at Wilkey Church and at Stetson Middle School. Law enforcement must do its part, but if the faith community likewise does its part, our future will be hopeful. The kids need to believe it, too.

Indicators Matter: Design a Community Barometer

It is critical for community partners to develop a barometer of community health. A gauge can be collaboratively designed and objectively assessed to give city and community leaders a way to evaluate neighborhood-directed initiatives. We can do more than simply seek to displace illicit activity. A community health barometer would measure the effectiveness of programs compared to an agreed-upon baseline. It might include the following:

1. total participation at all organization events (not just the traditionally counted worship service);
2. church membership resident-to-commuter ratio;
3. church participation resident-to-commuter ratio;
4. number of youth involved in programs, pools, parks, and clubs;
5. number of youth-specific programs operated;
6. employment statistics;
7. number of prostitution arrests;

8. number of reported violent crimes;
9. number of vacant lots;
10. number of abandoned vehicles;
11. quality-of-life perceptions interpreted through drawings;
12. number of graffiti occurrences;
13. number of businesses open;
14. number of faith-based organizations open;
15. teacher attendance;
16. student attendance;
17. high school graduation rate;
18. number of volunteer participants in programs;
19. uncollected trash incidents reported;
20. police response times;
21. fire response times;
22. violent crimes reported

A panel of community leaders would aggregate and analyze this data periodically, comparing them to other community or regional data and quality-of-life measures. This information would be made available in a way that would offer feedback to the entire community.

Recall the story of the Good Samaritan (Luke 10:25–37). Central to the story are the priest and the Levite who pass by the wounded stranger. Data collectors in the Samaritan's day would have loved to explore improved street lighting, while others would have invested in signage to warn of danger or set up task forces to better police the highways. But it was the Samaritan, the unexpected hero, the outsider, who stopped, and helped, and made a difference. The church has an opportunity to discover and then execute meaningful engagement that goes beyond collecting numerical or narrative data. The sunrise spreads its eternal and life-giving light not to the few but to the many.

5

Revolutionary Transformation

Figure 8

Ontario Presbyterian Church rebranded itself as Wilkey Memorial Presbyterian Church in 1940. About that time, the then very popular Mayflower Donut Shop's slogan gave advice this way: "As you travel through life, brother, Whatever be your goal; Keep your eye upon the donut, And not upon the hole." Transformation is like that. If you want a revolution, you must focus on the goal of transformation.

Process of Transformation

Transformation takes many forms but fundamentally concerns itself with what is missing, what is not right, what needs to be different, what isn't there. Transformation endeavors to put the hole back in the donut! It begins with the explicit understanding that a standard has not been met and the implicit suggestion that there exists a way to meet it. Transformation is a process, moving from where you are to a more authentic, healthier place.

From the very beginning, God noticed something was missing. Genesis 1:1, "In the beginning God created the heavens and the earth," affirms the reality that something needed to be done, something was not complete, namely, God's plan, and God went about in God's own sovereign way remedying the situation, using the agency and facility of the ultimate relationship, that of the Godhead, what we have come to know in the Bible as Father, Son, and Holy Spirit. "Renewal," says Richard Lovelace, concerns itself with "the infusion of spiritual life . . . by the Holy Spirit."[1] When God's Spirit "was hovering over the waters," renewal happened. "The goal of authentic spirituality is a life which escapes from the closed circle of spiritual self-indulgence, or even self-improvement, to become absorbed in the love of God and other persons. For the essence of spiritual renewal, spiritual transformation, is 'the love of God . . . poured out within our hearts through the Holy Spirit' (Rom. 5:5)."[2]

Places like Nazareth need transformation. Kensington needs transformation, too. "Now to God who is able to do immeasurably more than all we ask or imagine, according to God's power that is at work within us, to God be glory in the church and in Christ Jesus throughout all generations, for ever and ever! Amen" (Eph 3:20–21). Transformation begins with God.

Personal Transformation

Once upon a time in a village high up in the snowy Swiss Alps where my family name originated, there was a town in chaos. The ancient and dependable clock in the middle of the square had stopped. People did not know when to work, or prepare meals, or even milk the cows. Children were late to school and never knew when to do their chores. Workers were sought from the surrounding villages but no one could be found to fix the clock, though they tried day and night to find a solution.

Months had passed when one day a stranger entered the town and walked up to the bench near where the workers were having lunch. With their blessing, he borrowed a few tools; they watched as he entered the clock tower and climbed the tall spiraling staircase to the top. Some time

---

1. Lovelace, *Dynamics of Spiritual Life*, 21.
2. Ibid., 18.

went by and the stranger was almost forgotten by the resting workers. Suddenly some noise was heard, and some clanging, and then a few moments later the clock chimed the hour again! The entire town frantically made their way to the square to see what had happened. "Who fixed the clock?" everyone wanted to know.

The stranger returned the tools and began to leave the village. All were clamoring in praise but bewildered as to who fixed their beloved clock. A small child ran up behind the stranger and tugged on his pants to stop. All fell silent as they heard the child gleefully ask him how he had done it. "That's an easy question to answer," the stranger replied, smiling and holding the child in his arms. "I'm the one who built the clock, so I'm the only one who could put it back together again."

To put it another way, "Unless the Lord builds the house, its builders labor in vain. Unless the Lord watches over the city, the watchmen stand guard in vain" (Ps 127:1). My family name, Yoho (spelled Joho on the European continent), comes from a village like the one I imagined for my story, high up in the Swiss Alps. This story visualizes for me the awesome nature of God's loving interest in our life and the incredible power God releases in reconciliation and transformation.

My spiritual clock, which affects and is affected by every other component or aspect of my life when looked at as a whole, is at times in need of repair. Scripture speaks of this kind of essential renewal in terms of reconciliation; I need to be "set right" with God.

Instead of an artificial separation between the spiritual and the physical, the human experience is to be fully integrated, more aligned with Shalom in the Jewish, biblical sense of wholeness (physical, spiritual, emotional, etc.). This comprehensive view of an integrated life is mission-critical and essential to the possibilities of God's transformation of individuals and communities.

There is a difference between a "turnaround" and a "transformation." Jesus spoke to this distinction when he used the metaphor of the wineskin in Luke 5, and parallels in Mark 2:22 and Matt 9:17. The familiar wineskin image was used in Ps 119:83, Jer 13:12, Hab 2:15, Josh 9:4, 13, and Job 32:19. A turnaround is isolated, while transformation is connected. I like Lovelace's appeal for a lasting gospel presence in more than just the West when he decries the lack of Christian effectiveness and societal transformation in other nations: "But it seems that the millions of Muslims and Chinese should gain something more than a brief glimpse of a flare shot off over another country."[3] The flare is an event. What is needed is a process of transformational engagement that ensures mission effectiveness.

As church leaders it is easy to be jaded by repetitive appeals to the great days of church growth in the United States that occurred between 1930 and 1960. They point to the buildings (event), the programs (event), worship service attendance (event), and youth group and Sunday school activity (event). If these events defined the whole Christian church experience, I wondered why the church's effectiveness appeared increasingly muted and even absent from public discourse. What seems to be overlooked is that the church detached itself from the community and ignored the process of transformation, which resulted in modest spiritual depth and growth. Event-focused turnarounds have little that is of lasting value in the end. Transformation is a work of God. Let's consider the transformation journey by considering the practices of the early church as recorded in Acts.

> They devoted themselves to the apostles' teaching and to the fellowship, to the breaking of bread and to prayer. Everyone was filled with awe, and many wonders and miraculous signs were done by the apostles. All the believers were together and had everything in common. Selling their possessions and goods, they gave to anyone as he had need. Every day they continued to meet together in the temple courts. They broke bread in their homes and ate together with glad and sincere hearts, praising God and enjoying the favor of all the people. And the Lord added to their number daily those who were being saved. (Acts 2:42–47)

The coach of the Green Bay Packers was disgusted with his team's conference game performance at halftime. Everyone in the locker room expected Vince Lombardi to scream and humiliate his team. Instead, the room was hushed when he quietly lifted something high in the air and said, "This is a football."[4] Back to basics is the credo of transformation. A turnaround describes an event, while transformation describes a process. Now, events are important and useful, but events can frequently be self-contained, one-time experiences. This distinction speaks to the need for transformation in ministry and mission, too. The inscription on the

---

3. Ibid., 425.
4. "Gentlemen, This Is a Football," para. 2.

Clock Tower of London reminds us of the need for transformation: "No minute lost comes back again. Take heed and see ye nothing do in vain."

Transformation is an outcome of an intentional process of restoring health in several domains.

The Domain of Location

Transformative mission, and particularly the ministry God has given to me in serving the neighborhoods of Kensington, is localized as cohabiting a space. Initially, the spiritual life force from God describes "God and Me" connecting and sharing space. "To them God has chosen to make known among the Gentiles the glorious riches of this mystery, which is Christ in you, the hope of glory" (Col 1:27). This placement of the Spirit of Transformation within the believer is the beginning of authentic transformation. "Any viable strategy for church renewal must start with the unique personality, setting, history, and challenges of the particular church," asserts Howard Snyder in *Signs of the Spirit*. "Principles of renewal are valid only to the extent that they are not only scripturally sound but also sensitive to the particular place."[5] A theology of location is at the heart of ministry transformation.

In his seminal work *God With Us*, Joseph Haroutunian describes the nature of the church as a living thing in relation to Christ. Living things are connected. "'The body of Christ' is no institution [technical], with its claims upon men's 'loyalty' because of services rendered [function], but a company of people gathered around Jesus [personal, corporate], joyful with him and one with another, hearing his words laden with God's grace and happily breaking bread together [being] in thankfulness [dynamic]."[6]

The church expresses itself as a local organization that reflects the spiritual organism's life as the body of Christ. The very nature of the church is covenantal and community-oriented, not individualistic. "Biblical salvation creates a new Christian community," says Ron Sider. "We will not be satisfied as isolated saints and overlook Christ's new redeemed community of disciples."[7] We are, as the church, a people called by God to believe. Jesus did not call individuals as if in a vacuum to follow him—an unfortunate impression formed by scores of hymns that center around

---

5. Snyder, *Signs of the Spirit*, 189.
6. Haroutunian, *God With Us*, 243. Words in brackets added by the author.
7. Sider, *Genuine Christianity*, 27.

an almost isolationist "Jesus and Me" theme. Jesus' method of ministry was in a group context. Forming groups is an intrinsic component of the creation mandate. It reflects the very nature of the Triune God expressed as Father, Son, and Holy Spirit. We can now understand that the "I" and "Me" theologically narcissistic emphasis can be idolatrous, ignoring the group and community and thus the very nature of God connecting church and community. "In short," Haroutunian writes, "traditional Christianity and its theologies have been dominated by an individualism that has made the church theologically all but irrelevant."[8]

At a church leadership team meeting an elder remarked, "We do get some new people, but unfortunately we need ten new people to make up for one old-timer moving away, retiring, or dying." Another agreed. "The building is consuming 90 percent of our offerings, but these young people today don't give like we do. Can't get them to volunteer, either." These struggling leaders were trying to make sense of their church experience, a model for doing ministry that had served the greater church well for hundreds of years. They were expressing their lack of ministry satisfaction and essentially admitted they could not afford to grow. They were stuck in their building, out of reach of new and (especially) younger people. Mission endurance is not the same thing as mission longevity. Neither should it be confused with the persistence of our buildings and programs.[9]

While the church is not a building, it does require a tangible presence in the neighborhood to effect transformation. When we hear Jesus say (by means of a wonderful and supernatural eavesdropping event) in his Gethsemane prayer, "May they be brought to complete unity to let the world know that you sent me and have loved them even as you have loved me" (John 17:23), we are compelled to develop cooperative neighborhood ministry. The church is not a program, but it is gathered and sent to engage the world to transform the world. The church is not confirmed by race, color, language, tradition, form of government, or theological formulas, but it comprises people from all races, cultures, paradigms, and denominations.

---

8. Haroutunian, *God With Us*, 95.
9. Yoho, "Mission Endurance," 20.

The Domain of Destination

Without a compelling vision, the people will perish (Prov 29:18). Jesus knew the power of claiming and envisioning a future, when it is said of him, "who for the joy set before him endured the cross, scorning its shame, and sat down at the right hand of the throne of God" (Heb 12:2). I challenged Wilkey's session to do something bold. I envisioned a community where the church building was the setting for all kinds of ministry to the whole person, within the community of the whole. A place where it would be safe to worship and pray, to learn and be challenged. A central point of mission would result in the opening of its big red doors to the community. Dozens of caring, sincere disciples of Jesus Christ would reach out with deeds of compassion and service. It would be a vital ministry where God unconditionally met the needs of people, not just on Sunday but Monday through Saturday, too. It was the kind of vision Ron Sider shared when he wrote, "I long for the time when most Christians are in congregations where each month they experience the joy of hearing about new people who have just begun to taste the goodness of salvation. I yearn for the day when most Christians are in congregations that walk with the needy, say no to prejudice, and reach out to heal broken communities."[10]

The best way for church leaders to foster deep connections with the community is to take intentional walks before, during, or after their in-neighborhood programming. The purpose is not to advertise or solicit support but to actively engage and pay attention to what God is doing around them. "Walk with me" is a phrase that should be heard more often in our churches as leaders find ways to interact and learn outside the building.

While physically walking the streets is very effective, "digitally" walking around the community is useful, too. I recommend Mission-Insite's demographic tools.[11] Many regional denominational and nonprofit organizations purchase MissionInsite contracts for their member churches and organizations. When subscription demographic services are not provided, you can get basic demographic data from the Census Bureau[12] and the Pew Research Center[13] free of charge. These resources

---

10. Sider, *Genuine Christianity*, 96.
11. See http://missioninsite.com.
12. See https://www.census.gov/ces/dataproducts/demographicdata.html.
13. See http://www.pewforum.org/religious-landscape-study/.

can reintroduce your leadership team to your community, stirring the possibilities of transformation and blessing. When the church becomes more deeply connected to the realities in the neighborhood, it is also connecting to many hopeful possibilities in the neighborhood.

Some of us in the church still seem predisposed to think that the community owes us something, such as showing up at our church events, while we struggle to make real connections. I challenged the session to take a walk in the neighborhood, which motivated several of our key leaders to conclude that we had a responsibility to do more to improve the quality of life there. The clear vision to reclaim and restore, to reneighbor and rebuild, became shared in the context of our faith community. While we didn't require everyone in the church to agree with the vision, thankfully, our key leaders did agree.

The Domain of Process

We embarked on a journey of recognizing the value of paying attention to the right metrics as a means of experiencing God's grace. When we take our neighborhood walks with interns and visiting leaders, we note observations and provoke prayer requests. To bring the core value of our walks to those who were not able to participate, we ordered an aerial photograph of the Kensington section of Philadelphia, which we prominently displayed at the front of the sanctuary. These walks reminded me of several ministries I witnessed in New York that take seriously observation and physical movement in the context of community.

Resurrection Church in Brooklyn, New York, is representative of faith-based organizations with roots in Pentecostal theology. The core deliverance ministry, prayer walks, spiritual mapping, houses of prayer, and public gospel rallies are expressions of their connecting. The leaders of Resurrection Church understood the reality of spiritual forces in high places, which affect our ministry in the neighborhood. Presbyterians can easily neglect this spiritual dimension and ignore the spiritual battle being waged. Resurrection Church's mission model is centered on the power of God to set right what is upside down.

During lunch with the staff, I learned they characterized their neighborhood as a battlefield. It was the place where good and evil met and where the eternal destiny of souls was at stake. The seriousness of the mission of Resurrection Church was humbling. Though they spoke of a long-range plan and objective in their strategy, the ministry had a sense of urgency about it. It was clearly a tactical mission. They offered the verse from Matt 24:14 where Jesus says, "And this Gospel of the kingdom will be preached in all the world as a witness to all the nations, and then the end will come."

The Calvinist confidence in God's providence is often a substitute for an urgency in proclamation. It might be depicted this way: since God is in control, what's the hurry? Take it easy. God will do what God wants, and we are just along for the ride. I still see utter dependence on the sovereignty of God as being true encouragement for evangelism, but we too often discount an expectation for results as worldly or lacking faith. We are indeed partners with God, who is in total control, inviting us to confront principalities and powers in high places with the same resolute determination Jesus showed when he confronted Satan in the wilderness. This ministry image was Resurrection's gift to me.

As pastoral leaders, our responsibility is to call the congregation to its history, not reinforce nostalgia, which is powerless to evoke change. Truth is a powerful motivation. Spiritual transformation must be honest and accurate in its portrayal of God's grace as well as our sin and experience of sin's effects, personally and corporately, in the neighborhood. We are discovering that there can be no vital, working congregations in a neighborhood that is not working. That is to say, a truly indigenous congregation, made up of the people in a particular neighborhood, will truly reflect the economic woes and brokenness of the neighborhood and bring the hope of Jesus to that real context. Little else is needed. Thus, the congregation is called to embody the vitality of living with Jesus Christ not merely in the sanctuary but in the streets as well.

Thomas Chalmers (1780–1847) served in several parishes in and near Glasgow in the early nineteenth century. He knew how necessary it was for congregational mission to achieve impact in the community. He became the father of modern social work in his capacity as pastor to urban and rural people alike. For Chalmers, the Gospel was the basis not only for spiritual reform but also for societal reform. His writing ministry included such topics as education, housing, national debt, and the controversial Corn Laws, among other closely related issues. The majority of his economic views were expressed in his *Christian and Civic Economy of Large Towns* (1821–26). His publications challenged the community at large, while as a minister he influenced not only those who heard him preach but also those who witnessed his incarnational ministry, which communicated the heart of the message of Christ.

While in Glasgow, Dr. Chalmers wasted no time in ministering to what he considered a critical need of his day, especially in light of the new technologies being introduced into the factory: poverty. Although by today's criteria his views were paternalistic, in his day he was considered a radical by the conservative segment of the church. He became quite familiar with the English Poor Laws during his visits to England and through extensive correspondence with William Wilberforce and others; he concluded that the poor laws caused more trouble than they alleviated. Since the state was then in charge of meeting temporal needs, he noted the insufficiency of distributing resources without gaining insight into the family's needs and developing a plan to prevent the poor from remaining poor. Class distinctions were also made more apparent because the rich were the main ones supporting the burden of the agencies. This, Chalmers was convinced, caused the poor to become dependent on society in an unhealthy way (it could almost be said he foresaw the fatal flaws of the modern U.S. welfare system now being dismantled).

In 1819, Chalmers began the nearly impossible task of visiting every family in the Tron parish of Glasgow, which had a population of more than eleven thousand. Chalmers discovered that more than one-third of the families had little connection with any Christian church, and the thought of children growing up without any footing in Christian truth disturbed him greatly.[14] Approximately one hundred years later, a similar effort was being made in Kensington at Wilkey Church.

Robert Lupton is right when he argues that the quickest way to diminish a neighborhood's quality of life (and create a ghetto) is when the neighborhood's most resourced people leave as soon as they have the means to do so. Just ask several of our leaders who recently moved back into Kensington after moving away fifteen years before. Reconnecting to the community is not easy to do once the church and its participants have demonstrated a pattern of community abandonment. Lupton offers a new definition of gentrification when he writes, "Gentrification with justice—that's what is needed to restore health to our urban neighborhoods."[15] This suggests a paradigm for building leadership for the new millennium. Gentrification, as seen in our urban century between 1830 and 1930, radically displaced the majority of less educated, less resourced people (and often depleted existing housing), with more educated and financially capable individuals supplanting them. Lupton's view is to wel-

14. Young and Ashton, *British Social Work*, 88.
15. Lupton, "gen-tri-fi-ca-tion (jen´tre-fi-ka´shen) noun," para. 8.

come intentional relocation of resourced persons into a neighborhood (i.e., redeemed gentrification) among those who have fewer resources. He calls this positive reneighboring "indigenizing." Nevertheless, this effort alone will not build leadership. If a proactive indigenizing (moving in and staying in) could be a catalyst for servant leadership from within the neighborhood, then trusting relationships and community partnering could become an effective combination. The pastoral leader can contribute to this process of investing resources into the neighborhood mix. We are experimenting with Lupton's indigenizing model more than we first thought was possible.

The great act of the Creator coming down to where we are defines what is meant by incarnational ministry (Phil 2:6–11). The Apostle John wrote that "the Word became flesh and made his dwelling among us" (John 1:14), using the Greek word σαρχ, which is rendered "flesh." *Incarnational* describes an in-flesh, in-person ministry. It is more than a method; it is a core understanding of orthodox theology.[16] The process of incarnation is inextricably bound up with the whole salvation story of the good news.

Cardinal Suhard, the archbishop of Paris in 1940, knew the call of neighborhood transformation had been issued to the church. During that same period, Ontario Presbyterian was changing its name to Wilkey Memorial, in honor of the two wealthy sisters who had never stepped through its doors. A kind of symbolic permission was given to dozens (and later, hundreds) of our members to make their flight from the inner city to the outer bands of the suburbs, buying houses with mortgages that would soon come through the G.I. Bill. "In the 1950s, aided by federal government policies favoring suburban development, Philadelphia's expansion became regional in nature. New housing construction boomed in the towns and boroughs surrounding the city."[17] On the wall of the Lisieux seminary in Paris were written Cardinal Suhard's words: "I have not to search for the subject of my meditation. It is always the same. There is a wall which separates the Church from the masses; the wall must be broken down at whatever cost to give back to Christ the crowds who are lost to Him."[18] Breaking down this wall cannot be accomplished in

---

16. The Nicene Creed states, "And in one Lord Jesus Christ . . . who, for us men and for our salvation, came down from heaven, and was incarnate, by the Holy Ghost, of the Virgin Mary, and was made man."

17. Philadelphia City Planning Commission, *Vacant Land in Philadelphia*, xi.

18. Quoted in Shenk, *Write the Vision*, 25.

a vacuum. To reconnect with the neighborhood requires the stranger to become the friend, that is, to *reneighbor* in the deepest sense of that word.

Church newsletters typically recount glowing stories of success and growth when attendance is down and the church's financial health is in decline. We rarely take an honest accounting that reflects the true state of the church or the struggles it faces. Leaders often avoid deeper conversations with denominational and regional authorities, as Eugene Peterson recounts his memoir, *The Pastor*.[19] Are we saving face? Why are church annual reports more like wishful thinking? Our lack of insight and willingness to engage in evidence-based discernment has impeded our learning and impaired our mission's success. Russell Crabtree of Holy Cow! Consulting explains that "evidence-based discernment for ministry is a process of discovery that integrates organizational intelligence, core values, and an inspired imagination to generate a course of action."[20] Our misunderstanding of our own work as God works within us is at the bottom of this fantasy theology. Our God is too small. The God who loves the whole world invites every leader in a church, mission community, or other faith-based organization to pay attention to what is actually going on. If transformative leadership is to occur, leaders also need to pay attention to their own actions and how the community is impacted by those actions.

Corporate Transformation

No church, no organization can remain a silo, no matter how well intentioned that organization may be. Even if a church works hard on its own mission, and other churches do the same, with the city and business sectors all trying to do their part, they will not be able to create a sustainable community because, as Peter Block observes, "parallel effort added together does not make a community. Our communities are separated into silos; they are a collection of institutions and programs operating near one another but not overlapping or touching."[21] We do not need "silo" mentalities, "self-referencing" leaders, or congregations obsessed with "self-preservation." The health of the whole affects the health of the parts.

---

19. Peterson, *Pastor*, ch. 22, "Appreciation and Foolery," especially 266.
20. Crabtree, *Owl Sight*, 16.
21. Block, *Community*, 15.

> The way God designed our bodies is a model for understanding our lives together as a church: every part dependent on every other part, the parts we mention and the parts we don't, the parts we see and the parts we don't. If one part hurts, every other part is involved in the hurt, and in the healing. If one part flourishes, every other part enters into the exuberance. You are Christ's body—that's who you are! You must never forget this. Only as you accept your part of that body does your "part" mean anything. (1 Cor 12:25–27 MSG)

Transforming a congregation with a silo mentality into an authentic community partner requires a gradual, intentional process that respects the community system. A given church cannot decide one day to stop being a silo and expect the community as a whole to reciprocate instantly. Partnership and collaboration is a mutual process. If you want to go from the lobby in your hotel to the twelfth floor quickly, pressing the elevator button repeatedly will not make the elevator doors open faster. The elevator (thankfully) moves at a perfect, predetermined rate. (Imagine if it didn't and you were inside when an impatient guest kept pressing that button!) A lot of really smart designers and engineers make sure that the elevators are convenient and safe and that they get the job done. Getting somewhere fast is sometimes not the best objective when safety is a concern.

A congregation, like the human body, can be represented by its resources, values, and priorities. But the change a congregation can experience is developmental and is governed by the capacity of its members to learn and grow. Consider when you get to your hotel after a long, hot day and want to cool your room to 68 degrees quickly. You may set the thermostat to 50 degrees, but setting it to 50, 60, or even 70 degrees isn't going to reduce the temperature in the 85-degree room any faster. Air conditioning systems are designed to blow cold air into a room until the room hits the number set on the thermostat; then it stops. There's no "instant" change. Can you imagine what would happen if the temperature actually went from 85 degrees to, say, 60 degrees instantly? How would your body react? A great team of engineers designed the modern air-conditioner to adjust the air temperature in a way that adheres to the laws of physics and human design to get the job done right.

God created humans to be partners and producers, not mere consumers. We are sent to till the ground, make things, produce things, help people, heal sickness, and invest energy in relationships and systems to

God's glory. God is in the redemption business. Joining in with God's flow of possibilities is the way we embrace God's emerging future together.

Transformation, therefore, is not individualistic. Jesus called twelve disciples to be together as leaders of the new transformational movement, called them to be with him, then to be sent out to preach, teach, and heal the world in his name. Following Jesus' resurrection and ascension, leaders of "the Way," as the movement was called, convened in groups to make decisions and to support each other in mission. To get the right jobs done, to bless the world. In the church's early days, councils were formed. The New Testament speaks of leadership in the congregations as the shared work of spiritually graced men and women who form the body of Christ. Examples abound of people who were recognized for their contributions to the mission as they expressed love, concern, and servant and spiritual leadership to others.[22]

Church governance was not created in a vacuum. The Presbyterian Church, for example, connects its polity to what it understands to be clear biblical foundations, illuminated by confessional understandings, and has succeeded as just one form of government among many others to order a particular community of believers. It has evolved over three centuries based on the real-life experiences of women and men of faith. It affirms the importance of the local congregation to its members and to Christ's mission—but also the importance of empowering congregations to understand they are part of Christ's church. A council of churches, or a denomination's regional organization, is greater than the sum of its parts and sets the vision and mission of the whole—to build up, nurture, discipline, and guide. Administrative commissions, installation commissions, committees, teams, and staff—all are spiritual tools, resources God may use to build us up in Jesus Christ. Transformation is a process, and it takes all of the parts to continue the historic tradition within the church that we all need to learn, grow, and change together.

Guided by the Holy Spirit, gifted individuals who are called in faith, love, and common mission can accomplish much more through a spiritual synergy than any one person alone. We honor and glorify God best when we express the body of Christ together. We gather in celebration of Christ's life in our midst, and we gather for worshipful discernment to

---

22. Agosto, *Servant Leadership*, 121. Especially note E. Earle Ellis's analysis of shared leadership in the life of the Apostle Paul that enumerates dozens of leaders Paul affirmed for their contributions to the larger work of the mission.

ensure that every worshipping community has the resources it needs to fulfill God's unique call.

We need consolidated mission, not isolated ministry. When "silo" spirituality substitutes for true renewal in the local church, our wellness is impaired. This means that brokenness is not addressed through prayerful confession or mindful correction. God's grace is essentially ignored. When this impairment becomes a pattern, it leads to the death of vision and a diminished witness. Healthfulness, on the other hand, remains elusive and just out of reach. This cyclical pattern, like that experienced by Israel during the time of the judges, can be summed up by the words, "But when the judge died, the people returned to ways even more corrupt than those of their fathers, following other gods and serving and worshiping them. They refused to give up their evil practices and stubborn ways" (Judg 2:19).

We need to call the church back being a connected people. "The church gets into trouble whenever it thinks it is in the church business rather than the Kingdom business," observes Howard Snyder.[23] We need people with a capacity to think about building the kingdom and correct the notion that their church building or their ministry is that kingdom.

In the business world there are two realities—one is sales, the other is market share. Sales are short-term, an event, and thus tactical. Market share is long-term, a process, and thus strategic. The core business of the church is telling, living, and incarnating the good news to the world in truthful, authentic ways. However, we need to be less concerned with sales than with market share. Membership or even worship attendance does not measure the effectiveness of a congregation. Instead, being accountable and measuring the mind share and heart share of your neighborhood can be empowering.

This is the call we hear when Paul says to the church in Rome, "First, I thank my God through Jesus Christ for all of you, because your faith is being reported all over the world" (Rom 1:8); and also, "Do not conform any longer to the pattern of this world, but be transformed by the renewing of your mind. Then you will be able to test and approve what God's will is—his good, pleasing and perfect will" (Rom 12:2). Faith that matters has the confidence to say,

> All this is from God, who reconciled us to himself through Christ and gave us the ministry of reconciliation: that God was reconciling the world to himself in Christ, not counting men's

23. Snyder, *Liberating the Church*, 11.

sins against them. And he has committed to us the message of reconciliation. We are therefore Christ's ambassadors, as though God were making his appeal through us. We implore you on Christ's behalf: Be reconciled to God. God made him who had no sin to be sin for us, so that in him we might become the righteousness of God. (2 Cor 5:18–21)

The personal mind share is affirmed when Paul says, "All over the world this gospel is bearing fruit and growing, just as it has been doing among you since the day you heard it and understood God's grace in all its truth" (Col 1:6). The entire ministry of Asian believers spoke to the lasting effects (process) of renewal towards transformation, personal and cultural, when the apostle wrote,

> For we know, brothers loved by God, that he has chosen you, because our gospel came to you not simply with words, but also with power, with the Holy Spirit and with deep conviction. You know how we lived among you for your sake. You became imitators of us and of the Lord; in spite of severe suffering, you welcomed the message with the joy given by the Holy Spirit. And so you became a model to all the believers in Macedonia and Achaia. The Lord's message rang out from you not only in Macedonia and Achaia—your faith in God has become known everywhere. Therefore we do not need to say anything about it, for they report what kind of reception you gave us. They tell how you turned to God from idols to serve the living and true God, and to wait for his Son from heaven, whom he raised from the dead—Jesus, who rescues us from the coming wrath. (1 Thess 1:4–10)

The call to transformation requires a big God. A big God is needed when God brings the truth of sin and brokenness to light; in our own quandary, trying to reconcile this truth on our own, it is God's grace that points us to Jesus Christ. A redeemed relationship with God leads to a new paradigm shift and a hopeful future. The paradigm we are concerned with is one of forgiveness and transformation. This theme is evident in Scripture from Adam to Noah, from Abraham, Isaac, and Jacob to Moses and, finally, Jesus, a dead man who got up and walked. So will we.

God is in the news business. God doesn't give advice. Wilkey Church's congregation needs transformation from the inside out, and that "inside out" doesn't stop with their physical/spiritual person. So now, we have renamed the church office "Mission Control," identified by a big sign on the wall and door. We are developing a mission statement and pledge to the neighborhood. The future has been a tough sell to this congregation, which a few years ago would just as soon have closed its doors. Sustainability of vision and its ability to take best practice mission to scale cannot be undervalued.

The story of Nehemiah would offer our people at Wilkey Church a much-needed new paradigm. As J. Oswald Sanders observes, "Nehemiah exhibited keen foresight. He knew that opposition was sure to arise, so he secured letters from the king for safe passage and for the resources to accomplish the task, 'to make beams for the gates of the citadel . . . and for the city wall' (2:8). He carefully planned his strategy."[24] We are in the urban rebuilding business, too.

God confronted my own lack of faith and judgmental attitude when I realized that the elders were not simply stalling, but were truly stuck. Because strategy had to do with the future, and after many years of internal stasis and external change with rapidly diminishing resources, the people became accustomed to failure. They were, to borrow from Einstein, "doing the same thing, over and over, and expecting a different result." They had no space in their minds, or hearts, or calendars for thinking beyond next month's bills and programs. Consumed with fighting today's battles (short-term thinking), they ignored the past and seemed incapable of envisioning a hopeful future.

A truthful view of the incredibly awesome God of the universe must inform our thinking and our giving; it needs to animate our hands and feet and compel us to face the neighborhood that most of our drive-in members disparaged. Transformation in the congregation is both individualistic and corporate, clerical and lay, old and young, male and female, inclusive of all ages, ethnicities, languages, and economic diversity, for there are no shadows cast where the light of Christ shines. The Light reaches all of life, from the smallest part to the whole, from worship and economics to mission:

> But everything exposed by the light becomes visible, for it is light that makes everything visible. This is why it is said: "Wake up, O sleeper, rise from the dead, and Christ will shine on you." Be very careful, then, how you live—not as unwise but as wise, making the most of every opportunity, because the days are evil. Therefore do not be foolish, but understand what the Lord's will is. Do not get drunk on wine, which leads to debauchery. Instead, be filled with the Spirit. Speak to one another with psalms,

---

24. Sanders, *Spiritual Leadership*, 164.

> hymns and spiritual songs. Sing and make music in your heart to the Lord, always giving thanks to God the Father for everything, in the name of our Lord Jesus Christ. (Eph 5:13–20)

Through creative Bible study and authentic and intentional conversation I began to discover ways to affirm everyone's spiritual giftedness with interactive capacity assessments. If we were to turn the corner, we would have to do so together. Renewal is transforming us into the image of Jesus Christ. Now there is room on our congregation's calendar for tomorrow as well as today. There is room for God's emerging future! The past has come back to bolster and affirm our course. I reminded the leaders of the words in the church's charter, which says Ontario Presbyterian Church was founded so that "the children would not have to cross Kensington Avenue to go to Sunday school." Our future mission was rooted in our past. It may sound odd, but for the people of my congregation, God was actually getting bigger!

Promise of Transformation

> Because the church is a formal organization made up of policies, programs, practices, and people, it cannot by itself give a person any deep, permanent security or sense of intrinsic worth. Living the principles taught by the church can do this, but the organization alone cannot.
>
> Nor can the church give a person a constant sense of guidance. Church-centered people often tend to live in compartments, acting and thinking and feeling in certain ways on the Sabbath and in totally different ways on weekdays. Such a lack of wholeness or unity or integrity is a further threat to security, creating the need for increased labeling and self-justifying.[25]

Stephen R. Covey's insight quoted above resonates forcefully with Scripture (2 Cor 5:17; 6:16; Col 3:17; 1 John 2:6) and highlights the critical path for transformation in the church: alignment of spiritual energy. When our resources, processes, and values remain unaligned (or worse, misdirected) the congregation's impact is diminished and will likely be dismissed by the community it intends to serve. Transformation of the community depends on an effective worshipping and witnessing community that experiences its own authentic transformation.

---

25. Covey, *7 Habits*, 125.

"Church-centered" people, as Covey calls them, are not necessarily Christ-centered people, or God's-mission-in-the-world people. When the church itself is the mission of the church, our witness is diluted, and that may explain our lack of impact in the neighborhood. We have none of the peace, none of the integration of life conveyed by the Hebrew word *shalom* (שלום). Shalom is more than the external ordering of home and work, task and function. Shalom refers to the inner life of balance that necessarily affects our community and the outside world. Shalom was the proactive presence of wholeness, body and soul (later, for the Greeks, it included the mind as well). In a ministry of shalom, there would be no compartmentalizing, no silos, no exclusivity.

My experience of church begins with God and me and moves on to God and us. God is expressed as a Trinity of community, communion, and relationship. Though it is common to observe spiritual conversion as a singular act of God as experienced by an individual, such a spiritual transformation is not solitary. As with the ark in the Genesis story, salvation of the world is inextricably bound to community (Gen 7:1). That is where it all starts; the church, the εκκλησια, the "called-out ones." It is not merely descriptive, but prescriptive of the relationship, communion, and community, which does not dance back and forth from religious to secular, from holy to profane, from active to passive. God's life-giving spirit is in all and cannot be isolated (see Ps 139:8; Col 3:11). When the church community is not embedded in the greater community every day, from Sunday to Sunday, it denies its purpose and the power of God's Holy Spirit.

Our Sabbath talk must inform our weekday walk. (Jesus surely loved to make this point, as he healed on the Sabbath as recorded in Matt 12:1, Mark 3:2, and Luke 13:10.) If I read the Easter story correctly, a dead man got up and walked. Jesus came back to life again to build a new community, as "members together of one body, and sharers together in the promise in Christ Jesus" (Eph 3:6). Because of this truth, my commitment to be an agent of transformation in my parish, in my neighborhood, city, and world is not only expressed in community but is defined by community. My mission in Kensington as a servant leader is fundamentally defined by my participation with community, real community, that will help us look more like Jesus—Monday through Saturday as well as on Sundays. This, then, is the function of my Institutional Support Group, namely, to engage with me in doing business with God and with each other in the community. As Augustine said, "Without God we cannot; without us God will not."

6

Connectional Design

Figure 9

Building successful and sustainable connections rarely happen without intention. Authentic connections, in which all participants express and realize mutual respect and wellness, require intentionality and design. This is true of families and work teams, and is certainly true in an urban community. How do you reconnect a faith community or church with its context? Can the trends of community disconnection be reversed so

Reneighboring the Congregation

A church's loving relatonship with its neighborhood is analogous in some ways to the marriage relationship. Paul said,

> Husbands love your wives, just as Christ loved the church and gave himself up for her to make her holy, cleansing her by the washing with water through the word, and to present her to himself as a radiant church, without stain or wrinkle or any other blemish, but holy and blameless. In this same way, husbands ought to love their wives as their own bodies. He who loves his wife loves himself. After all, no one ever hated his own body, but he feeds and cares for it, just as Christ does the church—for we are members of his body. (Eph 5:25–30)

Love, sacrifice, care, support, improvement, provision, nurture . . . How can a congregation give up everything in service of a neighborhood it does not love? Will a neighborhood receive the tangible benefits of the church's ministry if the congregation does not love and serve it? From Torah and prophetic mandates, included in the "neighbor" laws (e.g., Lev 19:18), to admonitions to care for the orphan, the widow and alien (Exod 22:21–22), to Jesus' redefinition of "neighbor" (Luke 10:27–37), Scripture again and again exhorts God's people to make a difference that can be felt locally, regionally, nationally, and globally. The Great Commission was not called great because it was a great idea but because it encompassed all of life as God's people went forth in the power of the Holy Spirit to be Jesus' witnesses "in Jerusalem, and in all Judea and Samaria, and to the ends of the earth" (Acts 1:8). Robert Lupton, who pastors a reneighbored congregation in Atlanta, writes, "Withdrawal to places of privilege with no concern for those we have left behind is the American dream devoid of a social conscience. And when the church and the society it is to influence disengages from the practice of loving our neighbor, there is little reason to hope that benevolent mechanisms will fill the void."[1]

The past often enables a mighty power for transformation, while the present often obscures redeeming history and potential. Dr. Ray Bakke affirms this principle when he recounts the history of "old first" churches,

---

1. Lupton, *Return Flight*, 48.

which applies to any institution or association, from an entire neighborhood to a specific congregation. We experienced the truth of this when we began the ethnography of the parish, which unearthed an immense amount of data from the past and is now enabling discovery and action in the present. The past will give permission to the present to reclaim once again the physical space God gave to a few followers of Jesus to love our neighborhood a long, long time ago.

> For these reasons, unlocking memories is a way of affirming people and their church ... Recovery of the historic vision and the affirmation of great acts of God and God's people in the heart, together with the creative celebration of them in the present will eventually produce a congregational climate where expectant change can and will take place. People who have no memories can set no goals. The way forward is first a creative look back.[2]

It is also important to accurately understand what it means to love a neighborhood, and how loving a neighborhood is entirely different than loving the congregation itself. This distinction affects the perceived and actual roles of the pastoral staff in a significant way. In loving the congregation, the pastor functions as the flock's shepherd, but in loving the neighborhood, the pastor acts as a community chaplain. These two different but admittedly connected job descriptions for the pastoral staff must be equally owned and intentionally addressed in the mission. When these two roles and loves are left unaddressed, the neighborhood is not well cared for, while the congregation remains estranged from the streets the church calls home.

Aryeh Cohen tells a rabbinic story in his insightful *Justice in the City* about the gatehouse in ancient times. If a neighbor builds a gatehouse in your shared community space, you are obligated to contribute towards its construction and upkeep. The social expectation of reciprocity is a core community value. The gatehouse would be understood to provide protection and facilitate commerce and connections. However, if your neighbor builds a gatehouse intending to isolate your community from the cries of the poor, you must not assist in its construction, but rather insist that the gatehouse not be built. The principle at stake is central to the legal tradition—one must be able to hear the cries of the poor. Cohen convincingly suggests that a community politic should create a

---

2. Bakke and Roberts, *Expanded Mission*, 32–33.

"community of obligation,"[3] a reciprocity that begins with a practice of connecting, listening, and seeing. Church doors cannot become barriers and must not be gatehouses that suppress or ignore the cries of the community. "If one can hear the cry, one can choose to be like God. Precluding the possibility of hearing the cry of the poor is itself a choice—a choice to be like Pharaoh."[4]

Here is a way to understand the tipping point when your church may be dangerously close to a severe mission disconnect. When the number of drive-in attendees at a church is disproportionately larger than nearby attendees, it is difficult, if not impossible, to effectively listen to the cries of the poor right outside the gates. Walking on the streets of our neighborhood allows us to pay attention. Our practice of piety inside the building leads to political practice outside the building, which causes the city as a whole to engage the larger questions of justice, poverty, and homelessness. The community prospers and everyone is blessed. "Make yourselves at home there and work for the country's welfare. Pray for Babylon's well-being. If things go well for Babylon, things will go well for you" (Jer 29:7 MSG). If you want things to go well for your church, then make it your business to make your home there and work for your community's welfare.

As part of my doctor of ministry program, I had the opportunity to meet the Reverend Johnny Ray Youngblood of St. Paul Community Baptist Church in Brooklyn during a weeklong site visit to the boroughs of New York. He spoke passionately about the community he sought to serve and said he would partner with anyone who could help. His congregation loves their neighborhood. They love it so much they would do anything to make it better. "We need to be busy in providing real service to people, meet real needs," Youngblood offered. These real services translated into action as his board started the Nehemiah Project housing business. People needed affordable housing. They paid attention to neighborhood context because they also lived there, invested time there, and were part of that neighborhood's present as well as its past. What's more, the congregation was committed to being an integral part of that neighborhood's future—and the community knew it. In the words of Pastor Youngblood, "Economic development is hell, but you gotta do it."[5] Risk-taking was an

---

3. Cohen, *Justice in the City*, 17.
4. Ibid.
5. Ibid.

understood aspect of their mission. To build the community's capacity, the church bought out damaging and dangerous businesses, including liquor stores and porn shops, to eliminate their negative impact on the neighborhood at large. The evidence of that depth of commitment motivated many residents to participate in ministries and services of the growing church. Thanks in part to Reverend Youngblood's leadership, a community-wide collaboration ensured the sustainability of a variety of different transformational ministries.

Engagement blesses neighborhoods. Randy White, an urban pastor in Fresno, California, and his family undertook a life of "downward mobility" in the inner city. "Once we had worked through the myths and stereotypes surrounding the city, we were ready to really see what was happening there. Once we were able to see what was happening there, we became more inclined to enter relationships with people who were vastly different from us," White observes.[6] "The very act of involvement created love of neighbor. Love of neighbor led to the ability to identify not only the needs of the neighborhood but also the resources that already existed there. And once this happened, we were ready to treat our neighbors as partners in the healing of the neighborhood."[7]

There is a great power that is unleashed when reneighboring the church. John Perkins of the Christian Community Development Association invites churches in a loud voice to relocate themselves in neighborhoods of need. Though he admits that relocation is not for everyone, he does encourage a wide audience to consider the sacrifice, saying, "Jesus didn't just relocate his heart. We are all grateful that he came to earth in the flesh."[8] Fundamentally, Perkins understood that relocation is just one part of a three-pronged effort where relocation (making the area that God has called you to serve your home) connects with the ministry of reconciliation (calling people into relationship with one another), which is then attached to the goal of redistribution (sharing skills and resources to break people out of the cycle of poverty). Using a similar approach, Bob Lupton of FCS Urban Ministries in Atlanta speaks right to the issues that face Wilkey Church in North Philadelphia. The response to urban flight is the return flight. Lupton's three *R*'s of community development are

6. White, *Journey to the Center of the City*, 62.
7. Ibid.
8. Perkins, *Restoring At-Risk Communities*, 12.

- reneighboring (actual street-level connecting with the neighborhood);
- rebuilding (both the inner spirit of the neighbor and the structure of the neighborhood); and
- re-harnessing market forces (creating sustainable economic systems in the neighborhood).

Denominational executives considering new church development frequently forget that a faith-based organization cannot be expected to be economically self-sustainable if it is located in a neighborhood that is economically unsustainable. New, creative, and paradigm-shifting models must be developed where effective mission can be undertaken without the traditional congregation-funded financial base. If worship cannot support mission, then mission must be funded through other means. Alternate monetizing models for congregational ministry must be a mission priority for regional church mission agencies.

While economies of scale achieve significant impact in communities, the small indicators, the still, small voice of God, for example, deliver powerful messages, too. Robert Lupton urges the church not to overlook that "inner spirit" factor in community ministry.[9] The inner spirit of our members resonated around personal safety. As you entered our building on Ontario Street, you were greeted by a large, hand-drawn wall sign that read, "Remember to lock the door behind you." We acted like our church was a fortress in the neighborhood. The walls protected us from the desolation outside. While offering access to the insiders, the large red doors were our drawbridge that excluded outsiders from entering. That sign might as well have read, "Beware: the neighborhood is our enemy." Every time we read it, we reinforced its judgmental message of detachment and isolation. Many times I considered removing the sign myself. My role as the pastoral leader, however, prompted me to resource my own congregation's learning. Through conversation, modeling, and the transformational experiences ahead, I began to invite the congregation to take responsibility for its view of the neighborhood. I wanted them to relate to neighbors, not ministry targets, and certainly not enemies. We would begin to set aside our presumption as the teacher or expert and instead develop a humble posture as co-learners with the community. Every citizen-neighbor deserved our respect and love. Then we would

---

9. Lupton, *Return Flight*, 21.

understand the message that the sign conveyed was incongruent with an authentic urban ministry. I anticipated that when that transformation occurred, our leaders would not only take that sign down from our wall but remove it from their hearts and minds, as well.

To become present for others is a pretty simple task. Just be there. Be there in the morning. Be there at noon. Be there at night. Be present on weekends. Be there during the week. We needed to be present. Our presence would tell a neighborhood stigmatized into the bondage of worthlessness that God loved it 24/7. Not just for an hour or two on Sunday mornings. We opened those red church doors and our gym and let kids from the community reclaim our assets as their own. Not a few of our older leaders shuddered nervously at what we were trying to do. To them, it must have felt like removing protective slipcovers off their favorite old couch and inviting the children to take a seat. Our building and playground represented social capital we could invest back into the community. We came to understand that our God-given assets could and must be deployed for the common good.

I developed new ways to connect our congregation to its original charter—to provide a safe place for kids to have fun and hear about the God who loved them. Through Bible study, worship, and prayer, we reinvested in a new, emerging Ontario Spirit. Our neighbors were just as surprised as we were when, instead of driving away after Sunday worship, informal groups of two or three members would take walks around the block and introduce themselves to the neighbors. Our neighbors connected to our efforts. After-school and recreation programming earned us the right to validate what the world had deemed invalid. Kensington could be a place of hope. And all this was done with limited money. It confounded us that we often received more useful assistance from the Rotary Club or the corner market, for example, than from faith-based entities in the suburbs, or even from our denomination. We sought out partnerships to fund our initiatives, and within two years we built a collaboration of energy that surprised us even more than it did our detractors.

We must let the neighborhood hear, see, taste, touch, and smell the sincere love God has for them. In the words of St. Francis of Assisi, "Preach the Gospel by all means, and if necessary, use words."

Reneighboring through Modeling

"Here is the church, here is the steeple, open up the door and see all the people." I came to dislike that children's rhyme because it too easily identified the church as a building, with the people of God localized inside. But if the church is people, not a building, where are the people between Sundays? The majority of members who worship in the church's neighborhood make their home in a different, distant neighborhood. What core values are at work to make this church the church?

In the suburbs, traveling by personal car is commonplace. A typical church in the suburbs may draw from a radius of five to ten miles. Some large churches in the city may also draw large suburban crowds to its programs in the city. However, in the inner city, local church ministries must focus on the needs of the immediate neighborhood.

For our MissionWorks urban plunge, our invited suburban kids are sent on an urban walk and train ride. One of the things I ask them to consider as they travel is the condition of city churches and whether or not those churches have an attached parking lot. City churches typically do not have parking lots. In rare cases, a parking lot was added to the original building plan at a later time in the church's history when more and more of the parishioners commuted in from the suburbs for worship. Therefore, for neighborhood mission, a parking lot represented a missed opportunity for forming connections. Wilkey Church's "mom-and-pop" model is prevalent in the city. Most people either walk or rely on public transportation, and the neighborhood church really lives up to that name and serves the neighborhood. The large "supermarket" model of church ministry operates more successfully in the suburbs.

There are several critical issues to be resolved when members of an inner-city church relocate to the suburbs. First, the relocated members are now removed from the context of the primary neighborhood mission. To what degree can members effect change in a neighborhood in which they no longer live? How can they win the right to be heard? What do the neighborhood's residents think and feel when they see people arrive on Sundays and perform their duties, racing into their fortresslike building? An hour or two later these same people get back into their cars and leave. How can a neighborhood be reached effectively for the Gospel when the neighbors clearly don't care how much you know because they don't know how much you care?[10]

---

10. Barna, *Index of Leading Spiritual Indicators*, 66.

As disturbing as all this is, there is an equally tragic consequence of the displacement—members are likewise detached from effective ministry in their live-in neighborhood. When ministry opportunities arise in the new neighborhood, the displaced members have no localized reference point for evangelism, follow-up, discipleship, service, and accountability. The often desperate plea of many pastors—"invite a friend to worship"—takes on a entirely different meaning when the friends of the displaced members are miles (and maybe social classes) away. The displaced members wonder, "Why should I bring a friend down there?" since the only reason they are "down there" is that they and their family have remained down there.

Membership flight takes its toll in two areas. First, displaced members cannot earn the right to be heard in the church building's neighborhood resulting in an ineffective ministry. Second, displaced members cannot connect with the neighborhood they actually live in since a large aspect of their focus remains in the church itself. This is what has happened at Wilkey and scores of other previously neighbored churches across our country.

Nehemiah offered a solution to the dilemma of the displaced disciple: "Now the leaders of the people settled in Jerusalem, and the rest of the people cast lots to bring one out of every ten to live in Jerusalem, the holy city, while the remaining nine were to stay in their own towns. The people commended all the men who volunteered to live in Jerusalem" (Neh 11:1). After presenting their tithes to the Lord, they tithed themselves back into the city center in order to repopulate it. According to Ray Bakke, 10 percent "is enough" to make it work.[11] After the walls were mended (remember that they took only fifty-two days to build the wall to half its height), they knew that life had to be planted in the city, so they tithed people. Moreover, those who were selected were considered favored to live in Jerusalem! Ministry in Kensington cannot be done at arm's length, either. It cannot be done unless we live in the neighborhood, or at least have a constant presence, or at least a majority presence. Incarnational ministry requires it. The hope of the people depends on it. All of us should feel indebted for people who long ago presented themselves as living sacrifices to live and claim the neighborhood for God.

In order to love its neighborhood, the congregation needs to live in the neighborhood. Members should consider buying homes in close

---

11. Bakke, *Theology as Big as the City*, 111.

proximity to the church building. Neighbors already living nearby need to feel welcome to worship there, and effort must be expended to ensure that their needs are being met. The cycle of outward mobility must be replaced by one of inward mobility—an intentional plan to keep resourced, visionary people in the neighborhood.[12] We need to encourage talented and visionary people to remain in the neighborhood.

Proximity Matters

Our neighbors can't be expected to want to go into buildings that, like many of our churches, appear unwelcoming. Some churches look like medieval fortresses and are about as inaccessible. (Consider this: is the actual entrance to your building clearly marked? If it is, does it look welcoming?) The "job to be done" by individuals in our communities is likely not, "I want to be churched! Show me the way." I do think our neighbors are trying to get the following jobs done, one way or another: "I want to feel hopeful. I want to be treated with dignity and respect, and I aspire to a life of spiritual meaning. I need to ensure the safety of my family, have opportunities for meaningful work, and a sense of joy and peace in my community." I wonder what would happen if, instead of arbitrarily excluding our neighbors as outsiders, we intentionally provided ways for these kinds of jobs to get done through our worship, witness, and mission? It starts with listening and walking across the street.

Our neighbors notice people driving in and entering our church buildings one day a week, maybe two. In reality, it doesn't matter how many times a week people drive in. Neighbors see us driving in, then driving away. Community-facing ministries including food and clothing distribution, youth programs, or other needed and welcome services are offered seasonally, or multiple times each week. The point is that residents still observe people they don't know driving in and then driving away like so many weekday commuters. It's tough to build successful and sustainable relationships in this way.

One example of a faith-based organization building sustainable community wellness is found in Portland, Oregon. Compassion Connect[13] is partnering with other nongovernmental organizations and faith partners in the community to build neighborhood health and

---

12. Lupton, *Theirs Is the Kingdom*, 52.
13. See http://www.compassionconnect.com.

wellness through programs like the Apartment Complex Initiative and Compassion Clinics. Located in the communities served, impact is authentic and effective. Local churches can align their worship, witness, and mission by investing relationally in the lives of neighbors, creating a holistic sense of community.

A congregation in which a majority of active participants drive in from a distance is at risk of becoming a stranger in the community. God has moved in. Mission proximity matters. Move in and make positive love-in-action changes in your neighborhood.

God's story states that God "moved into the neighborhood" (John 1:14 MSG). This describes the incarnation (God, a spirit, becoming flesh and blood)—God became fully human in Jesus by moving in (not driving in) to our real world. This residency model of Jesus is incongruent with our drive-in, commuter-church model. Wilkey Church discovered the necessity of taking our community seriously.

You can become more present in your community. Start with the following homework. When your church is "home" again, the community will truly notice and be blessed.

Homework

1. Recall a time when you felt more "at home" in your church's neighborhood. What contributed to those "at home" feelings? What changed?

2. Explore the story of when your church was founded at your current location. Try to understand why "this" neighborhood was chosen over so many other options.

3. Read a copy of your church's charter. Why was your church established?

4. A few months ahead, choose a worship service designated "[Name of your town] Sunday." The worship focus of the gathering is to celebrate God's blessings and the community's many assets.

5. In small groups, collect lists of community assets. Consider domains represented in your community: faith-based organizations, volunteer groups, businesses, local government, health care, media, arts, parks, schools, libraries, etc. With a spirit of gratitude, identify gifts that bless your community. Don't forget to add your own church to

the list! Celebrating community gifts can inspire a deep reconnection and restore a feeling of "at home" not only for you but for your congregation, as well.

Reneighboring through Personal Interaction

Jesus knew a lot about the hearts of people. "For where your treasure is, there your heart will be also" (Matt 6:21). He knew that whatever treasure we value, no matter its location, our heart will be there, consistently and completely. My heart is in that neighborhood at H and Ontario.

I was called to be the pastoral leader at Wilkey and the Kensington Parish by the regional council called Philadelphia Presbytery. My mission was to explore the future sustainability of the church's mission. The presbytery's leaders made it clear to me that I was asked to put the congregation to sleep, peacefully. Wilkey Church was in a cycle of decline that nothing could reverse, or so they thought. Since Wilkey Church was a recipient of mission dollars, the presbytery wanted to be assured that their investment was prudent. Perhaps I would be the last pastor they had before closing their doors for good. However, what is important is that authentically being present in a place can result in deeper connections. Hearing the cries of the underprivileged and under-resourced cannot leave you the same again. Recall the image of tears streaming down Jesus' face as he looked over the walls of the city (Luke 19:41–48). What did he see? He must have seen into the homes and hearts of the people as his donkey carried him into Jerusalem. With this in mind, I became convinced that an effective neighborhood mission could be established. Sider correctly observes, "Most churches today are one-sided disasters. In some suburban churches hundreds of people come to Jesus and praise God in brand-new buildings, but they seldom learn that their new faith has anything to do with the wrenching, inner-city poverty just a few miles away."[14]

Robert Linthicum rightly cautions, "The need is not the call"—one must differentiate between the call of God on a person and mere heart-tugs of emotion.[15] So it is not out of guilt, or unresolved inner needs, but a determined heeding of the Spirit that compels the leader to reconnect what has become disconnected. How can followers of Jesus who live in

---

14. Sider, *One-Sided Christianity?*, 25.
15. Linthicum, *City of God*, 238.

the shadow of our cities ignore the tragic state of neighbors a couple of miles down the road? How can they pretend there is no connection? We can say our prayers, then drive from our zoned neighborhoods to a distant, moderately or exceptionally well-paying job. There is often a spirit of disconnect and confusion in the suburbs. By definition the schools are located in one area, the housing tracts in another, the offices and buildings in yet another. Suburban planning does not engender a holistic view of life. We are supremely detached from even the pieces of our own lives.

For us at Wilkey, establishing connections was essential, and not just between the members and the community, between the community and the church, and between the neighbors themselves; the ministry also needed to build connections with other organizations, both to share what we were learning and to benefit from resources they had to offer. MissionWorks was developed to support multiple connections. We designed a logo and promoted our site as a place of relationship-building and engagement.

Figure 10

As a direct-ministry effort, MissionWorks provided an effective way to connect partner organizations from the suburbs and across the country.

We strongly believed that it was a sin to bore a kid with the Gospel. Our mission theme of "I Can Do That!" underscored the importance of servant leadership based on the prophet Nehemiah's ministry to the city.

Figure 11

Nehemiah 2:18

Biblical reflection, asking hard questions, discovering joy in the city—these activities were woven together to do more than a standard religious curriculum or typical mission trip can do . . . all in just a few days. Though the focus was on serving the neighborhood, the participants would experience transformation, too. By inviting suburban kids to the city for our urban plunge, we intended to give away a part of Philadelphia, the city's possibilities, and its promise as a community of hope. Since the majority of the world's population live in cities, we accepted our responsibility to our suburban and rural sisters and brothers to build connections. Why is it that, despite knowing that most people today live in urban areas, many continue to ignore urban ministry? The whole world is present across the street in our urban neighborhoods.[16]

The MissionWorks crew included about a dozen young people between the ages of thirteen and eighteen, with four or five adult leaders. When a church from Rochester, New York, heard about MissionWorks,

---

16. Bakke, *Theology as Big as the City*, 73.

they initiated and funded their trip to our church during the summer. Our responsibility was to provide housing in the church by converting classrooms into reasonably comfortable accommodations. Our church leaders supervised logistics and the preparation of meals with the trip leaders, and provided around-the-clock on-site support and security. At least two of our adult leaders were embedded with the crew to provide hospitality and context by building relationships with the youth and facilitating the interactions between the youth team and hundreds of neighborhood kids. Conversational Bible study, prayer, and guided small group learning ensured that the experience was spiritually and educationally enriching. Trips to other churches and neighborhoods and visits to historical sites across Philadelphia were planned during a typical five-day MissionWorks session.

Local neighborhood youth prioritized neighborhood projects the MissionWorks crew participated in. Collaborative sweat and tears generated energy throughout the entire neighborhood. After-school programs, playground activities, repairs, and various improvements and chores at several city locations were coordinated in concert with neighborhood kids and adults. We were committed to designing an urban plunge experience for learning and improving the youth's leadership skills and deconstructing the mission arrogance and paternalism found in many other church programs. It did not take long to recognize that a suburban and urban collaboration can excite and challenge suburban and urban kids alike in incredible ways. The energy of one MissionWorks crew from Wisconsin helped make the start-up of our Ontario Spirit sports program a success. MissionWorks generated relationships with several churches, and Wilkey Church plans to host new MissionWorks crews.

It is important to understand how suburban isolationism (besides racism, classism, ageism, and some other "isms") feeds the "compartmentalized life" mentality. We segregate everything. We close our eyes to the poor. We would rather salve our guilt by sending a couple of bucks overseas or a busload of kids to build a house in the dessert than get up and hear the cries of hurting people in the inner city. Paul said in Eph 6:12, "For our struggle is not against flesh and blood, but against the rulers, against the authorities, against the powers of this dark world and against the spiritual forces of evil in the heavenly realms." Spiritual realities are reality. There is a God. God is present. Jesus disrupts what is not working, while the Spirit connects all of us to what is working, not just in a vocational sense but a locational one as well. Nehemiah demonstrates the importance of a transformed community being salt and light in the world. Keeping in mind Paul's use of the phrase "flesh and blood" in Ephesians, consider this narrative from Neh 5:5–12:

> "Although we are of the same flesh and blood as our countrymen and though our sons are as good as theirs, yet we have to subject our sons and daughters to slavery. Some of our daughters have already been enslaved, but we are powerless, because our fields and our vineyards belong to others."
>
> When I heard their outcry and these charges, I was very angry. I pondered them in my mind and then accused the nobles and officials. I told them, "You are exacting usury from your own countrymen!" So I called together a large meeting to deal with them and said: "As far as possible, we have bought back our Jewish brothers who were sold to the Gentiles. Now you are selling your brothers, only for them to be sold back to us!" They kept quiet, because they could find nothing to say.
>
> So I continued, "What you are doing is not right. Shouldn't you walk in the fear of our God to avoid the reproach of our Gentile enemies? I and my brothers and my men are also lending the people money and grain. But let the exacting of usury stop! Give back to them immediately their fields, vineyards, olive groves and houses, and also the usury you are charging them—the hundredth part of the money, grain, new wine and oil."
>
> "We will give it back," they said. "And we will not demand anything more from them. We will do as you say."
>
> Then I summoned the priests and made the nobles and officials take an oath to do what they had promised.

The church sees as its birthright a pattern of life that puts a priority on personal needs and location. The church that forgets its core mission to reach the neighborhood ceases to be the church God has called to that place. By embracing the neighborhood, choosing to love it, the church becomes a witness to the goodness of God and the hope offered and accessible through Jesus Christ. Once the church chooses to care, chooses to spend time on the streets again, chooses to invest its treasure and resources in the lives of people in the neighborhood, then and only then will a neighborhood see God's love and know its origin.

Reneighboring through Expression of Faith

As John Perkins points out, "During more than thirty-five years of ministry, we have discovered that one of the needs we can love people around is their children. As we love their children, the parents begin to respect us and to look to our spiritual motives."[17] The call of Christ to a worshipping, witnessing, mission community is to love all. No thinking disciple of Jesus would argue that. The leaders at Wilkey would agree with that, too. We loved singing the chorus, "Red and yellow, black and white, they are precious in his sight, Jesus loves the little children of the world." However, we do not adjust our behavior or allocate our resources in light of its truth. We ignore Jesus' efforts to reach the poor, the outcast, widows, orphans and women, stigmatized groups such as the Samaritans (John 4:4ff.), and even people of influence such as Zacchaeus (Luke 19:2ff.). In our northern Kensington neighborhood, the early conflict came within the same ethnic group—that of the Orangemen (Protestant Irish) and the Irish Roman Catholic. Members of the church have related stories to me about anger, resentment, fighting, and feuding as they were victimized by Roman Catholic neighbors. Now the racial mix is changing to include Hispanic (24 percent) and African-American (29 percent), among other groups.

As incredible as it seems, the cutting edge of faithful witness at Wilkey Church is the rediscovery that God loves us exactly where we are. I know that does not sound profound, but it is simply the truth. Not because of who we are racially, socially, or ethnically, but because of whose we are as human beings, created in the image of God, belonging to God, citizens of God's kingdom, coheirs with the Christ of the nations, with access to God's emerging and hopeful future as residents in Kensington. Its this simple story that merits a retelling.

Reneighboring through Collaborations of Faith

We prayed not only for our own programs but also for families and children, police officers, teachers and schools, and the few businesses still healthy enough to function. We prayed for other churches in our Kensington community and across the city. We sent teams to serve other neighborhoods. Most significantly, Wilkey was selected to participate

---

17. Perkins, *Restoring At-Risk Communities*, 19.

in a national model for youth violence reduction called the Youth Violence Reduction Project, referred to by its acronym YVRP.[18] We eagerly showed our story of transformation to anyone willing to see. Each week, I participated in the steering committee convened at the Philadelphia Safe and Sound offices. John J. DiIulio Jr., later the White House director of faith-based initiatives, was the senior advisor at Public/Private Ventures (P/PV). P/PV invited community leaders to play a critical role in designing the start-up whose mission it was to keep safe those youth deemed most likely to kill or be killed in the next six months. The tragically increasing death toll among our city's youth was highest within the 24th and 25th police districts, and Wilkey Church was at the center. The intensive intervention needed community leaders and safe places where the youth could gather. City officials, school administrators, community leaders, clergy members, and justice, law enforcement, and probation teams formed a strong partnership to keep kids "alive at 25," a motto of the group. I served as a member of the Operations Committee due to my church's proximity, community connections, and volunteer work (at Stetson Middle School, for example). Clergy contributed to YVRP's design and early implementation. According to the final report, YVRP's close collaboration with community organizations "produced promising results—namely, an increase in the number of young people 'alive at 25.' It bears repeating in high-crime neighborhoods around the country."[19]

Why do churches disconnect from their neighborhoods in the first place? This displacement is complex and can even be demonic. It can also be historical and political, racial and financial, personal, generational, and spatial. In our post-Christian, post-church culture we rarely invest our best assets in places with the least resources. If we did, we would understand a theology of location as much as our other theological containers and amusements. If we really got it, we would be putting skilled and funded teams of transformational leaders in strategically critical urban areas to build collaborative ministries. It takes time and faith to earn the love and respect of a stranger. What's more, it takes courage.

We have incredible social capital to reinvest in our urban places. Sure, people in our suburban and rural areas face many of the same problems as do those in the city. But the tragic fact is that despite (or because

---

18. McClanahan, *Alive at 25*, 36.
19. Gary Walker, foreword to McClanahan, *Alive at 25*.

of) the challenges of scale, the places where need is greatest receive the fewest resources.

The church often deploys well-meaning leaders and pastors with little experience and woefully inadequate competencies, compensation, and support to enter a world that does not exist anymore. Many seminaries equip our pastors with anachronistic tools, with methods and skills that are ill-suited to the challenges of a media-rich, experience-driven, technologically connected and entertainment-seeking culture. Our world, for all its craving, longs for meaning and authentic spiritual awakening—yet it is the church that often seems least equipped to add value to the search. Tragically, our councils, despite their valiant attempts at reorganizing and restructuring, seem perpetually unable to change from the inside out. Even worse, our congregations languish in the untreated trauma of their decline and with their last gasps fumble for an elusive fix, finally throwing their hands up in dismay. In their pain, they blame the leader, the church, the community, or even God for insufficient resources and unsustainable results.

We should think twice before closing a vital neighborhood resource like a connected congregation. At the same time, we should not hesitate to close ineffective, unable-to-be-reneighbored congregations. Reallocating their resources to strategically sustainable mission is better than ensuring the comfort of a few. Denominations, councils, and other governing bodies must not hesitate to start new, neighborhood-based worshipping, witnessing, and mission teams in the shell of a repurposed former church site, or boldly acquire, design, or build a site to meet the missional needs of a connected, sent-out gathering of worshippers. Better to build successful and sustainable transformational models at a few strategic sites in the city than to be burdened with ineffective and outdated buildings. Congregations can connect to their community in authentic ways and even collaborate with other neighborhood assets to explore partnerships with civic institutions, government, and the private sector.

Is Your Mission Working?

In Kensington we kept asking ourselves, how do we know we are connecting in authentic and meaningful ways? It is one thing for the worshipping community to feel good about their community-directed initiatives, for example, but if the community does not experience change that matters to them, then only the church wins (which is not really a win, of course). While a focus on mission deliverables is a good practice, a deeper understanding of the ministry's impact can be achieved by a focus on community receivables. How do you know you are connecting in authentic and meaningful ways? You can begin to answer this question by paying attention to the outcomes the community experiences.

I worked with the Presbyterian Church (U.S.A.) both as a regional leader and on their national board. I think a lot about the church's job to be done. Another way to think about your mission is to ask the question, what does your community hire your church to do? Or consider: what could families in your community hire your church to do for them? To answer these questions, you need to be in authentic relationship with your community.

Faith communities in the United States have been utilizing the same framework for their work for well more than one hundred years. Like other volunteer groups that value incumbency more than innovation, they have fewer and fewer people who continue to give their best, and they manage only to offer less and less. Regional councils exclusively listen to their largest membership churches and implement rehashed programs that promise greater growth, only to realize too late that they are missing other voices in the church and in the community. The incumbent church systems have too high a cost structure to innovate, let alone disrupt ministry models. Sadly, our ministry models do not produce energy, and they leave practitioners unsatisfied in their experience. Russell Crabtree makes this point when he says, "Evidence suggests that a church is vital and healthy when members bear witness to their experience in the body of Christ as one that is both satisfying and energizing."[20] Is it any wonder that more than seventeen hundred pastors leave the ministry every month?[21] We keep delivering our ministry as we always have, out of habit or convenience, expecting people to receive it and line up at the door, but for what? And why? What might be missing in your mission? Who is missing in your mission?

---

20. Crabtree, *Owl Sight*, 65.
21. Peters, "10 Real Reasons Pastors Quit," par. 1.

The Church's "Job To Be Done"

To more deeply understand the *why* of our mission, the "Job To Be Done" (JTBD) framework developed by Harvard Business School professor and author Clay Christensen can be useful. "When a company understands the jobs that arise in people's lives, and then develops products and the accompanying experiences required in purchasing and using the product to do the job perfectly, it causes customers to instinctively 'pull' the product into their lives whenever the job arises."[22] The church offers products, too, though we in the church may find this nomenclature unfamiliar or even disturbing. Our products can be programs like worship and after-school activities, or invitations to faith. Christensen defines the Job To Be Done as "a circumstance in which an individual is trying to solve a problem or accomplish a task. Companies find success when they make it easier or more convenient for customers to do jobs that they had already been trying to do. A product usually fails when managers expect their customers to prioritize something that they historically had not been trying to do."[23]

Church ministry as a job? Hiring the church? Aside from renting out the hall, what does that mean? I am not talking about renting out space in your building. I am referring to the core mission of your church (to show God's love and demonstrate the good news about Jesus Christ, as an example.) The thing is, the people across the street, shop owners around the corner, seniors, families, and digital natives in your community likely don't have a clue what your church could do for them. What's more, your community is looking to get jobs done, lots of different jobs, jobs that will, one way or another, get done but likely without you. The church has an incredible opportunity to understand how to "give yourself away" in authentic, transparent, and effective service in the name of Jesus Christ. Paying attention to our church's spiritual and social impact can lead us to consider how and why people choose to connect (or not) to our church.

Decades ago, many people could be expected to choose between multiple churches, deciding which of them to attend. The category (such as *a person who needs to go to church*) or the product (*attendance at a Presbyterian church,* for example) correlated with the action taken: "I choose *that* church." Most people attended a church or another place of

22. Christensen, Allworth, and Dillon, *How Will You Measure Your Life?*, 63.
23. Christensen, Anthony, and Roth, *Seeing What's Next*, 301.

worship many times each month. Churches just kept refining their offerings based on the feedback they received from people who already made the decision to attend. Church leaders did their best to meet the needs of current participants. What Christensen observes about education applies equally to the church—just substitute "churches" for schools and "neighbors" for students in the following sentence: "Our schools were improving themselves on dimensions of improvement irrelevant to the job that students are trying to do."[24]

As it turns out, trying to meet needs is a slippery slope. Needs just do not end. Furthermore, in recent years, there have been fewer and fewer people in the category of "looking for a church"—and even more revealing, they are not choosing between different churches. "Going to church" is not a task most people have on their job-to-be-done list. Instead, people are simply trying to accomplish things that matter, and their job to be done prompts them to hire services, activities, and perhaps churches that meet those goals. What could your neighbors hire your church to do?

The jobs to be done in your community might include these:

1. I want to get involved in the community.

2. I need help to better understand God.

3. I really want an opportunity to feel better about myself.

4. I am looking for a place where my family can feel safe.

5. I want to be more successful in my relationships.

6. I need a place to feel safe and accepted.

7. Where can I invest my interests in something worthwhile?

Of course, the best way to formulate this list of possible jobs is to listen to your neighbors—and to do that you have to get out and engage them. The single greatest opportunity we can embrace today is to take a walk. Walking is not just good for our physical health, it is essential for missional health, too. As simple as this sounds, those of us who gather inside church buildings each week seem to have forgotten what our neighbors actually see when they look at our place of ministry. It has been awhile since we paid close enough attention to listen with our neighbors' ears and see with our neighbors' eyes.

24. Christensen, Allworth, and Dillon, *How Will You Measure Your Life?*, 68.

If we want our true love story to become known everywhere, we can begin by thinking differently about who our neighbors already are in God's story, "For God so loved the world" (John 3:16).

Walking for Missional Health

Take a walk across the street and ask God to direct you to a neighbor you can thoughtfully engage in a brief conversation. In a neighborly way (think Mr. Rogers), ask if they would be kind enough to share what they "know" about your church. What's the neighbor's reading of the church's story? Be prepared to listen. Thank them for what they shared and let them know their opinions will influence your church's connection to the community. Remind them that God loves them—and so do those who gather at your church. Take proactive steps to share with your leaders what you discovered and boldly recalibrate your mission connections to write a new never-ending love story. Go back to Start, and repeat.

When we are alert to the spiritual and social impact of our activities (programs, services, ministries, etc.), we can learn what neighbors, families, and communities need to get done. Instead of incrementally improving what we already do well, or improving in areas we wish to improve in, we can realign our activities. Worshipping communities of every size could express their core mission as a servant in the community context. Being more attentive results in being more deeply connected, so that the church actually serves as it offers its services. Could the Job To Be Done framework help revolutionize your mission? We found it could.

Jesus told us, "Anyone who has faith in me will do what I have been doing. You will do even greater things than these, because I am going to the Father" (John 14:12–14). The Job To Be Done framework pushes the church forward to look at its mission in higher resolution. These connections of mission and context result in deeper satisfaction among those who are served, a greater sense of energy among those serving, and greater impact on the world.

When we look at the church from the perspective of our neighbors, we flip the focus from the church to the community. This shift is revolutionary because it offers the possibility that we can realign our resources, processes, and values to achieve the mission instead of preserving the illusion of a mission destined to crumble.

Questions for the Church to Consider

1. What is the use-case for your church?
2. Are you committed to growing and changing, adapting and learning, by discovering what the community is actually looking to "use" your ministry for?
3. What are your neighbors looking for that is currently and urgently missing from their lives?
4. What are the forces at play when a person chooses to visit any church?
5. What are the forces at play when a person chooses your church?
6. What spiritual needs do they express? How are they getting these needs met?
7. What schedules, budgets, and priorities do your neighbors manage that your ministry could address?

Exploring responses to these and similar questions within an adapted JTBD framework has provoked many leaders to think more critically about self-preserving, incumbent ministry models. Only then can leadership be released to imagine new possibilities for innovative ministry. Our leaders agreed to form a learning community to develop a missional, outward-directed response to these questions.

7

Community of Learning

A wonderful change occurred in the congregational outlook when we began addressing the reality of our underserved place and invited church leaders to form a learning group called the Ministry Learning Community, or MLC. It has helped identify biases, prejudices, and unintended stigma attributions such as sexism, racism, classism, genderism, and ageism, not in the community at large, but in our worshipping community. You cannot make a congregation love a neighborhood, but you can model the behaviors of loving a community and resource their learning.

Like a Good Neighbor, Discipleship Is There

Leaders in the religious community are typically well trained. Many pastors have postgraduate degrees. We should take responsibility for our church syllabus, then, our mission statement. For example, we know that Jesus had twelve disciples. We may also recall that the word *disciple* (from the Greek, meaning "student") was used to describe any student, particularly those who were following a teacher or a philosophy. Discipleship, then, is a behavior, and it did not originate with Jesus. Jesus' disciples were learners, modeling their practice after the master.

What have you learned lately, or in what ways have you grown emotionally and spiritually through your involvement at church? Our institutionalized Christian education programs have substituted the dynamic, behavior-based, life-giving learning relationship of teacher and student with church content that primarily reinforces church identity and beliefs. We aspire to teach discipleship—a good thing—but reduce it to little more than content acquisition. While we seem to train good disciples, we have failed to train good citizens. How can we be faithful disciples of Jesus in public spaces if we remain disconnected in our private spaces? You cannot have good discipleship without good citizenship.

As the pastor, modeling the love for the neighborhood and engaging the congregation in thoughtful and serious Bible study, prayer, and relationship-building activities can have a profound impact. Individuals report greater satisfaction in their work and more energy in their efforts. Incredibly, once we shifted our focus from how to save our church to how to help save our community, much of the complaining ceased. Even those leaders who habitually saw the darkness alone began to move out from what were their own shadows into the light. The light was outside and the source was blazingly bright. "I am the light of the world," Jesus said (John 8:12). Below are Four Reneighboring Steps we developed at Wilkey. If they can be implemented there, on the corner of H and Ontario Streets, then they can be implemented in your community, too.

Reneighboring, Step 1:
Love Your Neighborhood More than Anyone Else Does

If a congregation does not love God and people, then it will be unable to love the neighborhood. Though there may be nothing lovely or lovable about the neighborhood, whether in the inner core or the suburbs, the people there are of inestimable worth to God and to God's people. Luke 15 includes a cascading set of parables telling of the worth the seeker places on the lost sheep, the lost coin, and the lost son. Each parable of Jesus has similarities, but the key ingredient apparent in the first two parables—the seeker actively goes in search of the lost—is obviously lacking in the last. The man of the first parable cared for his sheep, and the woman of the second parable cared for her coin, but the older brother cared nothing for his own flesh and blood. He was less concerned for his younger sibling's well-being than he was for his own comfort. There was no love in his heart, nor was there any compassion—and when through a grace-act of God the younger son returned, the older brother became angry and refused to celebrate. Reconnecting a congregation to its neighborhood is primarily a matter of love.

Reneighboring, Step 2: Make Love Visible

Putting that love in action is another hurdle that must be overcome. Actively participating with others in our Kensington Ministry Partnership and the monthly prayer breakfasts we established was a constructive way to build vision-based cooperation in the community at large. Soon our people could hear and see what God was doing in the neighborhood through the eyes of other Christians as well as link with community development staff, business associations, media, and local educators.

Reneighboring, Step 3: Leverage the Past

We are beginning to understand our past and are rediscovering the passion and energy of our founders. I have undertaken to become a master of the past, bringing others on historical journeys to understand not just the *what* but the *why* of mission and program efforts. I love to tell stories I have read, or—even more exciting—stories I have heard from older members of the congregation as they recall the passion of the prior generation.

Reneighboring, Step 4: Make Community Connections

We linked with community institutions and initiated ministry programs such as MissionWorks and a literacy and training center to meet immediate needs, giving away ministry that balanced our commitment to the broader church and to the local neighborhood.

The congregation can become complacent in its mission; the downside of long-range planning is that it may never come about. Our church began to show urgency in reneighboring, since our love for people in Jesus' name could not remain inside the fortress we had become self-conscience of. Our essence is no longer "fortress" but "resource." We realized that the land, the place, does not belong to us—it belongs to the neighborhood. We released our gifts and resources for God's use on behalf of our neighbors, and the neighborhood responded in demonstrable ways.

The sign reading "remember to lock the door behind you" is still the first thing you see as you enter our church, but the seeds of its removal have been planted. In addition, I intended to wait patiently for a church member to suggest its removal. But sometimes the long view must be sacrificed for the bigger picture. My graduate school chose our church as the site for a New Year's convocation. The purpose of the event was to recognize academic achievements and the transformation Wilkey Church was experiencing. I spoke to one of my leaders a few weeks prior to the event and shared my particular consternation regarding the sign's message. She agreed, obviously, because a few days later the sign was gone. I was also delighted that the sign did not make it back up on the wall.

Most of our leaders expressed a commitment to be connected to the neighborhood. Moreover, that circle of love for the neighborhood was big enough to include the folks within the church family who dared not expand their vision. It was not easy. Nevertheless, the journey we started in simple faith, to act out on the street what we believe in the pew, was not one that we regretted.

God Is the Model Maker

As Bill Veltrop rightly observes, "Today's change initiatives are primarily based on a problem-solving view of organizations and change. They usually ignore the potential for generative change. Generative change is change designed to be life-giving—change that builds in the organizational capacity not only to continuously improve what is but also to make evolutionary leaps to what's possible."[1] Veltrop's contribution to our learning community was practically a paradigm shift in and of itself. Establishing a ministry learning community began as an exercise in problem-solving. I needed a team to learn with me, to ask the hard questions, to determine the metrics for mission success, to learn and grow together. It sounded simple. It wasn't. "Not so fast," I heard that still, small, inner voice whisper. The futurist Veltrop argued that there was a better motivation for change than mere problem-solving (dealing with what we have), something far greater—generative change (believing that we can become something better.) Veltrop's generative change idea was powerful, but when that idea was integrated with the actual agent for lasting and truthful change, namely, God, the idea became transformational. For Veltrop's model, the words *evolutionary* and *generative* speak of something that comes from within the self, group, or organization alone. We had a different focus. In our model of transformation there was indeed a focus on

---

1. Veltrop, "Discovering a Generative Path to Organizational Change," in Gozdz, *Community Building*, 117.

capacity not deficiency, but the primary agent of renewal and any paradigm shifting that would occur, the source for capacity change, was the reality of a dynamic, life-giving relationship with God. Instead of being content with the possible, we could actually experience the impossible.

A model is a symbol representing an idea that has three dimensions. It typically moves in more than just two dimensions. Our *Sitz im Leben* frames the model, a convergence of relationships around the Wilkey Church. The notion of a ministry model was initially difficult for the leaders to visualize until they understood their role to be that of model maker. I was inviting them to co-create an intervention (the model) that could transform not only the community but also their own experience as a community of faith. Every ministry must align with the work of the Maker. We are participants with the Creator in building God's mission in Kensington. We are guards, watching and building the neighborhood with the Lord. As I began to visualize the model for our MLC, I knew it was an important task, for we would welcome and engage with the Spirit who connects us to the possibilities of success. God is the model maker.

Community Is the Focus

We began by formulating guiding principles that would build on the idea of God as the model maker. We would affirm the worth and value of each participant committed to the process. The purpose of the MLC was not just to help mold a model for mission. When called together as a group of people to be the MLC, it was to be a ministry with them. When Jesus called his disciples, Mark 3:14 records, "He appointed twelve—designating them apostles—that they might be with him and that he might send them out to preach and to have authority to drive out demons." The priority was that we might be together in our diversity but with a common mission.

There were twelve unique individuals called apostles who would somehow make a mighty team. Jesus saw a capacity in each of them to learn, grow, and lead that they and others did not at first comprehend. He saw that Peter was a rock when Peter's parents saw only a pebble. He saw mighty thunder in James and John when the crowds saw only complaints and reckless energy. In doubting Thomas, Jesus saw a "Thomas of faith." In Matthew, Jesus saw not a cheating tax collector but a future storyteller of the promised King. Even at the last hour, Jesus loved Judas—who would in futility betray him.[2] The city would be our mission field, which required a team to function with or without their pastoral leader. John W. Gardner underscores the idea of leadership capacity when he writes, "A community has the power to motivate members to exceptional performance."[3] Gardner adds that "a clear part of the problem—particularly in our cities—is the fragmentation of leadership. Most leaders are One Segment Leaders, fattening on the loyalty of their own little segment and exhibiting little regard for the city as a whole."[4] We do not need more fragmentation in mission; we need mission focus and a commitment to the larger picture. We called together a group of people who would build more than Kensington, as Nehemiah exhorted the families to take responsibility for their section so the whole could be completed.

> The men of Jericho built the adjoining section, and Zaccur son of Imri built next to them.
> The sons of Hassenaah rebuilt the Fish Gate. They laid its beams and put its doors, bolts, and bars in place. Meremoth son of Uriah, the son of Hakkoz, repaired the next section. Next to him Meshullam son of Berekiah, the son of Meshezabel, made repairs, and next to him Zadok son of Baana also made repairs. (Neh 3:2–4)

The MLC's task was to listen to the voice of God, to see what God sees, to build God's City. Community building was the point of mission.

The Learning Community

The pastor's role is a diverse one, and the MLC offered support and encouragement in the midst of my ministry at Wilkey Presbyterian Church, and as coordinating pastor for the three-church Kensington Presbyterian Parish. The MLC evaluated the developing model and provided needed accountability and assistance.

---

2. John 13:26 reads, "Jesus answered, 'It is the one to whom I will give this piece of bread when I have dipped it in the dish.' Then, dipping the piece of bread, he gave it to Judas Iscariot, son of Simon." For the host to offer the first piece of bread in this way was regarded as an act of honor. Though identifying his betrayer, Jesus extended his love toward him. Sadly, Judas took his own life as Jesus died on a cross for his sins on the other side of the mountain.

3. Gardner, "The New Leadership Agenda," in Gozdz, *Community Building*, 283.

4. Ibid., 292.

Second, the MLC was a unit of ministry, striving to experience community and evoke giftedness and shared ministry among its members. As a unit of ministry it served the broader church as a catalyst for change and growth.

Third, the MLC was a bridge to the neighborhood. The commitment to congregational transformation and renewal is inseparably connected to community impact. Representatives from the community, both young and old, who were not directly involved in the church would be recruited to serve on the MLC. Two young people from the neighborhood kept our MLC process honest as our focus on youth ministry strategically bridged into families. The MLC served as the ears, eyes, and feet as we engaged the community.

True community, as M. Scott Peck observes, is not something the faith community easily attains. We use the word *community* for "a town, a church, a synagogue, a fraternal organization, an apartment complex, a professional association—regardless of how poorly those individuals communicate with each other. It is a false use of the word."[5] Community, then, is not just a descriptor of a place—the community in one town versus another. Community is an organic and living experience of individuals who come together to achieve something meaningful. But the vision that brings together a group or team, or even a neighborhood, is not the only thing that matters. "What gives power to communal possibility is the imagination and authorship of citizens led through a process of engagement," writes Peter Block. "This is an organic and relational process. This is what creates a structure of belonging. This is more critical than the vision and the plan."[6]

Six individuals were initially recruited to form the Ministry Learning Community. We started with individuals known at least superficially to one another. It was difficult to introduce new members from the community, especially the youth who were not known by the group. This discomfort was understandable due to the persistent congregational detachment from the neighborhood. Most in the church were not familiar with their neighbors. In our "family model" congregation, the gathering around the table was familiar and comfortable. The congregation was enthusiastic about the program since I introduced the idea in the fall of 1996 and I was sure these people would be a good ministry group for

---

5. Peck, *Different Drum*, 69.
6. Block, *Community*, 109.

my MLC experience. I was sure I had a diverse learning environment, and the Learning Styles Inventory (LSI)[7] provided useful questions with responses tagged to different learning styles. I pictured each team member in my mind's eye, attempting to correlate how they fit with the other members. I learned that the MLC was resistant to the "testing nature" of the inventory, and my suggestion that we use it was not unanimous. The LSI was an aid to understanding the group and deepened our understanding of one another. Eight individuals eventually made up the MLC, with a learning style distribution of three Accommodators, one Diverger, three Assimilators, and one Converger. The tool affirmed our differences, and that began an enriching and productive discovery in its own right.

The participants began right away to get to know one another on the MLC in a deeper way than they initially enjoyed as members of the congregation. It was a good group of both affective and directional people. Two were married couples; the remaining two, both women, were unmarried. All had been involved at Wilkey for more than twenty years. The young person (and often his little brother) remained in the MLC loop, and though they did not regularly attend the formal MLC meetings, they attended worship and participated in our Ontario Spirit sports programs. The qualities I was looking for were enthusiasm, commitment, perseverance, and a love for the people.

We had previously spent about two months studying Nehemiah, and as our MLC began to take shape we enjoyed the metaphor of taking a walk with Nehemiah to describe our process. Our journey together represented the possibility that God was bringing us along a process that would stir our spirits and affirm our gifts. We tried to more deeply understand how to be a community of faith within, and a partner to, the community at large. We agreed that our MLC was a kind of mission experiment and we were all in.

Teams first experience what Peck calls "pseudocommunity": "In pseudocommunity a group attempts to purchase community cheaply by pretense."[8] While unintentional, a team that is just trying to get along withholds the truth; the important and often disquieting facts are ignored to avoid conflict. "Pseudocommunity is conflict-avoiding; true community

---

7. The Learning Styles Inventory proved to be a highly useful instrument with two key attributes: (1) it was easy to administer since it was self-scoring, and (2) it unlocked a deeper understanding of how individuals learn and how a diverse team can be enriched by members' differences.

8. Peck, *Different Drum*, 104.

is conflict-resolving," Peck writes.⁹ At our first meeting it was difficult to resist the focus on the positive—how we were all in this process together and how encouraging it would be. Building a sense of community with a leadership team is not an easy task. Being guided by M. Scott Peck's *Different Drum*, we learned that there were stages our Ministry Learning Community could expect to experience. As I pondered the stages of community, I recognized from our first meeting that I kept the group in pseudocommunity! I acknowledged no problems or concerns, and since I did not expect any, I realized I must have unwittingly looked the other way when conflicts came up. I needed to affirm the process and be honest about the steps along the way. I had an opportunity to exercise my ability to admit and communicate difficulty (as opposed to blind optimism).

The MLC's experience of pseudocommunity led the group to politely ignore hurtful words or misleading assumptions offered by certain members. Biases and preconceived attitudes, like racism and classism, were left unaddressed—unaddressed until, after a few meetings, one member or another began to say something risky, admitting, for example, that they hated what the neighborhood had become. While difficult for the team to process at first, several other members tentatively agreed, whereas others did not, which in the community formation process led us to the second stage: chaos.

"In the stage of chaos," says Peck, "individual differences are, unlike those in pseudocommunity, right out in the open."¹⁰ At times the group seemed to linger in that chaotic place, only to be drawn back as if by an invisible magnet to what we might call political correctness. Crabtree correctly diagnoses our experience when he writes, "We characterize low-satisfaction, high-energy churches as chaotic systems."¹¹ The stages of community building are not sharply defined, and after a time of processing it was back to chaos when truth emerged, whether in the form of attacks on the neighborhood, or me as the pastor, or the process itself as expressed in statements like, "What is the point of trying to help the community when we can't even get along!" Finding ways as the leader to affirm the courage of expressing truthful feelings and facts allows the chaos to ebb and flow until a channel of energy on the team begins to lead to the third stage Peck identifies: emptiness.

9. Ibid.
10. Ibid., 108.
11. Crabtree, *Owl Sight*, 67.

"As a group moves into emptiness, a few of its members begin to share their own brokenness—their defeats, failures, doubts, fears, inadequacies, and sins," Peck explains. "They begin to stop acting as if they 'had it all together' as they reflect on those things they need to empty themselves of."[12] Several of our MLC meetings did not end well. As the leader, although I well understood the stages of group building, coming to an end point, to the "death" of the group, as Peck describes it, was painful. It was in this place of emptying that I came to the realization that our intervention would not work as we had hoped. Intellectually I got that. Emotionally and internally, my ego resisted it. We came to accept our defeat as we recalled Jesus' own experience of defeat, dismay, and discouragement in his encounters with persistent obstacles, resistant followers, and his own suffering. The MLC found a special place of emptying peace when it reflected on Jesus' own emptying:

> Think of yourselves the way Christ Jesus thought of himself. He had equal status with God but didn't think so much of himself that he had to cling to the advantages of that status no matter what. Not at all. When the time came, he set aside the privileges of deity and took on the status of a slave, became human! Having become human, he stayed human. It was an incredibly humbling process. He didn't claim special privileges. Instead, he lived a selfless, obedient life and then died a selfless, obedient death—and the worst kind of death at that: a crucifixion. (Phil 2:5–8 MSG).

The MLC traveled the first three stages of community building in several iterations. Sometimes we found ourselves back in a place of psuedocommunity, but at last we learned and we grew so that those jumps back were just check-ins that were quickly vacated in chaos that once again led to a humble place of acceptance. It is there, after emptying, that "something almost more singular happens. An extraordinary amount of healing and converting begins to occur—now that no one is trying to convert or heal. And community has been born."[13]

Emptiness was for us a gateway, not a barrier, to our eventual effectiveness as a team. Our experience was a process that could not have been achieved during a quick overnight visit.[14] It took an investment of

---

12. Ibid., 109
13. Ibid., 122.
14. Gozdz, *Community Building*, 90.

time and energy. Though these resources always seemed in short supply, the possibilities that we imagined were realized.

We scheduled several MLC retreat mornings during which the MLC gathered either alone or in collaboration with the broader leadership of the three-church parish I headed. The story of Nehemiah provided the primary biblical frame for our Bible studies, which added interactive discussion and even songs that were correlated to the stages of community we were experiencing together.

Pseudocommunity in Nehemiah

> We are one in the Spirit, we are one in the Lord,
> We are one in the Spirit, we are one in the Lord,
> And we pray that our unity might one day be restored.
> They will know we are Christians by our love, by our love.
> Yes, they'll know we are Christians by our love.

Nehemiah knew the community he started with was inauthentic. They were not being true to themselves because they had forgotten their citizenship, their core identity. In the biblical narrative, he got the word from travelers that Jerusalem was in shambles and the walls had been torn down. The weight of this news brought Nehemiah to weeping and then to confessing to God the sins of the people, forgetting the city and their homeland. It is was if Nehemiah, rummaging through his belongings, came across his long since forgotten passport. To his utter amazement, he saw he was a citizen of another country. Not Babylon, but the promised land. He underwent a paradigm shift—a shift of destination and location. Because Nehemiah realized he wasn't located in the place God wanted him to be, he made Jerusalem his destination. Nehemiah remembered. Remembrance restores the vision.

Chaos in Nehemiah

Nehemiah then was in chaos. He was living in the wrong place, removed from the city of his ancestors. He knew God was love, and he was ignoring that love by failing to show the love he should have had for his people and land. Our MLC experience included the singing of this familiar chorus:

> Love, love, love, love
> The Gospel in a word is love.
> Love your neighbor as your brother,
> God is love.

For many years, the Jewish people lived in a foreign country. The people lived a lie. As soon as Nehemiah shared the vision with the people, they knew they were not who they had pretended to be—as if they too ran home and found their own long-forgotten passports, which revealed they were in fact aliens in an alien land. They did not belong there. They had neglected their neighborhood, they had forgotten their language, they had fallen in love with the enemy. They, too, knew chaos. They honestly dealt with each other and with their God. Anger. Disappointment. Fear. Nehemiah shared the vision and they all remembered. Remembrance restored the vision. The people began to see Jerusalem as Nehemiah saw it, as God saw it. They became broken, and God put them back together again.

> We lay down and wept, and wept, for thee Zion.
> We remember, we remember, we remember thee Zion.

There was an emptying, a sense of repentance. They embraced the vision. They shared the hurt and pain. I believe the MLC members connected with this emptying stage of Nehemiah. They knew they could do nothing in the city without God and without one another. They, too, remembered what once was. As the process unfolded, we together made a commitment to rebuild the walls. We would begin to focus on our capacity for praise and offer to God all that we had.

In Nehemiah's story, the people by the river became the people of the march. They made up their minds to go on the trip and make a difference in their lives and the lives of their children, whom they took with them.

> Praise the Lord together, singing,
> Hallelujah, hallelujah, hallelujah.

Community began to take shape. They would know pseudocommunity again, chaos and emptying, but the struggle affirmed the path they were on and it led them home. Nehemiah had resources, as if he had the credit cards of the king. Plus, he had a leave of absence and a team ready to make the trip back home. The walls were restored in only fifty-two days. True, they were built to only half their height, and there was much more to do that Ezra and others would do later, but each family took their share of the wall and creatively worked within the constraints of their context. The book of Nehemiah begins with remembering and ends with remembering. In a marvelous act of commitment to ensure the sustainability of the reclaimed city, the community tithed themselves back into the urban center. The last words of the book are these: "Remember me with favor, O my God" (Neh 13:31).

After our mini-visits with Nehemiah, we routinely divided into small groups and discussed the ministry God had given to us. We recalled that there was pain all around and we were on a path to courageously seek after the heart of God and discern as best we could how to respond as God would respond. M. Scott Peck advises that "it is better to let groups struggle toward community without giving them a detailed road map at the beginning which will guide them through the various stages, telling them all the pitfalls to avoid."[15] We reflected on Nehemiah's struggle, but it was not yet our struggle. That would come later. The Nehemiah story was for us an event we shared in, and as such it shaped our community, as if we were actually observing Nehemiah and his struggles through the four stages.

After we reviewed the Nehemiah "rebuild the wall, reneighbor the city" model in conversational settings as a larger parish and separately as the MLC, we attempted to see our own views of the church in the neighborhood using the Church Models Grid and the Church Model Evaluation Chart.[16] The Church Models exercise invited comments and ideas from each MLC member. At first they could see only a few models and offer limited examples. By the end of the meeting they were seeing all kinds of models, sharing how a type of model can influence how they view the pastor's role, the place of outreach, and the use of resources in the church. Recognizing the deficiencies in the models challenged their point of view. Reflection on what we were learning occurred frequently. Through the MLC experience, we achieved authentic community, which empowered a collaborative engagement in mission.

---

15. Peck, *Different Drum*, 131.

16. The Church Models Grid, Church Model Evaluation Chart, and other resources are available at the author's website, http://www.crayonsforthecity.com.

Resource Manual and Tools for Learning Community Transformation

The MLC model was meeting the objectives set for it. We needed to remain focused on vision-building as a way to identify common beliefs and values. I wanted to build an MLC that was focused on the future that God was bringing into view more and more each step of the way. It was also important for us to develop the means to accommodate an MLC member needing to retire or a new member coming in. These were issues the MLC must wrestle with. I did not want to impose my own views on the group. At the outset I set the stage. Now my role was to affirm the group's own identity as an MLC. But the purpose of the group remained the same. Each member affirmed the same purpose in the MLC support covenant. As our relationship in time grew invested in study and prayer I wanted to ensure shared ownership of the group. To do this I chose to be in the background more and allow the Spirit to build a community. It's like planting a tree. The tiny seedling is nourished and planted in prepared soil. Some could ignore its diminutive start, but as the roots begin to take hold, the tree starts to grow. I would like the group to envision its own purpose, including the features and framing the statements to still meet the original objectives and learning covenant, but still uniquely theirs.

Resource 1: Church Models Grid

Figure 12

Instructor: Dr. Kevin Yoho • email: kyoho@nbts.edu

CHURCH "FACE" MODELS • "What if your church looked like a..."

STEP 1 Consider if the church was like a...	STEP 2 1. How does the model to the left affect your view of these areas? 2. What is the observer's perception?					
	Community	Message	Mission	Leadership	Membership	Funding
Fortress	Hostile	Invasion	Claiming	Inherited, Birthed	Tiered, Hierarchical	Inside
Lighthouse						
Family				I		
School 1 Public 2 Special 3 Private 4 Parochial						
Restaurant 1 Fast Food 2 Diner 3 Cafe 4 Fancy						
Embassy						
Fitness Center/Spa						
Entertainment/Party						
Health Care 1 Free Clinic 2 Emergency 3 Hospital 4 Doctor's Office						
Bank						
Shopping 1 Mall 2 Department Store 3 Mom & Pop 4 Online						
Network/Internet						
Water/River						
Wireless						

The MLC spent four sessions exploring and discussing the Church Models Grid. The MLC's strength lay in its ability to consider various points of view and probe the possibilities of paradigm shifts. The Models Grid enabled the participants to consider the church from many different points of view, gaining from the dialogue and affirming our differences while building a spirit of community.

To use the Church Models Grid, begin with Step 1 (the left-hand column), "Consider if the church was like a . . ." Then proceed down the column and choose a church model—the image that corresponds with the community's perception of the church. For Step 2, consider the question, "How does the model to the left affect your views of these areas?" For example, consider a church that conveys the image of a fortress in the neighborhood. As a fortress, what is the church's view of the community (column one)? What is the church's view of its message (column two)? Proceed across the chart to the right. As a fortress, what is the church's view of its mission, its leadership, its membership? And where does the majority of its funding come from?

When "fortress" is selected in Step 1, the Church Models Grid might look like the following:

Community	Gospel	Mission	Leadership	Membership	Funding
Hostile	Invasion	Claiming territory	Inherited, birthed	Tiered, hierarchical	Inside

Take another example. Consider that the church conveys the image of a lighthouse. When "lighthouse" is selected in Step 1, the Church Models Grid might look like the following:

Community	Gospel	Mission	Leadership	Membership	Funding
Dangerous	Rescue	Saving lives	Trained, specialized	Trained, certified	Outside

Using the Church Models Grid can provoke a deeper conversation about a congregation's neighborhood image and the implications of that image for its mission.

Figure 13

Page 1 of 2
Instructor: Dr. Kevin Yoho • email: kevin@newarkpresbytery.org

CHURCH "FACE" MODELS • "What if your church looked like a..." ©1997, 2013 Dr. Kevin Yoho

STEP 1 Consider if the church was like a...	STEP 2 1. How does the model to the left affect your view of these areas? 2. What is the observer's perception?					
	Community	Gospel	Mission	Leadership	Membership	Funding
Fortress	Hostile	Invasion	Claiming	Inherited, Birthed	Tiered, Hierarchical	Inside
Lighthouse	Dangerous	Rescue	Saving	Trained, Specialized	Trained, Certified	Outside
Family	Familiar	Fellowship	Protecting	Patriarch, Matriarch	Married or Born	Inherited
School (1. Public 2. Sprout 3. Private 4. Parochial)	Ignorant	Education	Teaching	Headmaster	Students	Tuition
Restaurant (1. Fast Food 2. Diner 3. Café 4. Fancy)	Hungry	Satisfaction	Feeding	Head Chef	Host, Hostess	Itemized
Embassy	Foreign	Peace	Tolerating	Ambassador	Outsiders	Outside
Fitness Center/Spa	Out of Shape	Discipline	Exercising	Most fit	Athletes	Dues
Entertainment/Party	Bored	Fun	Entertaining	D.J.	Players	Advance
Health Care (1. Free Clinic 2. Emergency 3. Hospital 4. Doctor's Office)	Sick	Wellness	Healing	Expert	Employees	Insurance
Bank	Needy	Safety	Conserving	Board	Investors	Deposits
Shopping (1. Mall 2. Department Store 3. Mom & Pop 4. Online)	Hungry	Consumption	Selling	Manager	Clerks	Outside
Network/Internet	Disconnected	Participation	Connecting	Shared	Inclusive	Distributed
Water/River	Parched	Refreshment	Flowing	Source	Molecular	Included
Wireless	In Range	Connection	Broadcast	Multi-layered	Tuned In	Available

Resource 2: Church Model Evaluation Chart

Figure 14

CHURCH MODEL EVALUATION • "My church is like a..."			©2013 Kevin Yoho, adapted from an idea by Dr. Ray Bakke
Identify a model that fits your church...	Write the model type here in this box, then discuss the questions below.		
In what ways does the chosen model fit your church, program and ministry?			
How does your model differ from conflicting images held by others? What do you do about managing conflict?			
What issues affect the families in your neighborhood?			

WHAT ARE THE TOP TEN PROBLEMS...			
...facing your neighborhood?		...facing your church family?	
1.	2.	1.	2.
3.	4.	3.	4.
5.	6.	5.	6.
7.	8.	7.	8.
9.	10.	9.	10.
HOW DOES THE CHURCH MODEL ABOVE HELP SOLVE THESE PROBLEMS...			
...facing your neighborhood?		...facing your church family?	
1.	2.	1.	2.
3.	4.	3.	4.
5.	6.	5.	6.
7.	8.	7.	8.
9.	10.	9.	10.

What other images of the church does your neighborhood need to see?

For three sessions, we used the Church Model Evaluation Chart to consider the congregation's relationship with the neighborhood. The neighborhood, after all, is the reason we are there as Christ's people to begin with. Understanding the Top 10 Challenges Facing the Neighborhood, for example, becomes not just an opportunity to deliver a program to address these challenges but also a humble alignment of the church leadership with the community itself so that it is not an us-them conversation. The MLC affirmed the importance of the neighborhood and their commitment to connect with it, because the members of the MLC were becoming a part of the neighborhood itself. We reviewed early church documents that helped us connect with bearers of our faith in the Kensington community.

Resource 3: Multi-church Consultation

Because our congregation shares ministry with two other Presbyterian churches in a parish relationship, I wanted the MLC to understand the systems that affect our neighborhood. The only way to reach a neighborhood is to work hand in hand with other followers of Jesus. If authentic ministry is to be done, we must find ways to bridge the gap between the community of faith and the community at large.

Resource 4: Kensington Ministry Partnership

Figure 15

If God loves Kensington... How will Kensington know?
Mission Leaders Prayer Breakfast
10/05 8:30 Penn Home 215.739.2522
1401 E. Susquehanna Ave. 19125

We convened a monthly all-Kensington prayer breakfast hosted at various locations with leadership from area churches in attendance. The purpose was to share what God was doing in our midst and the vision for renewal in faith and life. This fueled a broader conversation of renewal in the neighborhood as we offered the resources of the church, spearheaded by the MLC, as a servant in whatever way was required.

The MLC developed the following affirmations that represented what we were learning about community-directed ministry. You may want to invite your leadership to create their own affirmations.

> I will be renewed in my commitment and love for God and others. At the completion of the program I will be more in love with God and will have grown deeper roots into his word and ways, more confident of his presence, calling, and spiritual vitality. I expect to be different at the end of the program than when I began.

I will be an agent of renewal at Wilkey Church and in Philadelphia Presbytery. I will do all I can to give ministry away, to help equip others to do the work of ministry right now, right here, in the Philadelphia region like there was no tomorrow.

I will improve my skills in renewal ministry. Through God's renewing work I will discover gifts and abilities, identify mission critical resources, and learn to identify and minimize my impediments to effective ministry. I will enhance my perception of people, ideas, and programs, formulate biblical mission strategy and relevantly connect with the culture to proclaim the Good News in good, new ways.

I will positively contribute to the learning and growth of other program participants, my institutional support group, my session and ministry team and colleagues in ministry. I am committed to living out my faith in community.

The commitments for change and renewal at Wilkey Presbyterian Church included the following:

- We offer ourselves as servants to the community.
- We will become visible in the community.
- We will become a preferred community center destination.
- We will proclaim the good news we experience in new, tangible ways that are relevant to the community.
- We will listen and be open to new possibilities in God's emerging future.

Watch Your Language

Our language and our words should align with our true and transparent mission. Our values should reflect the life-giving actions of Jesus Christ. Jesus' mission eschewed the language of insiders and outsiders. Jesus disrupted the status quo of brokenness and reconnected humanity with the Creator. The one who came from Nazareth . . . "What good could come from there?" said Andrew to Philip. Jesus did not exclude anyone. Jesus was in the disruption business.[17] When Jesus proclaimed the Gospel, it was not the standard set of beliefs and practices that many today understand it to be; it was not meant for incumbents and insiders. Walls (whether of

---

17. See my article titled "Reciprocity in Action" at http://bit.ly/reciprocalrevolution.

the temple or of the spirit) were to be reduced to rubble so that all could connect, listen, and experience life in abundance. The other, the stranger, would remain so no longer. Why would the church do any less?

People cannot be deconstructed to little more than ministry targets. The community cannot be dismissively reduced to or objectified as a mere ministry target. Those who do not gather with us in our places of worship are not the "unchurched," either. It is time to eliminate this disparaging and unfortunate term that we too frequently use to describe the other.

I realize we use words like *unchurched* with good intentions. It is time for us to think more deeply about the language we use and consider how our language is understood by the community at large. And I cannot help recalling the proverb about good intentions. As good as our intentions may be, they are said to "pave the road" to a very unpleasant place! Since our neighbors are people whom God loves, we must carefully consider the impact of our language and our behaviors. We recognize that our language and behaviors should respect our community's diverse amalgamation of stories, ethnicities, values, and languages. Our diversity represents amazing opportunities.

> Diversity, generally understood and embraced, is not casual liberal tolerance of anything and everything not yourself. It is not polite accommodation. Instead, diversity is, in action, the sometimes painful awareness that other people, other races, other voices, other habits of mind, have as much integrity of being, as much claim on the world as you do . . . We are meant to be here together.[18]

Church insiders may (unintentionally?) use the term *unchurched* as a kind of shorthand to describe outsiders. This self-referencing label is an irony, of sorts, since insiders presume that outsiders want to be churched to begin with. In using our "unchurched" language, we are implying that our goal is to transform the unchurched into the churched. Is that really our mission? Is transforming outsiders into insiders the transformation we seek—the transformation of lives, congregations, communities, and the world? I don't think we mean that at all.

Our communities are neighbors, not others. Admittedly, it is sometimes difficult to feel this neighborhood connection when so many of us live some distance away and must drive in to church. We may feel

---

18. William M. Chase, "The Language of Action," quoted in O'Brien, "Diversity in Action Is . . . ," par. 1.

more emotionally "at home" with the church building or its history than with the people whose homes surround the church. It is understandable that in our sincere desire that others should discover the abundant life we have found through Christ we assume that they will find hope and experience God in the same way we do, and in the same place. We would be wise to test our assumptions.

As satisfying as our church experience is to us, others may not share that experience. What's more, they may have chosen long ago to stop connecting "hope for a better spiritual life" to a church experience. We have a persistent, well-practiced behavior of using us-and-them language. No wonder many recoil when they hear our references to reaching the "unchurched," or the "lost," no matter how these terms seem to fit our theological biases or aspirations.

Most of our neighbors do not want to be churched in the first place. Could we simply stop using these off-putting terms? If we get to know our neighbors better, we may discover what it is they really want in life. Plus, we might in humility and authenticity begin to respect them. We can choose to stop labeling them as "un-" people and instead affirm that they are citizens and members of the community that God loves.

8

Engagement, Act 1: Reneighboring the Congregation

Figure 16

Ethnography of Church Leaders

To get connected, we must start where we are as a community of faith. "It is much easier to work on all these things from a position where members feel good about themselves and energized about what they are doing."[1] Achieving community impact as a strategic neighbor requires the worshipping, witnessing, and mission community to grapple with its own identity, a deeper and more authentic sense of self. The church is the worshipping and witnessing community of disciples of Jesus Christ, across the centuries and around the world. These diverse voices offer visible expressions of the kingdom of God that proclaim the good news of Jesus Christ. The Gospel, representing the entire witness and experience of the written and living Word of God, has not changed (Jude 3). Paul instructed Timothy, "What you heard from me, keep as the pattern of sound teaching, with faith and love in Christ Jesus" (2 Tim 1:13).

Though the ancient story has not changed, the containers, vessels, expressions of that story change and adapt to new contexts. The Holy Spirit authoritatively reveals God's love story in the biblical record that points us to the message of God made real when Jesus "moved into our neighborhood" (John 1:14). Jesus is the image of the invisible God (Col 1:15) who transforms individuals, congregations, and communities to bear witness to Jesus in whatever language, form, or container is necessary to build connections for worship, confession, repentance, forgiveness, re-engagement, and service. As the Christian church is transformed, changed, it in turn becomes a change agent in the world, giving evidence of God's justice and righteousness. The community church in Asia "became a model to all the believers in Macedonia and Achaia," as the "Lord's message rang out" and their faith in God became "known everywhere" (1 Thess 1:7–8).

The church in Asia did not become known everywhere without effective relationship-building behaviors and authentic community connections. Every church has a story to share, and the story of those gathered "inside" (active participants or members, for example) intersects in one way or another with the stories of those "outside." Authentic connections between the church and the community are nurtured when the individuals gathered in the community of faith have frequent interaction and public engagement, shared values, common norms of behavior, and experiences. These systems of meaning within the community vary not only between churches but also across the life cycle of a given church.

Ethnography would prove to be an effective instrument in better understanding the church's historical and future capacity to engage with the

---

1. Crabtree, *Owl Sight*, 69.

northern Kensington community. An ethnography describes a method of collecting and studying stories about individuals' beliefs, morals, culture, and daily activities that can inform a deeper understanding of the processes and values of the groups and associations to which they belong. By conducting an ethnography, any overlap or disconnect in the systems of meaning between the church and the community could suggest ways to align priorities and improve engagement, increasing the congregation's capacity to be a transforming agent.

The ethnography project began by interviewing, in focus-group style, eight leaders from the parish. James P. Spradley, professor of anthropology at Macalester College, offers a word of caution regarding a member of the group also being a subject of the study.[2] Yet being a member of the group that one sets out to study does have some advantages. One advantage is that there is more observing than participating when the researcher is a participant in the group. But "this role also has disadvantages," states Barbara Kawulich, "in that there is a trade-off between the depth of the data revealed to the researcher and the level of confidentiality provided to the group for the information they provide."[3] A word of caution as the pastor invites the leadership into a deeper conversation about their historical transitions and experiences: it is important that the pastoral leader not allow dysfunctional behaviors to be normalized. The health of the entire group, the entire church, must remain a priority of the process. As Russ Crabtree observes, an effective leader must keep "dysfunction from metastasizing throughout the church. If the leadership misreads this as, for example, the anger stage of loss and encourages its expression as part of the healing process, tremendous damage can result. When dysfunctional behaviors are normalized and excused as grief reactions, it often does not result in insight, it tends to incite."[4]

By inviting leaders of the church to grapple with their own stories historically, sociologically, politically, theologically, and relationally, they can begin to recognize their place in their own timeline of meaning.

---

2. Spradley and McCurdy, *Cultural Experience*, 2.

3. Kawulich, "Participant Observation as a Data Collection Method." "By way of advantages one can list: the researcher has firsthand knowledge of the group, its language, jargon, traditions, history, and so forth; firsthand knowledge can lessen the time required to conduct the study; and firsthand knowledge can lessen the chance of misunderstanding an aspect of the group under study" (North).

4. Crabtree, *Owl Sight*, 142.

"Ethnography can be the basis for social change."[5] Inviting the leadership of the church into a focus group to remember the significant events of their collective history may empower them to face their future with renewed energy and purpose.

Focus Group Rationale

The congregation's worship attendance of forty individuals represents 10 percent compared to forty years ago. Only 6 percent of the membership (revealed in the ethnography) lives near the church building.

A simple walk around the neighborhood has a purpose and can be referred to as contact work. This contact provided not only a great deal of information about the church but also insight concerning the community's perception of the church. During a contact work experience, I introduced myself to the neighbor living right across the street from the stone church building. With a dazed expression on her face, she responded, "What church are you from?" Gesturing right over my shoulder toward the building, I answered, "Wilkey Church." She had no trouble seeing the church building. She was not disoriented, either. She simply concluded that nothing of value had ever come from Wilkey. Her remark was an indictment of a church that had become a stranger in its own neighborhood. I spoke to other neighbors who would express a similar judgment by saying, "I thought that church closed years ago."

It became clear that the mission of our congregation was being undermined by our absence from community life. The church was essentially invisible. Research of old church session, trustee, and Sunday school records, accessed on-site and at the Presbyterian Historical Society depositories in Philadelphia, revealed an interesting fact about neighborhood presence.

A frequent practice had been to record the addresses of church leaders in the minutes of the session. Plotting these locations on a map, I took note of the distance from the church officers' residences to the church building. Though elders lived within two or three blocks of the church in the early 1920s and throughout the 1930s, by 1940 church leaders had begun relocating greater and greater distances from the church building, and that trend would continue in subsequent years.

---

5. Spradley and McCurdy, *Cultural Experience*, 4.

According to church documents from 1908, the church was established "so children did not need to cross the busy avenues to go to Sunday school." From its inception, the church was intended as a neighborhood church, located in the neighborhood to serve the neighborhood. Over the years, this deep connection eroded, a condition reflected and reinforced by members moving farther and farther away from the neighborhood. With less frequent and less effective community engagement, the church's mission as a transforming agent was impaired.

Understanding historic dynamic changes prepares the pastor as the observer-participant to maximize the value of ethnographic interviewing. In our particular history, one very dynamic change occurred in 1940, when Ontario Presbyterian Church became Wilkey Memorial Presbyterian Church. This name change story suggested a hypothesis concerning the residency of members, the presence of local neighbors at worship, and how these relationships may correlate to the name change. Primary historical information puts seemingly isolated facts in their context. The focus group would be invited to recall the most significant events they could remember. The process of recollection would test the hypothesis and suggest other connections. If ethnographic discoveries surface in the focus-group setting, a more complete understanding of the root cause of the congregation's decline could emerge. Even more importantly, the participants in the focus group would be in touch with some very powerful feelings that could be redirected productively.

Classic ethnography often relies on taped interviews, earning Spradley's "strongly recommend"[6] endorsement, and are often expected in the interviewing process.[7] The optimal setting for the focus group should provide sufficient open space that provokes openness in the conversations and access to the stories captured on newsprint. "Physical space is more decisive in creating community than we realize. Most meeting spaces are designed for control, negotiation, and persuasion."[8] Ethnographies are large group methodologies that benefit from an optimal, open, conversational space. "They are more than simply tools; they are the means of creating the experience of democracy and high engagement, which we say we believe in but rarely embody. As this thinking and practice grow,

---

6. Ibid., 55.

7. Weiss, *Learning from Strangers*, 61–62.

8. Block, *Community*, 197.

they have the potential to fundamentally change the nature of leadership, which would be a good thing."[9]

Newsprint overspread the longest wall, more than twenty-five feet in length. This visual workspace provided the real estate to capture the stories to be shared. Before the focus group started, vertical markings along the newsprint established a horizontal timeline. The participants were configured in a semicircle. Since a focus group is as much a data collecting process as a storytelling process, notes supported the formal scribing of the participants' responses on the newsprint. As the direct interviewer, I prepared questions to be posed to the group.

Though the participants in the focus group were members of the church, this was a distinct and unfamiliar setting. Participants' brainstorming sessions[10] produced specific, significant events along a timeline, ensuring that our discussion was "focused" from the beginning.

About six months prior to the focus group sessions, the participants were informed of the process and told that they would be invited to share stories about their congregation. Most of the people were eager to participate and agreed to do so if invited. I had several informal conversations with likely participants and described the process ahead. They understood their stories would explore their life experience as it connected to the church, including pleasant and unpleasant memories. "The pastors have all been just great," one person volunteered, and almost apologetically offered, "The neighborhood just changed, that's all." How prophetic this statement would be.

Focus Group Event

As the pastoral leader, I appreciated and welcomed the gift each participant represented. In selecting individuals to form a team, I looked for a balanced representation across several engagement criteria based on their responses to the following: (1) duration of time in the congregation, (2) depth of relationships in the church, (3) influence in the community, (4) engagement in the ministry of the congregation, and (5) demonstration of mutual respect and trust with those who would constitute the team of eight individuals.

---

9. Ibid., 37.

10. As explained by Andrea Fontana in her article titled "Interviewing," in Denzin and Lincoln, *Handbook of Qualitative Research*, 365.

The venue selected for the off-site event was an assisted living facility well known in the community. In our large room I attached five sheets of newsprint to the wall, arranged side by side. On the first I wrote the word "World," the second I left blank, on the third I wrote "Community," the fourth I left blank, and on the fifth I wrote "Church." A well-designed ethnography ensures that the participants control the story and ascribe a value to that content. The discussion focused on categories placed as headings on the sheets of newsprint. I invited the group to tell me about the significant events they had experienced in each of these three areas.

Focus Group Discovery

After a brief introduction to the ethnographic method, the stories began to take shape on the newsprint, framed as clusters of words or more detailed narratives. At this initial stage the participants were guided to describe their experiences in their own words. The group began with stories recalling the time when Kensington was its own city, independent of Philadelphia, at the turn of the twentieth century.[11] The "World" sheet focused on world happenings they considered significant. "World War II," one offered. "Yes, put that up . . . 1941!" another said. I wrote "WWII" with the date to its left, about halfway down the sheet. All agreed that was significant. I could sense their energy building as they moved forward in their seats.

Seeking to connect the energy to an adjacent category, I posed the question, "What was going on in a significant way in the community when the war started?" The participants gave animated responses. "A lot of good men left the country to fight . . . we had to start finding other work to do when the war started, no more chocolate was made at the candy factory around the corner, and I had to move in with my aunt." "We pulled together." I linked their stream of comments to the category marked "Church" on the newsprint.

I asked, "What was going on at the church in 1941?" "We were big then" one said. "Lots of activities and youth programs" offered another. Then one person blurted out, "We changed our name." Suddenly everyone was quiet. Their faces had the look of recognition and awareness.

---

11. A few group members confirmed that the Northern Liberties section of Philadelphia, just south of Kensington, was called Liberties because the city tax was not collected there; because it was just outside the city, residents from Center City frequently went to the Northern Liberties neighborhood to purchase goods free of city tax.

The name change event resonated with the group as they reflected on its significance.

It is true that many of the events might have been available in an ordinary church anniversary booklet. But that booklet represented a collection of facts and stories aggregated by others at a different time. Likely, church documents capture events that are significant to the writer of the booklet. The ethnographic process captures an entirely different storyline. Not only does the ethnography connect stories with events, but it is also a self-discovery experience, not an edited one. When guiding groups on a more thoughtful journey of self-understanding, posing questions that require them to connect their experience to their motivations empowers learning. The newsprint sheets captured real-time connections as each individual contributed to the group's story.

While the world was at war, the community was adjusting to the changes associated with maintaining the war machine, and our church was changing its name. "Not everybody wanted to change the name," someone offered. "No," affirmed another. "So the name issue was significant?" I asked. All agreed that it was—some said yes, others nodded in the affirmative. I added, "What other events do we need to get up here?"

The participants were enthusiastic. On the "World" sheet we recorded "Immigrants—1900." The group was clear that Kensington was part of the great immigration story that connected to the corresponding "Community" sheet, where they listed "Scottish, Irish, German" immigrants. The neighborhood then did not include many African or South American immigrants, earning Kensington the nickname "White Town."[12]

The "Community" sheet captured the conflict between Catholic and Protestant neighbors. Immigrants from Ireland (Roman Catholic) and Northern Ireland (Protestant) settled blocks apart. The "Community" sheet captured significant identifiers, including "papal school" (referred to in a rather pejorative manner) and the neighborhood challenge that the religious zoning brought. Jewish storefronts were remembered and linked to a successful Kensington during the years 1920 to 1930. Even despite the unrest brought about by the Depression, participants remembered their Jewish neighbors in Kensington fondly; it was recalled that their strong family and economic contributions benefited the entire community. "When did they leave?" I asked, knowing that the Jewish population in Kensington was then less than 2 percent. There was a pause,

---

12. *Whitetown USA* is the title of Peter Binzen's excellent book about Kensington.

and then one participant suggested that many Jewish families benefited economically from store ownership. They began to relocate several miles away, to Northeast Philadelphia, in the early 1970s. New waves of neighbors, including African-Americans, moved into the neighborhoods in the decade 1970–80. The group recalled the large synagogue on Allegheny Avenue and noted that it was now an African-American congregation. The stores once owned and "kept beautifully" (as one participant noted) by the Jewish merchants were in a shambles and part of the more devastated parts of Kensington.

Now focusing on the "Church" sheet, the group spoke fondly of their founding pastor, without mentioning any of the other five pastoral leaders the church had had since its planting in 1908. In 1941, the name was changed. "Anything significant about that time?" I asked. "We became Wilkey instead of Ontario because of the Wilkey sisters," said one; another chimed in, "We took their money and built a building, but we shouldn't have changed our name." That last comment was not corroborated. The group was very lively in this discussion.

Together the participants began to fill in the story of two unmarried women who wanted to leave a permanent mark on the Presbyterian Church by way of a church named in their memory. The sisters sent word to the presbytery (our regional governing council) that about $50,000 would be available to build a Presbyterian church on their property in Kensington. The Philadelphia Presbytery approved the request and received the funds with the understanding that a church named Wilkey Memorial United Presbyterian Church would be established. Before the church could be built, however, the sisters died, and somehow the land was sold to the city board of education. J. B. Stetson (as in the Stetson Hat Company) Junior High School was erected on the Wilkey farm property donated to the presbytery. Several of the participants confirmed this understanding as the discussion continued with a few interjetions of "Oh, yeah" and "That's right."

Any church could apply for the funds, the presbytery decided, as long as the church agreed to change its name in memory of the Wilkey sisters. Three congregations "rushed to get that money," as the participants recalled. (The focus group was now becoming more of a storytelling group. All were participating either verbally or through body language—nodding their heads, etc.)

Ontario Presbyterian Church was one of the congregations that applied—and in the end, the group said, Ontario won the court battle that ensued. The lawsuit was brought by the heirs of the Wilkey sisters against the presbytery and Ontario church for intending to use the money to establish a church some distance from the designated Wilkey farm site. When the litigation was resolved, Ontario and Philadelphia Presbytery won, though no details emerged to explain why or how Ontario won. The anticipated disbursement from the estate was effectively reduced to about half the amount after paying legal costs. For the sum of approximately $25,000, the name Ontario Church was changed to Wilkey Memorial United Presbyterian Church in May 1941. According to one church document, Pastor Lonsinger, the beloved pastor, "was against the name change from the beginning. He said we should never change the name." He resigned one month before the name change took effect, reportedly due to ill health.

Focus Group Pain

In our discovery, we wanted the focus group to better understand the correlation between the church's name change and the congregation's mission in the neighborhood. The group was asked, "Tell me how the actual residences of the church members shifted over the years since 1908. What percentage of the congregation is resident in the neighborhood?"

To track this information, I led the group down the list of dates on the "Community" sheet. "In 1908"—the year of our founding—"how many members lived in the neighborhood?" "100 percent, or close to it," one replied. "All of the members came from the neighborhood," another responded. We reflected on this information as I summarized: "In 1908, 100 percent of the membership lived in the neighborhood?" "Yes," the group affirmed.

Our conversations about successive decades explored the relationship between the neighborhood and the congregation. It was difficult in the middle years, 1940–60. They had no idea what the percentage might have been. I fast-forwarded to the present. "Okay, what percentage of the congregation lives in the neighborhood today?" One of the participants was the church's clerk of session, who would be familiar with this and other statistics. "Well, we have 43 members," she offered. Someone else began identifying people who lived within proximity to the church building. One, two, then three people. "Three?" I queried. "So 6 percent of the congregation is from the neighborhood?" "Yes."

This information was not encouraging. It was difficult for the group to look at the sheets and see how the membership had grown through 1940, and then again in 1950, and accept that the church had been in a tailspin since. They had not been aware that the church-neighborhood distance had increased since the 1940s. The attitude of the group remained good, however.

We identified other world events to add a larger context as we explored what was going on in Kensington. I asked them about their experience during the tumultuous years of the 1960s. They offered no response, as if they were not especially attentive to national issues from that time. Stepping out of my role as observer, I reminded them of the flight to the suburbs and of the civil rights movement, which was hard for them to recollect. The civil rights movement seemed to be regarded as "not significant" to this group. In the changing neighborhood context, European-Americans began to vacate urban neighborhoods, especially after World War II, just after the time when Ontario Presbyterian Church sold their church name for $25,000. During this period the white evangelical church dismissed the challenges of the city; their message was, effectively, "We and our Gospel have nothing to say." When racial conflict began to affect everyone in America, the church at large was silent and still. This moment gave us pause and engendered dialogue about "the then and the now" and how we are in fact in the midst of a struggle.

God's love for the world demonstrated in the incarnation of Jesus also disrupted the entire planet. When the Word became flesh and "moved into our neighborhood" (John 1:14), the neighborhoods he visited changed. Lives changed. Though nearly every congregation when it is established is connected to the neighborhood, too often (as evidenced by Wilkey Church) participants become disengaged from the community's life and move their homes outside the community; the church, then, is no longer a neighbor but a stranger. Those who are called into worship are to be sent out in witness and mission, to impact lives and communities. Good discipleship leads to good neighborship. When a worshipping community, a church, is effectively connected to the neighborhood, it is located *in* that neighborhood—it is a reneighbored church. Reneighboring the church, therefore, is essential for a community to see God's love authentically demonstrated with transformative power.

How to reneighbor our church emerged as a key question to explore during a later session. The church that does not connect to its neighborhood ceases to be a neighborhood church and withdraws its spiritual, social, reputational, and physical capital. Future focus groups would explore reneighboring along with other questions we proposed, including the following:

1. In what ways can we effectively reconnect the church to the neighborhood?
2. What messages do we convey to the community?
3. What messages are received by the neighborhood?
4. What are some ways in which the mission of Wilkey Church could build upon its historical reputation at H and Ontario?

Focus Group Reflection

Notes and responses covered the newsprint hanging on the wall, with descriptions of church and community connections. The two-hour focus group session was a "wonderful" experience, according to some of the participants. Many reported the joy of remembering, and they took pride in recognizing their place in the world. On these sheets of paper were also untold stories of challenges ahead as a ministry team.[13]

When the pastor embraces the role of ethnographer, an important relational and informational asset is added to the ministry. The ethnographer and the individual contributors can give voice to the group's experiences, and the discoveries made can provide useful information for better future ministry decisions. Learning together as a group resulted in a sense of accomplishment when the ethnography process concluded. The focus group of parish leaders from Wilkey Church became stronger and more determined than ever to keep linking the stories recorded on the three sheets of paper. Without this learning and visioning component,

13. I wondered what the responses would have been had I populated the group differently. Spradley discusses the characteristics of a good and bad "informant" and concludes that a good informant "knows the culture well" (*Cultural Experience*, 47). This is an apt description of our group members. However, he also observed that one who is too analytical will constantly "translate his information into concepts" (ibid.) that, as the interviewer, I may understand better and be more familiar with. I did notice that one of my participants tried to interpret the information consistently too soon, which at times might have skewed the natural flow. I kept the focus on the data sharing and tried to be intentional when we were doing a correlation or assessment. Something I observed during and especially after our session: I came to respect the power and sanctity of the focus group as a self-contained entity, a group living and interacting with itself and the world around it. I think Fontana is right.

little growth will occur, with even less community impact. Through our ethnographic experience, the church's internal stories became dynamically woven into a beautiful tapestry of the entire community.

Evidence of a Reneighbored Congregation

The newsprint bore visual witness to the inner work the group accomplished. The individuals on the team eventually emerged as an authentic group, with its own identity and with the sense that decades of ministry and accomplishments, including the more conflicted and distressful issues, were all part of their collective historical narrative. It became my story, too.[14] The team was prepared for the emerging future story.

---

14. As Fontana observes, the interviewer "no longer pretend[s] to be a faceless subject and an invisible researcher," but the researcher and subjects are "portrayed as individual human beings with their own personal histories and idiosyncrasies, and we the readers learn about two people and two cultures." "Interviewing," in Denzin and Lincoln, *Handbook of Qualitative Research*, 372.

9

Engagement, Act 2: Reconnecting the Community

Figure 17

Drawing to Give Voice

Leaders in the church and the newly involved adults and families were seeing the neighborhood as God saw it—as a place of value. "Place is so constituent of human being that perhaps this is one reason why it is so easily overlooked. But we desperately need to recover a sense of place and placemaking."[1] Earlier, before our intentional reneighboring efforts, the leaders resonated only with the neighborhood's own helplessness and the Badlands attribution. But now, the worshipping community was making connections with the broader community. Neighbors were attending activities for the first time in decades. It is important to note that the increased community participation correlated with the new behaviors of our worshipping community. Up until that time, it was felt that the reason people did not come to church was that they did not need our program content or they surmised that our forms of worship were outdated. The worshipping community was now visible and accessible in tangible ways. The reneighboring process produced tears of joyful relief with a renewed sense of meaning. Others discovered a newfound sense of energy. There was a new capacity to love the neighborhood with all of its complexities and challenges. The congregation was beginning to reneighbor itself to the neighborhood.

But what about the children, still bound as they were by the stigma of hopelessness and despair? Using the sociological lens provided by Goffman and Mead, I wanted the children to see a new, truthful view of themselves. To lift and remove the stigma, the children themselves needed a new view, just as the church's leaders did—an opportunity to be heard in their own voice. They needed the truth.

Jesus said, "Then you will know the truth, and the truth will set you free" (John 8:32). Since stigma bound and marked the children of Kensington with a false identity, including worthlessness and despair, we needed to enable them to see the truth of who they were as children of value in God's eyes rather than as children of stigma. Their physical location in Kensington certainly affected their perception of self-worth; their spiritual location as children of God should as well, we concluded. How could their relationship with their Creator become a transformative experience, one that would remove the stigma of physical location?

In *The Inner World of the Immigrant Child*, educator Cristina Igoa took on the daunting task of serving the needs of immigrant students in her school. Her goal of listening to them and taking them seriously, along with their families and their traditions, brought the children to a new place of authentic self-acceptance, academic achievement, and a "sense of feeling fully alive."[2] Her methodology could be applied to the children

---

1. Bartholomew, *Where Mortals Dwell*, 17.
2. Igoa, *Inner World*, 8. Igoa describes the attractively phrased "fully alive" to be

in Kensington ("all children can benefit from this approach," she writes).[3] By making art and media accessible, Igoa showed children "how to stand up for themselves, how to voice their thoughts intelligently and in a manner that could be heard"; she admits that "sometimes they were heard, sometimes not. But try we did."[4]

The use of drawings has been helpful not only in educational settings but also in clinical settings, where art therapy is used in interventions regarding a child's self-image[5] and in helping a child articulate their worldview, which is evident not only in what is drawn (shape) but in how the drawing is presented (color).[6]

There is wide acceptance that "self-expression through art is good for people and especially for unhappy people."[7] Art's therapeutic place in our urban environment is particularly striking since art expression is generally absent in everyday life. If the activity of drawing became an everyday activity, its significance in communicating the hidden or silent would be impaired. "It is only when folk art was on the wane and when established art traditions had lost their vitality that the art of children began to attract attention," Edith Kramer suggests.[8] Tim Ladwig, who through his beautiful illustrations sets Psalm 23 in an urban landscape, reminds us that art can be supremely relevant; he dedicates his book "to the children of Newark."[9] Art could become a method of voice-giving not limited by age, gender, intelligence, literacy, or skill. It could help us understand self-esteem, aggression, anger, and ambivalence. Through a transformative art experience the children could gain a clearer self-perception and see themselves as God saw them. Since the capacity of art as a communication medium was evident not only in the fine arts but also in art therapy, the prospect of using art in a pastoral intervention was clear.

---

a state achieved when "the child feels in balance with" the cultural, academic, and psychological aspects of herself or himself (ibid.).

3. Ibid., 9.
4. Ibid.
5. Canino and Spurlock, *Culturally Diverse Children and Adolescents*, 73–76.
6. See Kaduson and Schaefer, *101 Favorite Play Therapy Techniques*, especially Glenda F. Short, "Art or Verbal Metaphors for Children Experiencing Loss" (40–43); Barbara A. Turner, "Outline Drawings of Boys and Girls" (108–13); and Stanley Kissel, "The Picture Drawing Game" (114–17).
7. Kramer, *Art as Therapy with Children*, 1.
8. Ibid., 4.
9. Ladwig, *Psalm Twenty-Three*, i.

Igoa's Cultural/Academic/Psychological (CAP) approach to intervention included religious traditions in the cultural portion of her triangular model. The intervention gave children a voice through these intervention domains. The artful expression of a child depends on a few critical elements, including the use of a medium or technology appropriate to the child's skill level, the availability of the medium or technology, and whether it is feasible for others to view the medium or technology. Art became the tool for unlocking the voice of a child—and in our case, it could enable two-way communication along that corridor of expression. Igoa used celluloid film. I needed something more accessible.

After several personal visits with Dr. Michael J. Christensen and Dr. Victoria Lee Erickson, both from Drew University, I became certain of the usefulness of Igoa's theory, and the medium also became clear. Christensen had long been committed to extending acts of grace towards strangers. He had been invited to Belarus, Ukraine, in the former Soviet Union, to serve victims of the Chernobyl nuclear power plant disaster on behalf of World Vision. It took Russian officials six years to disclose the magnitude of the tragedy and belatedly ask the world for help after that fateful April afternoon in 1986 when reactor No. 4 exploded, sending radioactive gas to fall on 2.2 million people, including 800,000 children.[10] Chernobyl became a "dead zone." On the survivors—or more accurately, the "not yet dead"—was levied a mark of death, a stigma. Survivors faced the onset of leukemia, among other terminal conditions and cancers.

Christensen's intervention initially focused on the adults. Attempting to provide an activity for the children that would allow counselors to work freely with their parents, he gave the kids some paper and crayons. He discovered that drawing, instead of being merely a means of pacifying the children, gave rise to artful expressions that were therapeutic and deserved attention. I was shown many of the drawings and came to understand the power of giving voice to remove stigma. By being given a way to express with art what could never be expressed with words, the children were empowered to internalize their Chernobyl "me" (Mead) and embrace a new and certainly truthful God "me." I proceeded to design a similar voice-giving program with the children of Kensington and came to realize firsthand the power of a crayon to remove stigma.

---

10. Carter and Christensen, *Children of Chernobyl*, 4 and 184.

The Therapeutic Milieu

With the task of reneighboring the heart of the congregation back to the corner of H and Ontario Streets well underway, a ramp-up period began with the children in the neighborhood. Our youth outreach effort started with no children; after six months of work, we had involved more than one hundred children aged eight to eighteen. In Christensen's words, we were "visible in the community" and had a "reputation for service."[11] The ministry on the street centered around what we called the Ontario Spirit sports program. A developing theology of location demanded the inclusion of the name of our street in the program's title. Sports became a vehicle for mission, while crayons became its voice.

Transformative leadership is rarely done alone. We sought to establish collaborative partnerships with other community organizations, including churches. Though it takes a sustained effort to build trust, we achieved success when we shared the vision of a transformed community with other churches. After a year of mission storytelling—telling the story of a congregation becoming a good neighbor again—we created MissionWorks to promote our open invitation to other organizations to send their teams to work at our church in the city. MissionWorks was sourced in the reneighboring effort of the prophet Nehemiah, who sent teams back into the ravaged city of Jerusalem after a successful and massive wall-rebuilding effort (Neh 11:1).

Our kids had little, if any, relationship with a local church. Why would they? Up until that time, most of the community's faith-based groups had been strangers in our neighborhood. If the kids had any contact at all, it was with Ascension Roman Catholic Church a few blocks away. Ascension attracted people to its school, but like Wilkey Church, it seemed as inaccessible as a fortress and offered little neighborhood impact. There were no youth programs within a four-block area, which was home to more than two thousand people.

Our reneighbored church became an accessible church. Our leaders demonstrated their interest in the neighborhood through their presence in the mornings when children walked down the street to school, and again when they returned home in the afternoon. Authentic leaders remember their neighbors' names and will use their names in conversations and interactions, no matter how short those interactions may be. Being

---

11. Ibid., 87.

authentically present brings a knowledge of the neighborhood better than any knowledge one may gain from those who remain at a distance.

As an authentic leader, I came to know our church's history better than any of our members. I knew where the hurt was. I felt it, too. I became a friend to the neighbors. I learned to think about the street milieu and became more connected with it than many who lived there. It did not take long for me to earn the right to live into the role of the neighborhood chaplain. In a reneighbored church, the pastoral leader serves the community at large, not just the worshipping community that pays the leader's salary.

The Ontario Spirit basketball program, which took place on Saturdays, involved mostly boys. A few members of the leadership team assisted with the work, and parents began to volunteer. My research on Kensington had taken me to Temple University, where I met faculty and staff in the social work department. Dr. Erickson also put me in touch with several other resources, and within a few months our ministry benefited from the addition of several interns from Temple University's school of social work administration who multiplied our efforts in the neighborhood.

The children of Kensington rarely expressed much hope, but you could definitely see hope at the hoops in the gym at H and Ontario Streets. We had more than fifty kids involved by our third open gym night, with an "assist" from a great MissionWorks crew (from Gwynedd Square Presbyterian Church). The thirteen- to seventeen-year-old boys played some very intense half-court basketball, with about six teams of five playing with an energy (and physicality) similar to that of football. The younger boys and girls used the other half of the court, or did arts and crafts upstairs.

A new congregation of trusting relationships began forming as the ethnically and racially diverse children and their families participated in activities. The prayers and well-wishes of many caring friends and colleagues provided a spiritual environment in which to experience God's presence and empowerment. We were determined to love these kids, their families, and the neighborhood. The sports program not only provided the context to build relationships with kids. The Wilkey congregation began experiencing reneighbored connections like those they had enjoyed fifty years ago. It was a return of the former Ontario Presbyterian Church's spirit as a neighborhood community church. I often mused to myself at the conclusion of one of our Saturday activities, "We're back!" The neighborhood welcomed us because we were the neighborhood.

While the boys did what they referred to as the "hoop thing," we began exploring ways to involve the girls, who did not want to play basketball. I asked the girls what would interest them and an idea emerged. Why not start cheerleading teams for the girls? I walked around the neighborhood and asked kids about the idea. Ascension Catholic School had offered cheerleading teams in the past. Sheridan Middle School provided no after-school activities at all. A cheerleading team became an important opportunity.

In conversations with colleagues in the community, I discovered that Wendy, the head nurse at the assisted living facility where we held the ethnography sessions, was also a part-time professional cheerleading coach. I approached her about the cheerleading idea. If she would organize a neighborhood cheerleading team, I would gladly start one. She was ecstatic. She did not even ask when or how—she simply said, "Yes!"

I was not aware at that time that Coach Wendy had been intending to give away twenty cheerleading uniforms that she thought she no longer needed. The very day I asked her to help with the cheerleading program she returned to my office and told me about the uniforms. They were purple and just the sizes we needed. What's more, already embroidered on the front was this team name: SPIRIT. God was executing an unexpected transformation plan.

Halfway through the Saturday afternoon program, I invited the guys to take a break while the cheerleaders joined us in the gym. Each week, I gathered the kids in the same way for a twenty-minute period I called FloorTalk (fig. 18).

Figure 18

FloorTalk served as an entertainment, a community meeting, a prayer meeting, and a Bible lesson all rolled up into one interactive event. It provided a safe place for kids in the community to express their joys and concerns, fears and hopes, with prayer, songs, and a message about Jesus and God's presence in their neighborhood. This became a new worshipping community linked to the Wilkey congregation. As the neighborhood chaplain, I had earned the right to care for these kids. Between sixty and one hundred kids crowded the corner of the gym for each thirty- to forty-minute FloorTalk. I related stories about the kids and the neighborhood, and I always invited the kids to share prayer requests or concerns, which they did. Everything they shared was welcome and meaningful, and I led a short prayer for whatever came up. A sick pet, problems at school, a shooting, drugs—whatever the concern, we prayed about it. Then, in the remaining ten minutes or so, I told the kids a story about Jesus from the Gospels.

I reminded the kids each week, in one way or another, that Jesus knows what it is like to live in their neighborhood. I told them God cared about them. I told them that God was here with them in the good times and the bad, that God was loving, powerful, and worthy of our attention, the good news being that God was paying attention to us. God would never leave them or forget them, and neither would we. Of course, words were one thing. But my presence, and the presence of a team of caring adults who were being drawn together as leaders in the congregation, brought these words and affirmations to life. Storytelling became a core experience to make God's love and presence accessible to every child and family.

Mission Storytelling

The Apostle Paul excitedly proclaimed the power of story when he wrote, "But how can people call for help if they don't know who to trust? And how can they know who to trust if they haven't heard of the One who can be trusted? And how can they hear if nobody tells them? And how is anyone going to tell them, unless someone is sent to do it? That's why Scripture exclaims, 'A sight to take your breath away! Grand processions of people telling all the good things of God!'" (Rom 10:14–15 MSG).

Storytelling is as old as language. I imagine you can recall stories from your earliest memories. We know how wonderful it is to tell stories.

Songs, poems, and rhymes are delightful ways to share stories with our children. In the beginning, created in the image of God, we had our voice. God sent us on a mission so important that images, symbols, music, and words were all employed to help us tell God's story—our stories. Stories of hope, joy, and triumph. Stories of pain, sorrow, and death. Stories conveyed life, growth, and framed the emerging future.

God's story of life and purpose became a story incarnate in Jesus Christ. With the incarnation (recall *Face Loved* in our Transformation Paradigm) the Logos (total expression) of God became human. The story was visible, audible, and transferable. Shared with groups identified as the Twelve, the Seventy, and the thousands, Jesus' story became a story of power built on the cascading events of Jesus' death, resurrection, ascension, appearances, and promised return. The Spirit's indwelling at Pentecost ensured that empowered storytellers would keep the story going.

We intuitively recognize the power of story. Now, science is helping us understand why storytelling is effective. Doctor Keith Oatley, professor of cognitive psychology at the University of Toronto, found that stories can produce a simulation of reality that runs analogous to simulation on computers.[12] We know how the performing arts, including theater, dance, and music, can engage the audience. Visual arts (such as cinema), digital gaming, and social media can be so completely immersive that the messages conveyed in the stories have real staying power, or stickiness. Effective storytelling engages people so completely that behaviors and emotions change—and futures too can change.

Jesus' story (like so many other stories in the biblical narratives) became the Apostle Paul's story because it was transformative. It was conveyed to Paul on the road to Damascus through blinding light, dramatic voice, and immersive experience, and it resulted in redirection. Paul was changed, and his story became the Romans' story, too. Paul persuaded the Romans to keep the story going. Jesus' message of good news constituted a life-saving relationship that changed lives. It was a story of impact, drama, and engagement. It was a story worth telling in every way possible.

FloorTalk welcomed our youthful participants to a safe intersection of their own stories with the larger transformational story that began and finds its ultimate fulfillment with God. FloorTalk affirmed all of the following:

---

12. Paul, "Your Brain on Fiction," SR6.

- The story is for everyone.
- The story must be deeply heard to be trusted.
- The story must be credibly told to be heard.
- The story must be clearly conveyed through a storyteller.

From the inception of the Christian church, history records the dynamic stories of many tribes within the faith community. For example, our Presbyterian tribe's story had tremendous impact on the world because Reformation leaders effectively harnessed the new technology of Gutenberg's printing press to tell their story on an incredible scale. Today, digital communication, social media, and mobile devices have enabled those of us in the church to increase the clarity, reach, and impact of the story God created us to tell. The Apostle Paul's vision is still being realized: "A sight to take your breath away! Grand processions of people telling all the good things of God!"

Storytelling is the task of the church. How can your story be more effectively conveyed to achieve measurable impact? How can your unique story intersect with and even become the story of your community, the story of individuals and families across the street, and even around the world?

Storytelling in Three Acts

When individuals gather as a congregation, the story of unique individuals becomes the worshipping community's story, too. How can we pay better attention to that story? Your church's story is more than theological or liturgical. It includes the story told through your building and grounds, visually and logistically. What feeling do people get when you welcome them inside? By improving the congregation's sense of satisfaction in ministry and its spiritual energy, the church represents the possibility of making the world different. Russ Crabtree, a well-known analyst and strategist for nonprofit and religious organizations and founder of HolyCow! Consulting, understands that an organization must do more than just hope to achieve ministry impact. "The evidence suggests that a church is vital and healthy when members bear witness to their experience in the body of Christ as one that is both satisfying and energizing," he writes.[13] As Yoda reminded young Luke Skywalker in George Lucas'

13. Crabtree, *Owl Sight*, 65.

Star Wars Episode V: The Empire Strikes Back, the church needs to take its mission seriously.

> LUKE: Master, moving rocks is one thing, but this is a little different.
>
> YODA (irritated): No! No different! The differences are in your mind. Throw them out! No longer of use are they to you.
>
> LUKE: (focusing, quietly): Okay. I'll give it a try.
>
> YODA: No. Try not. Do, do. Or do not. There is no try.[14]

To have life-changing impact, God's story must resonate deeply through your church's story using three components of persuasive storytelling: empathy (Greek: *pathos*), credibility (Greek: *ethos*), and logic (Greek: *logos*). There is no try.

Empathy—the Pathos of Your Story

Empathy is rooted deep within the DNA of your church, but it can be developed, and improved, through learning. Understanding and clarifying your church's values, and also understanding others' values, is essential to effective storytelling—storytelling that can transform lives. When the story is all about the storyteller, little empathy is expressed and impact on others is marginal. Self-referential storytelling is rarely interesting or effective. When the storyteller pays attention to others, however, and captures the experiences, emotions, and context of the listeners, empathy rises, which empowers life-changing behaviors.

> Don't talk to their minds, talk to their hearts.
>
> —NELSON MANDELA

Congregational Empathy in Practice: What is going on in your community? What do you see and hear? What are young people concerned about? What are business leaders concerned about? Gaining understanding, seeking answers to these kinds of questions, can increase the empathy expressed in your ministry. From the perspective of others, what one change or improvement would offer the greatest benefit that your church's ministry could be engaged with?

---

14. Kasdan, *Empire Strikes Back*, line 310.

Credibility—the Ethos of Your Story

Credibility is mostly learned and acquired but is connected to the church's experience. Some churches have accrued credibility from their historical community relationship. More than a few congregations are depicted on a town's official seal, for example, or represented on physical and digital community signs. Though historical integrity is critical, it raises the bar of expectation. If a congregation's recent credibility is not congruent with its reputation, significant challenges must be addressed.

Credibility refers to the church's character. Character is what we do when no one is looking. It is the story that is told when we are not setting out to tell a story. Credibility expresses itself in between the lines of our mission narratives. Obtaining credibility is one thing. Projecting it authentically is another. A church's credibility speaks louder than words.

> Preach the good news. If you must, use words.
>
> —ST. FRANCIS OF ASSISI

Congregational Credibility in Practice: How would you describe the internal pulse of your church? What is the level of satisfaction experienced by those individuals who are gathered and sent every week? What is the energy level of your leaders? What forces motivate your behaviors and inform your decisions, and how are they reflected in your worship and mission? In thinking deeply about your responses to these kinds of questions, consider how your internal assessment matches the perception of others. How is your inner life conveyed to those outside? Learning from the continuities and discontinuities in your character story can improve your church's credibility.

Logic—the Logos of Your Story

The Greeks highly valued logic, but their word *logos* was much more than connecting the dots and completing a thought. When the Gospel of John begins with the proclamation, "In the beginning was the Word, and the Word was with God, and the Word was God" (1:1), the message is that the Word was the essence of God's identity that pointed to a future destination, result, or outcome aligned with the essential character of God. The *logos* of a church expresses its purpose and gives evidence of its direction. Understanding is important, and credibility is essential, but when a church demonstrates it own *logos*, it intends to manifest a meaningful, aspirational, relevant direction. Your church's logic addresses the "Why?" for your church. In the incarnation, God's *Logos*—essence of intention—was incarnated (enfleshed, embodied) into our neighborhood for a particular purpose (John 1:14). God's story took up residence to accomplish something—many things, in fact. The incarnation was not a side trip to our planet but an intentional mission to redeem our home.

> We should try to be the parents of our future
> rather than the offspring of our past.
>
> —MIGUEL DE UNAMUNO

Congregational Logic in Practice: Why do you go to church? It may seem an odd question to ask, but when you consider the energy invested in your ministry and its outcomes, it should be clear why it is important to connect the dots—not just passively observing where they may be leading but intentionally connecting and reconnecting the dots so that your ministry achieves its unique purpose. Why do you serve in ministry? Why is your building on the corner? What does your budget reveal about what matters to you? Considering your responses to *logos* questions can help you connect the dots pointing to your preferred future. Understanding your church's purpose and the relevance of your ministry can inform your allocation of resources, align your priorities, and promote courageous storytelling.

There are many resources available to develop empathy, earn credibility through character, and ensure that your story is relevant—that it aligns with God's Story but intersects with the community's story. The height, breadth, and depth of this all-encompassing and never-ending story becomes an authentic expression of the greatest story ever told.

I shared stories while we gathered in the gym for FloorTalk. I told the kids about Jesus coming from Nazareth (a place like Kensington in some respects) and about his turning water into wine (most had never heard that story). I told them about Jesus healing the blind and those with leprosy. We talked about AIDS, about violence and fear, about Jesus showing us a better way of living, each day right here in the neighborhood. The kids listened. They listened because the adult leaders cared about them, and they knew it. They and their families knew that Wilkey Church was a safe place. They knew they were loved. They were shown that God loved them even more than they loved themselves, even more than a caring parent or guardian. They discovered in those brief FloorTalk minutes that God loved the neighborhood and wanted to help us rebuild it.

The content of FloorTalk messages progressed developmentally from stories about the life of Jesus to the work of reconciliation God accomplished through Jesus' suffering, death, resurrection, and ascension. The liturgical celebrations of Christmas, Easter, and Pentecost provided a framework for story engagement.

After several weeks, the FloorTalk idea took hold and a new strategic component was added. I asked the kids to draw pictures for me. I explained that I wanted to find new ways to show them God's love and that I was sincerely interested in what they thought about themselves, the neighborhood, the world, and God, too. This more intimate and expressive dimension of the intervention was met with enthusiasm based on trust. Thankfully, they agreed, and we began.

The Drawing Intervention

The neighborhood suffered a stigma others placed upon it. Could an intervention be designed that would give voice to the children in an authentic way and lift the stigma? We wanted to determine if direct intervention would be effective in lifting that stigma. We also needed an appropriate way to evaluate our weekly programs, summer activities, and summer camp experience. Those kids who gathered at Wilkey Church comprised the primary group, but a secondary group not directly involved in the intervention would function as a control group.

Ms. Lucy Rodriguez, the principal of Stetson Middle School, was supportive of the intervention project. After hearing the details during our first meeting, she introduced me to Mr. Bill Bowen and his class of fifth-graders. His thirty-two kids were from the general neighborhood of Kensington, with none involved in our Ontario Spirit sports program. Neither would they be involved in our summer activities. "Teacher Bill," as his students called him, invited me to teach his class twice a week. Though I asked for only fifteen minutes, he gave me an entire fifty-minute period—ample time to introduce the drawing topics and invite the children to draw.

Two groups were established. The Primary Intervention Group numbered eighty-five children who participated in the Saturday sports program. The Secondary Intervention Group was comprised of the thirty-two fifth-graders at Stetson Middle School. We established a large enough cohort of children to protect the validity of conclusions and our learning. When an intervention is designed that will utilize a control group, it is essential that each individual be invited to give his or her permission to participate. When these invitations to participate were given, I explained to the children that I was asking them to help me with my project. In addition, parental permissions were secured for each child participating in the sports program. No one declined. While gratifying, this positive response was rooted in the constructive and trusting relationships established with families in the community. I regard the entire drawing experience as a wonderful gift.

The topics for the drawing activity were determined in consultation with my mentor, Dr. Victoria Erickson (Drew University), and my project supervisor, Dr. Dean Trulear (Public/Private Ventures). Dr. Michael Christensen asked the children of Chernobyl to draw their world as they experienced it.[15] Igoa's children drew components of their culture.[16] Kramer's art therapy included topics depending on the specific nature of the intervention.[17] In each case, the objective was to give voice to the child's whole world experience. The drawing topics selected were as follows: Me and My Neighborhood; Me and My Friends; Me and My Family; Me and My School; Me and My World; Me and My Church (Mosque, Synagogue, God, or Religious Life); and Me and My Future. Our drawing journey began, then, with Me and My Neighborhood.

The order of the topical drawings was intentional. We began with a topic domain that was obvious and familiar. As they made their drawings the kids were on the floor, in the gym, in a church, on the street, in their neighborhood. I wanted to begin our drawing with what we had in common. Progressing through the orbits of experience closest to the children, we proceeded from the topic of Friends to that of Family and then to School. After engaging the basic local associations, we progressed to World.[18] The children would know how special their own local

---

15. Carter and Christensen, *Children of Chernobyl*, 160 and 166.

16. Igoa, *Inner World of the Immigrant Child*, 163.

17. Kramer, *Art as Therapy with Children*, 108. In Kramer's discussion, a participant named Clyde demonstrated extreme ego strength. She noted how he could dominate and interfere with another client's expressive drawing.

18. I had hoped to broaden the domain of "World" for the children by introducing

"world" was by asking them to think about the "local" world of others. The language of the Church topic was to undergo some modification. Initially, I framed it in terms of Me and My Church, only to have one of our kids who was Muslim initiate an important dialogue on the first day of drawing. It occurred to me that using the exclusive nomenclature of Church was restrictive and disrespectful of other faith traditions—and, for these children, stifling. I apologized for leaving Mosque out of the title and amended the drawing sheets to an inclusive title in succeeding sessions,[19] which was particularly helpful when I was with the students at Stetson Middle School. The final domain the children would be asked to draw was Me and My Future. It was here that I supposed transformation would be most welcomed, if not desired, as hope and faith are rooted in a view of the future.

The children and I began a journey—a journey to see each other more clearly and (hopefully) see ourselves through the eyes of God. As the psalmist pleads, "Keep me as the apple of your eye; hide me in the shadow of your wings" (Ps 17:8).

Protocol

The topics were drawn in regular sessions over a seven-week period, during the FloorTalk time of the Ontario Spirit sports program, limiting participation to kids in basketball or cheerleading. Permission slips were sent home for inclusion in the drawing project. The parents understood that I was asking the children to draw and invited their child's expression and discovery.[20] At the outset, the kids understood that their drawings

---

them to Christensen's children of Chernobyl via an exchange of drawings. Since both groups of children have been stigmatized due to their location (admittedly, the suffering of the children of Chernobyl was an order of magnitude more severe), they could benefit from sharing with others who also experience stigma of place. I contacted an agency in Minsk, Belarus, that was initially favorable to the exchange; however, subsequent contact was halted. I reconnected recently with the agency and hope the exchange will yet occur.

19. Not all the children attended every FloorTalk session, which necessitated distributing topic sheets from the previous week to anyone who had missed. Yes, it became an administrative challenge, especially since some of the children wanted to draw on *every topic* every week!

20. As with our previous activities, from vacation Bible school to the sports program, a permission slip return rate of 75 percent was achieved and deemed satisfactory.

would be coded to ensure security and protect their privacy, but almost without exception, the children autographed their creations as masterpieces in crayon. The coding was done but was in practice unnecessary.

Along with the pride of drawing, evident in their gleaming eyes even before I handed out the crayons, I realized that the kids loved what became their project. This transference and identification were not surprising. The more time I spent with the children and their families, the more meaningful the experience became. The project provided opportunities for self-expression, trust building, and discovery. The scope of the mission was redefining itself each time we met. It was our journey, and the crayon artistry was central to the intervention's design to give children a voice. I did not need to collect the papers to achieve the fundamental objective. Permission to display the pictures in public places was not even a necessary question! I asked, "Is it okay that we put up some pictures at the corner stores, in the windows or on the counters?" Hands shot up as the kids offered their works of art for display. Eventually, we also secured parental permission by adding a checkbox for including photos of the children and their "photos and creative writing" to the standard medical release forms used for our sports program. If we had succeeded at enabling the children to express themselves through their drawings, then it would be a greater success to let the community "see" their voices in their artwork.[21]

Technique

The drawing intervention required essentially two items, both of which I supplied each week: one box of twenty-four Crayola crayons for each participant, and one piece of standard white paper, 8.5 inches by 11 inches. Each child was assigned a number code (for tracking participation)

---

21. Displaying the drawings in store windows proved problematic. First, store window space was for merchandising, as I was told. On at least one occasion, we had drawings in three of the half-dozen storefronts around the neighborhood. We also displayed the drawings in the gym, along the hallways, and sent copies home to parents. Some of the kids were really impressed that "Pastor Kevin" carried their creations in two huge binders and "showed them every chance he could." Needless to say, the kids were overcome with joy when they learned that our intern, Pam Stump, scanned the drawings digitally so that I could display them on the computer, too.

and then was issued his or her own box of crayons[22] and a sheet of paper labeled with the same identifying number. The intent of giving voice involved affirming the children and their worldview, and then leveraging that experience into an opportunity for them to see themselves as God does. The sheet of paper was prepared in advance with the following information in the corner: topic, code number, and date. Later we added areas in which to record name, age, and location (Stetson Middle School or Wilkey Church).

The Primary Intervention Group, a.k.a. the "Kids in the Gym," was comprised of eighty-five boys and girls (the group was 38 percent female); approximately 35 percent were Hispanic, 30 percent African-American, and 35 percent Euro-American. The children lived within a few blocks of the church, most of them within a five-minute walk.

The Secondary Intervention Group, a.k.a. the "Stetson Kids," included thirty-four boys and girls (the group was 45 percent female); the racial composition was 45 percent Hispanic, 35 percent African-American, and 20 percent Euro-American. The children lived within six blocks of the school—less than a ten-minute walk. The twenty-minute sessions occurred during the first period of Mr. Bill Bowen's fifth-grade class at Stetson Middle School.[23] After the first few weeks, the children's excitement about their drawing activities became more widely known throughout the school. With the blessing of the principal, Mr. Bowen ex-

---

22. Within the scope of this project, the type of drawing—whether crayon, chalk, pencil, or ink—was irrelevant. However, since the effort expended by everyone was significant, I decided at the outset to include an array of variables for later, post-project evaluation.

One important consideration was color. It would have been more economical to purchase and distribute vast containers of crayons the children could choose from. When decoding the meaning of a drawing, however, one might ask, "Why did the child use that color to express herself?" or "What does the dominant use of that color mean?" So I decided to provide each child with his or her own box of crayons. If children wanted to use blue, for example, because it was their favorite color, they could—they would not have to use another color simply because it was all that was available. Accessibility to a range of tools, in this case crayon colors, ensured that the child's voice was authentically expressed. Though I have touched on it only briefly in this project, color interpretations have proved helpful in art therapy and clinical settings, as suggested by Leslie Hartley Lowe in her article "Scribble Art," in Kaduson and Schaefer, *101 Favorite Play Therapy Techniques*, 121–24.

23. Children from the H and Ontario neighborhood can and do attend Stetson Middle School, located at the corner of B and Allegheny Avenue, approximately eight blocks from Wilkey Church. Before these classroom visits, I did not know the students in this class.

panded the drawing time to a full period of forty minutes. The additional time allowed for conversation and sharing. The topics for the drawing sessions were the same as those for the Primary Intervention Group.

Process

The routine below was repeated with only slight modification for each session:

- *Describe the topic:* At the beginning of each session the topic for that week was explained. Sometimes the children drew freely about some other topic; other times the children did not draw at all but turned in a blank page. Some of the children asked for help in drawing their picture, which I generally resisted, encouraging them to try again.

    On several occasions, all the children could do was to express themselves with printed words, which I came to see as a drawing in and of itself, no less valuable than any of the others. I tried to show my deep appreciation for each child's effort.[24]

- *Distribute the supplies:* As the weeks ensued, it became harder to keep the crayons together. Replacements for broken crayons were made whenever possible. Despite our best efforts, involving at least three adults, crayons went missing and boxes were destroyed. By the conclusion of the project, more than two hundred boxes of crayons had been called into service.

    Then the fifteen-minute session began. In "neighborhood speak" this was translated as "more like thirty minutes, or however long it takes to collect the drawings." Thankfully, in the Stetson classroom, a more organized structure prevailed. The goal was not simply to adhere to a schedule but to ensure the inclusion of every child's contribution.

- *Drawing time:* Participants shared their drawing with the whole group. Most children, however, did not want to share with the entire group but instead shared their work with me or with another adult assisting in the project. I believe the noisy and acoustically

---

24. See Kramer, *Art as Therapy with Children*, 47. Kramer discusses the various art expressions and ways to understand their meaning in her chapter entitled "Art Therapy and the Problem of Quality in Art."

challenging gym precluded the children from sharing effectively. Ironically, it was in that cavernous gym that their voices as expressed through the drawings were given, seen, and touched, if not also heard.

We expressed our gratitude to the students for completing and sharing their drawings. This was mission-critical to the project. Generous appreciation is the cornerstone of worship, the mortar of mission, and the capstone of acts of kindness.

- *Collect the supplies*
- *Invitation to the next session*
- *Refreshments:* This was, needless to say, a highlight of the morning for the children.

Evidence of the Stigma Removed

More than three hundred drawings were collected from these sessions. We regarded them as three hundred precious and colorful gifts of life experience, stories that contributed to a larger cascading story. Often, the children's drawings were easy to understand at first glance, or after they had interpreted their work during a conversation following the drawing exercise. When we compared the children's attitudes and engagement at the inception of the drawing interventions to their attitudes and engagement at the conclusion, it was clear that a transformation was occurring. The leadership team conducted after-action reports following each drawing session, usually with the Ministry Learning Community and members of the Institutional Review Board. The after-action review provided continuity from week to week. Qualitative assessments suggested that the children were empowered to express themselves; the goal of "giving them voice" as the sessions progressed was achieved.

One child, whom we will call J, drew his neighborhood with the entire page blank except for the lower center (see fig. 19, J's neighborhood).

Figure 19

When asked about the drawing, J said it showed his street. His mom would not let him play outside because of the shootings that had occurred. "So you have seen a lot of shootings?" I asked him. "Yeah. [Pause] Drugs and fights about drugs is right there," he answered, pointing to the drawing. "Has anyone you know been shot?" I asked. A long pause followed as he nodded his head in the affirmative. J became a regular participant in the basketball program; his mother considered the gym to be a safe place. The stigma associated with street violence was at least diminished for J, since in this case the street led to Wilkey Church, a safe place.

A few weeks later, another child we will call K produced a drawing of his family that featured a large empty circle in the middle of the page (see fig. 20, K's Family).

Figure 20

Beneath the circle, two stick figures can be seen (see enlarged view of fig. 21, Family conflict disclosed in drawing).

Figure 21

K reported a dispute between his uncle and aunt who live with him. The nature of their relationship is captured in the conversation—the uncle says, "Get away," while the aunt defends herself and says "you," as in "You get away from me," K explained. I later learned that K had revealed this conflict to no one else. In this example, K was *given a voice*. I assured him of our support and offered to help in any way we could; all he had to do was ask. Stigma stifles openness and sharing as it repeats its monotonous message: "You have no value, and no one cares." Showing K a God who cares for him, a love demonstrated by all the adults at Wilkey, helped challenge and overcome the stigma that had left a mark on his community and his family.

A child we will call L presented a drawing on the topic of Me and My Neighborhood. What was his neighborhood like? We studied the drawing. It clearly depicted a simply drawn handgun in the center of the page. I invited L to say more about the drawing. "What have you drawn for us today?" I asked. There was no response. "Is this a gun?" I gently prodded. I could hardly refrain from asking for other details. I wondered if he was in danger and where the gun was located. Suddenly he motioned for the drawing to be given back to him. Thinking he was going to add further to his drawing, I returned it to him.

As we began to collect the other children's papers, L presented his updated drawing. It appeared to be a different drawing—at first glance, the handgun seemed to be missing. I saw instead a darkly drawn red cloud. I asked about the other drawing. It became evident to me that this was in fact the same drawing after all. L had obscured the image of the handgun with a whirlwind of red wax (see fig. 22, Child obscures depiction of gun).

Figure 22

I asked him where the gun had gone. He replied, "Pastor Kevin, a gun don't belong in church." I affirmed his respect for the church but gently tried to correct his assumptions: "L, thanks for your drawing, but if we can't talk about guns here, where can we? It's okay to draw whatever you want. You are safe to tell Pastor Kevin and the other adults here whatever you need to share." We both looked intently at the drawing. I could still discern the outline of the handgun. I later learned he drew the gun because his uncle had one and frequently waved it at his aunt.[25]

Additional examples of amazing revelations through artwork can be seen in the Me and My Neighborhood drawings of several other children. Child M colored a blue sky and, underneath it to the left, a big tree (fig. 23). To the right, a large yellow sun shines brightly above her house. Between the tree and the sun, in the middle of the page, M drew a trash can, overturned, with its lid on the ground to the right.

Figure 23

Notice how disproportionately large the trash can is compared to the house. Notice also that the home is a single-family dwelling. In Kensington there are only a handful of single-family houses, and none near the church. The vast majority of people live in row homes (see fig. 24). The

---

25. Later I was able to determine that L's uncle was no longer living in his home. As a mandated reporter, I expressed my concern to the mother, who assured me that the uncle had taken his gun with him and so that threat was no longer in their home.

row homes were built right next to the church, as seen in fig. 25[26] and fig. 26.

Figure 24

Figure 25

26. Notice the graffiti on the wall of the row home directly behind the church; later it would be transformed into a sign of hope. See the following chapter.

Figure 26

Child N included in her drawing of the neighborhood (see fig. 27) an incredibly large trash can half the height of her house.

Figure 27

The primary and secondary intervention groups displayed this same theme many times over.[27] The neighborhood's stigma is revealed not only

27. More crayon drawings and other resources are available from the book's online companion.

by the inclusion of disproportionately drawn trash cans but also by the fact that their contents are overflowing and scattered everywhere. The identifying symbols for our children in drawing the neighborhood were a tree or two, a house, and a trash can. The trash can's contents were an intrinsic part of the children's mental landscape of their stigmatized neighborhood.

A fire traumatized the neighborhood in winter and destroyed the home of eight-year-old Christopher and his mother (fig. 28).

Figure 28

With burns covering more than 30 percent of his body, Christopher was treated in the burn unit at St. Christopher's Medical Center for Children for several months and then transported to a rehabilitation unit in Delaware County. Before he could be rescued, he suffered from a lack of oxygen, which took a serious toll on his cognitive and motor skills. Thanks to God and to the medical teams, his injuries eventually healed. His family had no social group associations or faith community connections. They were known to stay indoors most of the time since Christopher's mom feared for his safety. When news of the fire broke, Christopher received daily visits for several weeks, though not from his family alone. While a few relatives visited Christopher periodically during his stay in the hospital, the neighborhood crossing guard stopped by on numerous occasions!

A caring crossing guard managed to visit Christopher on her own time. Leaders must pay attention to often forgotten and overlooked assets in the community, especially individuals who have a special job to do when accomplished with passionate dedication.

Christopher needed connections, a reminder of a welcoming place, a home to replace the one that had burned down. He and his mom needed not only a place in the community but also a place in God's arms. I introduced myself to his mother and offered my presence, a prayer, and expressions of encouragement. Until they could find a new place to live in, the neighborhood relationships offered a kind of emotional "place" for them.

The next Saturday I updated the kids on Christopher's condition. They were still talking about the fire trucks they had seen and the flames that had left yet another house on the block vacant (fig. 29).

Figure 29

Children expressed their own ideas of who was at fault, with shocking depictions of Christopher trapped inside the house while his mother, identified with the stark words "Christopher's mom," stood safely outside (see figs. 30 and 31).

Figure 30

Figure 31

One year later, the vacant, ash-ridden, burned-out home continued to bear witness to the flames of tragedy, which for many would be transformed into hope. We seemed to have faith to ask God to prevent a fire, but did we have faith to see God in the midst of a fire? During FloorTalk, I shared the biblical story of Daniel's three friends who were thrown into a fire because they trusted in God (Dan 3:17). I asked them to recall details from the story: "How many people did the king notice in the flames when he looked inside the furnace?" "Four!" the kids exclaimed.[28] "That's right, four," I said, "because God's angel was with them even in the fire."

A few weeks later the children drew pictures for Christopher as a community project (fig. 32).

Figure 32

Though months had passed, by the time the children were completing the series of drawings for the project, it was evident that they were still dealing with the tragedy. Everyone was interested in Christopher's condition and wondered when he was going to return home.

Good neighboring is a powerful and transformative force, something the children demonstrated in a colorful, crayon-drawn group project get-well card (fig. 32). Several of the children and their parents went with me to Children's Hospital during one of my several visits to see Christopher. The kids were not permitted to go any further than the waiting room, where they anxiously awaited news of their friend while I

---

28. Daniel 3 tells the story of Shadrach, Meshach, and Abednego. Note particularly the response of the king in verse 25—looking into the fiery furnace and expecting to find three bound, dead men, he exclaims, "Look! I see four men walking around in the fire, unbound and unharmed, and the fourth looks like a son of the gods."

personally delivered the card to Christopher's nurses in the intensive care room down the hall.

The stigma of their neighborhood told them, "God doesn't care about you in this place. Because you live here you have no value. People do not want to live here. God doesn't either." But through safe and trusting relationships with church and community leaders the kids learned that though the fire was bad, God had not abandoned them. God was with them right where they were and walked with them even in the fire. The children wondered, as the Israelites did, why Moses took so long on the mountain,[29] or why the disciples were alone on the lake during a storm.[30] The children learned about Jesus weeping over Lazarus when Mary and Martha complained that he (and hope itself) had arrived too late.[31] God is not absent, even though we sometimes feel abandoned and afraid. We are not alone. Though we may not be able to hear God's voice as loudly as we would like, God is not silent. We wonder where God was when tragedy strikes, but God is never late. God is always present. God always loves. The kids at H and Ontario Streets were beginning to experience these affirmations for themselves.

Stetson Middle School

The secondary intervention group at Stetson Middle School produced drawings that expressed ideas similar to those of the primary group at Wilkey Church. The drawing skill level was higher (see fig. 33). This was perhaps due to the older age of the class, or simply the fact the Stetson children had more time to draw than the Wilkey kids did.

---

29. Exod 32:1: "When the people saw that Moses was so long in coming down from the mountain, they gathered around Aaron and said, 'Come, make us gods who will go before us.'"

30. Matt 14:22ff.

31. John 11:21: "'Lord,' Martha said to Jesus, 'if you had been here, my brother would not have died.'"

Figure 33

At the outset, my hypothesis was that the Stetson effort would have minimal impact since the children were not involved in our weekly Ontario Spirit program. What I discovered was the opposite. Caring adults can make a significant contribution to the self-esteem and wellbeing of children, even if that contribution consists of only a few minutes each week.

Authentic connections will effectively reneighbor a formerly disconnected congregational ministry. When church leaders pay attention by investing their time and energy in community relationships, amazing outcomes will occur. For example, nurturing relationships in the community, meeting people all across the neighborhood, afforded the opportunity to become acquainted with Mr. Bowen, a caring schoolteacher. That teacher invited me to help with his class at Stetson. Were it not for my time hanging out in the community, building friendships over the course of months as an agent of hope, I cannot imagine how that opportunity would have developed at all. Building trust, being present—these are the key priorities of an engaged community church. From these mission emerges in an authentic and effective way.

The principal, Ms. Lucy Rodriguez, enthusiastically introduced the drawing program to Mr. Bowen's class. During the following weeks, several teachers asked if their classes could participate.[32] I received several duplicate invitations to school-based gatherings—one from my previous community contacts and another from Stetson mailings. I was invited to participate in the annual career day, which enabled me to share my story of being a pastor in the neighborhood with five different eighth-grade classes. I became acquainted with children in our neighborhood, many of whom then took part in our sports programs.

The fifth-grade class welcomed the attention brought by the crayon storytelling. The Stetson kids took pride in their artwork, asking to display it in the hallway for the entire school to see. Often, as I approached the third-floor class at the end of a long corridor, one child, then others would recognize me and call my name. To the casual observer, it might seem strange that the pastor of a church blocks away would even be present at the school to begin with, let alone welcomed by so many students. What's more, many of the children who greeted me were not actually in my class but had heard from their friends how much they enjoyed the drawing project. This recognition was not about me as an individual but the role I represented as a caring adult who invested time with them. The connection was made all the more significant because they also realized I did not have to be there at all. Volunteers who enter the classroom can have an incredible impact not just on the students they work with but also on those who observe the interaction.

Every drawing told a story that captured a range of expressions. Many of the children expressed messages of judgment concerning their environment (see fig. 34). Then children offered their own faith statements concerning loved ones (see fig. 35).

---

32. Drawing interventions were developed with several additional classes at Stetson Middle School a few months later. Mr. Bowen's teacher colleagues were impressed with the student engagement that seemed to improve the overall teacher-student relationship. They modeled the crayon methodology in their own classrooms. Not surprisingly, it was the art teachers who seemed to take a deeper look at the benefits of their own instructional goals as they saw artistic expression in ordinary classrooms.

162 *Crayons for the City*

Figure 34

Figure 35

Each topic framed the focus of their story, drawn with purpose and energy. Four boys in Mr. Bowen's class initially refused to draw but soon after began their own drawing projects like the rest of the class. Drawing was not a requirement, and I developed other means to invite their participation. I asked them to help distribute and collect the papers and crayons, for example, and before long they came to understand the value of their classmates' drawing efforts. Eagerly wanting to catch up a week or two later, they added their crayon masterpieces to the dozens of other drawings already completed. The children in the secondary intervention group responded to caring adults just as the primary intervention group did. We built rapport and established trust by respecting the children and the gifts they had to offer to one another, and through drawn stories gave them a way to express their own voice.

At Wilkey, we created a safe gathering place for children in their community, while at Stetson, children were met on their turf, in their familiar school setting. We took the children seriously and offered them a way to experience their own unique value, to recognize their place in their world, and to become more hopeful about their future.

As a trust agent, an ambassador of God, I received the children's drawings as sacred offerings. I did not need to assess them. I did not have to approve or disapprove of the content of their drawings. I was not there with an ulterior motive, as someone who wanted something. Instead, I wanted the children to discover something about themselves. It is a very powerful gift to invite someone, especially a child who has been stigmatized, to share his or her feelings and needs, despair and hope. And all in the class came to recognize the contributions of their classmates. We had wonderful conversations about religious faith, even in the classroom at Stetson, as children shared their drawings. It was their storytelling, not mine, that gave the crayon drawings power.

A frequent story revealed in their drawings was the anger they felt about their neighborhood and their situation in it. Using only their crayons, they brought forth the messages they had internalized in their stigmatized neighborhood, and I was the engaged and present observer. I went where they were in their drawings. I tried to pick out recurring images in the wax marks they made on the white paper, where reality and fantasy merged in a kaleidoscope of color. The layers of story and imagination included religious imagery, too, such as Jesus in a manger, a cross or a crucifix. Many of the children expressed how they began to see God's presence where they were—Jesus was not a relic or a statue but someone who could be known. I began to understand my role in connecting the children and the community to God's presence as similar to the role of the Apostle Paul, who wrote, "We are therefore Christ's ambassadors, as though God were making his appeal through us. We implore you on Christ's behalf: Be reconciled to God" (2 Cor 5:20).

For reconciliation to occur, individuals old and young and organizations such as the church must realign their life with God's life. "Faith is not a feeling or a capacity we conjure up, but trusting that God can act decisively in the world."[33] Authentic, meaningful, interactive connections must be accessible and understandable by a child. We tried to demonstrate that the children were important in their own eyes, and to us as well. We attempted to build experiences that demonstrated that they were important to their teachers and their parents. I showed them they were special members of their neighborhood and citizens of the city in which they lived. Truly, they were important to God, and God did not need me to establish that fact. But I believe that the community of faith must work hard to be an effective ambassador of the loving Creator God. In a nonthreatening and welcoming environment, the children could consider how their Creator viewed them. God could become for them an ultimate validation of acceptance, forgiveness, and hope, and an ever-present resource for ordinary and extraordinary life experiences. Their Creator could be the one voice they would hear that would lift the stigma and its effects.

The drawing intervention invited the children to articulate their vision of the world. We recognized that we need to articulate a vision for restoring hope. Summer camp, we concluded, would be the place for creating that vision. The children understood that Wilkey Church's caring adults did not want merely to send them away to a camp. We wanted to take them to camp with us! We made plans to attend Young Life's Lake Champion for a week in August.

---

33. Wink, *Powers That Be*, 145.

10

Engagement, Act 3: Restoring Hope

Figure 36

Camping with the Damascus Project

I began to observe that an emerging unstigmatized self was supplanting the former one, supported by improved self-esteem, respect for the neighborhood, and a generally more positive outlook. Our team grew more excited about taking the kids to camp with us. Our goal was to leverage our adult team's relationships with our multiethnic mix of middle school–aged youth, who would, we hoped, be empowered to become youth leaders in their own neighborhood. When I saw the kids, I envisioned a new generation of leadership for a new community. Before us was the solution to a lack of indigenous transformational leadership. Now was the time to embrace God's emerging future.

Not everyone understood the deeper transformation that was occurring in the lives of young people in Kensington. I was frequently asked, "How come the kids don't come to church?" My initial response was, "Why should they?" I did not think of it as a problem to be solved. I was continually amazed that the kids found a safe, nurturing place at Wilkey Church and that children actively participated multiple times a week for more than a year. I had to work hard to remove the "church kid" and "non-church kid" labels from our vocabulary. Even more difficult was the unfortunate "Christian kid" and "non-Christian kid" tags. These categories were not useful, especially to the leadership, and the young people definitely misunderstood them.

Many leaders in my denominational and regional council office seemed to be uneasy or even disturbed that one hundred-plus kids gathering on Saturdays were not being described by their preferred label of "church kids." I think I confused my colleagues when I described the children as "just kids from the neighborhood." Somehow, we as Christians became self-referential in a kind of spiritual arrogance, thinking we were the only point of reference. My focus was on building the capacity of a worshipping community that was achieving community impact. I understood our urban life experience to be more of a continuum of transformation than demarcated boundaries. The young people were beginning to understand worship as a verb and not as a time and place on Sunday mornings.

We believed that God wanted to impact the lives of kids over the course of their lifetimes. The opportunity to build a core group of neighborhood leaders who were spiritually connected came on nearly every day of the week but Sunday. To redirect the good intentions of a few denominational detractors, however, I consistently referred to these kids as neighborhood kids, not as church kids. Of course, I hoped that many would express faith in their own way, in their own time, but again, that was an outcome the person alone controlled.

Our Damascus Project objective was to provide resources to cover the cost of filling a charter bus to capacity with thirty-five young people[1]

---

1. About forty-three kids actually attended. A dozen more children wanted to go but, for various reasons, were not able to.

and six adult leaders. They would attend a weeklong summer camping experience at Young Life's Lake Champion, in southern New York. The project was designed for urban multiethnic, multiracial children aged twelve to fourteen.

The story of Paul's conversion in Acts 9 formed the mission rationale for our Damascus Project intervention. As Saul the rabbi might explain it, it was during his brief out-of-town visit to Damascus that he began to see things from an entirely different point of view.[2] As a result of his transformational experience with Jesus, Saul became Paul, a man of hope and promise. We wanted this same outcome for our kids. My firsthand experience with Young Life's outstanding camping program over many years reinforced the importance and potential of this effort.

As we learned through our research into Wilkey's past, names are significant. Names can empower or names can enslave. The renaming of Saul symbolized an incredible change, just as it did when Simon the Stone became Peter the Rock.[3] We were renaming things, reclaiming space and meaning—making sacred what was once considered the profane. In her discussion of the relationship between the profane and the sacred, Dr. Victoria Erickson argues that the sacred-profane dichotomy is a construct that ultimately must be cast aside in order to embrace something more divine. She correctly asserts, "In the stories of those considered 'profane' Jesus is often seen as ultimately inviting believers to give up the sacred, including himself as sacred object. For the oppressed Jesus points to God."[4]

The engagement intervention began with Act 1—reneighboring the congregation using ethnography as a tool to develop an authentic sense of mission rootedness in the church. This was followed by Act 2—reconnecting the community using crayons as a tool to to develop an authentic voice in the community. For Act 3—restoring hope, we would use an out-of-community experience to develop an authentic view of self apart from the physical constraints of the stigmatized neighborhood itself. This transformational journey was designed to restore the children's hope. They were invited to step outside the traditional boundaries of

---

2. Acts 9:1–31.

3. Matt 16:17–18: "Jesus replied, 'Blessed are you, Simon son of Jonah, for this was not revealed to you by man, but by my Father in heaven. And I tell you that you are Peter, and on this rock I will build my church, and the gates of Hades will not overcome it.'"

4. Erickson, *Where Silence Speaks*, 187.

the sacred-profane dualism into a continuum of divine space, a space in which they would be freed to see themselves with the stigma lifted. I wanted the kids to hear the words Lazarus heard long ago when Jesus called him out of the tomb: "Lazarus, come out!" The dead man came out with his hands and feet wrapped with strips of linen and a cloth around his face. Jesus then said, "Take off the grave clothes and let him go" (John 11:43–44). For us, the grave clothes represented the stigma to be lifted. The young people would return from their Damascus experience filled with possibilities and would become peer leaders for a new neighborhood-based worshipping community at Wilkey Church—seeds of hope for a community of despair.

The Ontario Spirit Street Leaders program invited kids who attended camp to opt in to further develop their relationship with one another and with Jesus Christ. Through personal one-on-one and small group experiences, team building, and learning exercises, they would integrate their personal life with their neighborhood, school, and community life. Twenty-one of the thirty-five young Damascus Project participants were to become Street Leaders. Spiritual formation would occur through an innovative approach I called *neighborship*, which extended the traditional, if not more narrowly focused, discipleship curriculum common in Christian churches. Our view was that you cannot be a good disciple without being a good neighbor. Our small groups also had a mentoring component as children and often their families participated together in conversational Bible studies. Our Ontario Spirit Street Leaders connected with similar street leader programs in Kensington, such as one operated by the Shalom House, and with Young Life in Philadelphia's Germantown neighborhood.

Community collaboration developed with the assistance of Charles Harris, director of Philadelphia Young Life. Young Life owned the Lake Champion property in New York. Charles was planning to take middle school–aged kids living in Germantown and West Philadelphia for a special urban emphasis week. Most of the three hundred kids attending that week would be from urban areas such as New York, Trenton, Baltimore, and Washington DC. We requested space for August 15–21. Initially, we had hoped to take thirty-five kids, but that became a challenge since more than thirty-five wanted to go. When you earn the right to be heard, capacity and energy naturally result. If the depth and reach of our ministry were significant enough, then parents would want their kids to go. If the trust we had built was worth anything at all, then God was about to do something incredible.

Most kids from our neighborhood had never been to camp before.[5] If they had, it was likely through the city of Philadelphia's department of recreation, or possibly with an out-of-city or suburban church. However, the Damascus Project would be uniquely different from most traditional camps precisely because caring adults were committed to going to camp with the children and, at the week's end, sharing a future in the neighborhood.

Based on the principles of the Damascus Project, we decided that kids were not to be sent to camp; they were to be invited to go with us. This was critical to our Act 2 objective of removing the stigma by giving a voice to youth through relationships and the tools of drawing. Most kids who go to camp are typically sent away alone to spend a week with a counselor they do not know; then they return home alone. What kind of authentic voice does that offer a child? In effect, you say to the child, "Go away where I can't hear you and come back again some other day." However, we were continuing a relationship and affirming the worth of the child by saying, "You're special to us. We care about your feelings and believe in your future. God loves you and we do, too. How would you like to come with us to Lake Champion for what could be the best week of your life?" The relationship exists before the camp, which gives the camping event the power to be a transformative experience.

Kids belong to a system of relationships, and we must respect those networks. They do not need to build a relationship with the pastor if that relationship is not connected to the rest of their world. Dr. Dean Borgman, the Culpepper Professor of Youth Ministries at Gordon-Conwell Theological Seminary north of Boston, sees "each individual as a product of several systems: family, community, schools, media, peers—and for some, church."[6] This means it is contrary to the systemic nature of individuals and neighborhoods to dislocate a child from her social systems and send her to camp. Whatever a camp may accomplish will be undermined, or at best diminished, because the systems of the child were not taken into account. Both before and after the camping experience I sought to be intentional about connecting with social and family systems.[7]

    5. Of the children who went to camp with us, twenty-eight (65 percent) had never been to a summer camp before.

    6. Borgman, *When Kumbaya Is Not Enough*, 107.

    7. Dr. Dean Trulear pointed me in this direction early on in my project. Borgman

A church cannot hope to be effective in spiritual formation training, typically called *discipleship*, if it is not a good neighbor, which requires the practice of *neighborship*. Parents and their children must be treated with respect by a church that is also a good neighbor. Being responsive to questions, beginning and ending our programs on time, ensuring the safety of the children, returning things we had borrowed (something as simple as a cake plate, for instance), meeting a child and their family in their house or on their stoop—all became touchpoints for affirming the value of the family system. I attribute the outstanding response to the trip to the authentic connecting with families we demonstrated consistently throughout the year.

Funding

With the date of the camp approaching, funding became a problem to be solved.[8] We needed $10,000 and the resources within the congregation were insufficient. In light of the limited means of our families, we asked that each family contribute at least $35. That was only a small portion of the per child cost ($225), but it was what most could afford. Though a general invitation to go to camp was offered to many, we also sought to target kids who we believed would be good candidates as future leaders. Some of the families could pay a bit more, so we established an informal scholarship fund to offset the difficulty others had in meeting the $35 minimum. When a child could not raise the money, we offered to have him or her earn the money by completing chores around the church and community. Several kids offered to clean the houses of elderly folks for

---

also underscores this point in his discussion of holistic youth ministry. Intervention must be led by those who are prepared to think critically and theologically about youth and their systems. Ironically, though Borgman sees youth ministers as "adult role models in the young person's growth process" (*When Kumbaya Is Not Enough*, xxi), he does not elaborate on being an adult role model to the adults in the child's system as well. This brings youth ministry into the mainstream of our efforts to rebuild a neighborhood and not only run a great youth program.

8. I was a bit reserved in talking about camp in the same breath as money, since I did not want to disappoint the kids if in the end we could not raise what we needed. I also did not want to "lose" face! My own faith was stretched as I prayerfully took my concerns to my Institutional Support Group, family, and friends, using all the systems I was connected to. Then, almost as soon as my faith and confidence in Christ and his work in the neighborhood was affirmed, I began to receive commitments from several people, including a professor, to help with the project.

a few dollars. Still others saved birthday money. Nevertheless, the balance needed seemed overwhelming to us. The camp funding goal represented about 50 percent of our church's operating budget for the year. God would provide. We were certain of that. If God were in this, funding would come in. After the last of the kids signed up and the permission slips were in hand, we received word from a benefactor that the remaining funding would come through!

Several months before we even knew we needed to raise the money, a colleague, the Reverend Tom Wray, shared our ministry with his church in Norristown, Pennsylvania. At their invitation, we presented our story of transformation that included a large aerial photograph of the neighborhood, ministry photos, and an invitation to become a prayer partner in our work, which they happily agreed to do. A few weeks later, when Pastor Tom discovered we needed additional funds for camp, we began to explore ways to secure it and eventually submitted a grant request to his church's missions committee. We were overjoyed and grateful when we received a seed grant of $3,300. Encouraged by their generosity, we submitted a proposal to the Mustard Seed Foundation in Virginia for a matching grant. With that approved, we were about two-thirds of the way to our goal. Young Life was exceptionally generous, too, in agreeing to reduce the net camp costs. The divisional director of Young Life, with whom I used to work, also offered to pay for a couple of our kids to attend. Finally, within two weeks of our departure date, we were fully funded.

The final list of kids who would actually go evolved during the months preceding departure. Some kids changed their minds; others discovered to their disappointment that some other trip or visit would interfere with their camp plans. Because of our commitment to respect systems, we ended up "inviting" more kids than the original target of thirty-five—if one child in a particular family were going to camp, then the sibling closest in age would need to go too.[9] We kept signing up kids. I would have to call the Young Life office in Philadelphia and then the camp itself to check on the quota allowed and to inquire about camp capacity. We were determined to get these kids to Lake Champion. If a child wanted to go, then we would do all we could to make that happen. When

---

9. I was reluctant to tell Charles Harris, but some of the kids who signed up were pushing the "not yet twelve" age. He found out about it soon enough, however. As it turned out, Charles was assigned to Lake Champion for the entire month of August as head counselor, a position that brought him face to face with our younger youngsters!

we reviewed the near-final roster, it provoked a deep sense of gratitude in our entire team. I think most of us, if we were honest with ourselves, were incredibly surprised that God actually pulled this off. How could a congregation of thirty-five members serving hundreds of young people and families every week in a resource-depleted neighborhood, a congregation with a $25,000 budget, send forty-three kids to camp for $10,000? We could not, but God could.

We recruited a team of counselors; most were leaders in our programs. I was thrilled to have Jonathan, my then twelve-year-old son, come along. He was frequently with me at church. Rozanne, a member of my ISG and an elder in the church, also committed to going. Stew, a colleague's college-aged son who, I hoped, would stay connected with our kids, balanced out our team. Since Young Life required a counselor-to-kid ratio of 6:1, we connected our many kids with additional capable counselors from Young Life's Germantown and West Philadelphia teams.

Finally the day arrived, and all the participants gathered for what promised to be an incredible adventure (see fig. 37).

Figure 37

This intervention was intended to restore hope. It centered on loving kids enough to ensure that they had an opportunity to see themselves and their world more clearly. Since that awareness could be unsettling and painful, this important experience was supervised and supported by caring adults who had invested time and energy in building relationships of trust. It was not just about a congregation, drawings, and a week at camp. It was about experiencing God's love together.

After taking a group photograph, with most of us in our bright yellow "Club Ontario Spirit" T-shirts, we boarded the bus that would take us to Lake Champion. The atmosphere was electric. "Hey, Pastor Kev, this isn't anything like the SEPTA bus!" one kid screamed as parents waved to send us off.[10] "This is going to be awesome!" another kid said quietly. The leaders knew they had not seen anything yet.

At Camp Lake Champion

The long bus ride was, well, long. As we got closer, only a couple of hours away, all forty-three kids grew impatient (way too impatient, it seemed), until finally we arrived. From the moment we rolled down the road into the wooded hundred-acre property featuring a huge lake, zip lines, jacuzzi and pool, game room, ropes course, and beautiful cabins,[11] the kids knew they were the most important people in the world. Young Life does youth ministry better than nearly any other organization. When it comes to summer camping, they are the absolute best. But restoring hope does not happen with a change of venue alone. Three important engagements were designed to help us achieve our objective.

Engaging in Action

When we arrived we were met by the program staff, who acted out a creative story that would set the stage for the entire week's program. On cue, but unknown to the delighted campers, the bus was abruptly stopped as actors pulled off in a Jeep with one of our kids. The rest of us, now screaming with delight, stayed in the bus till we reached another staging area. Suddenly we were escorted off the bus, with our luggage and gear still inside. (High school volunteers with the camp's Work Crew would take the luggage to our cabins for us.) We ran through a huge welcoming committee of Work Crew and college-aged Summer Staff up onto a stage. Unbeknownst to us, the stage was actually a trailer attached to a tractor—and once we were all on board it started to move! Out by the lake we went as program staff dropped from the low-hanging trees above us and continued the adventurous storyline. Music pounded, sounds were

---

10. SEPTA stands for Southeastern Pennsylvania Transit Authority, the Philadelphia area's public transportation system.

11. See the camp promotion sheet in the online Appendix companion.

all around, the camp looked immense, and all the while the kids looked astounded. The excitement of the first thirty minutes was intended to show the kids that they were special and to let them know that they were in a very cool place with people who cared about them.

Engaging in Relationships

Everything the staff does at Lake Champion, as at every other Young Life property, is designed to build relationships between the counselors and the children. (See fig. 38 showing our kids at the camp.)

Figure 38

Program and club gatherings, waterfront activities, river rafting, swimming, gym, the ropes course, the fantastic zip ride into the lake, meal times, cabin times—all of these combined to provide a setting for relationships to grow. Wilkey was connected to the neighborhood (reneighboring the congregation); the kids were connected to us (removing the stigma); now we could, as a third act, connect the kids to their Creator (restoring hope).

With their new self-perception, many of the kids explored areas of interest they had not explored previously. Some loved to make crafts, while others loved being in the pool so much that they looked more like prunes than middle school kids by the end of the day. The counselors, for their part, were run ragged. Up late and up early. The camp staff provided all the tools we needed to show God's love for our kids. The twice-daily counselor briefings kept us clued in on the activities and prepared us for the non-stop action. But the camping methodology was not just intense activity all week long. The pacing of the activities gradually declined during the week as small group interactions increased. Early in the week the activity was high and the message offered each night by the camp's program leader included short vignettes about the life of Jesus Christ. These talks were similar to the FloorTalk conversations back home. The crowd of four hundred kids enjoyed it all. As the week progressed, we came to know our kids in wonderful new ways. The message content each day built on the previous night's story, while during the day, activities engaged us in physical challenges. One of the events required the entire cabin to carry their counselors across the sandy beach at night in a race to the finish. The counselor team just loved being with the kids. And the kids knew there was something much more exciting than the camp experience (and even better than the sumptuous meals)—they were coming to understand in their own way the good news about a God who could make their future different.

Engaging in Transformation

During the week at Lake Champion, each kid engaged in whatever activities suited him or her. Some kids were active throughout the week, while others kept more to themselves. Still others began the week a bit disinterested but increased their participation later on. Respecting each child's place emotionally and spiritually was essential to the counselors and the camp staff. As the camper survey cards rolled in and we had our last-day conversations, we were humbled and grateful that all of our kids indicated they had a positive camp experience and were glad they came. Seventeen kids indicated they had made a first-time profession of faith in Jesus Christ during the week, their own Damascus experience, which was wonderful. At the closing meeting the kids heard a beautiful message of hope and love. The camp's director, Bo Nixon, began a time for those kids who felt comfortable doing so to stand and say what the camp experience had meant to them. We were thrilled that many of our kids responded. After the kid's "say-so," Bo recalled a story from his own experience and asked if there were any who had responded to Jesus in faith who would like to stand. Many did. As the wireless microphone passed from kid to kid, our own Antonio and his brothers Max, Michael, and Angel all stood up. Each in turn introduced himself and said in his own words that he had responded in faith to Jesus Christ and that he was from Kensington. Our entire group celebrated the fantastic week we had shared together, giving witness to God's transforming power.

Evidence of Hope Restored

On the bus ride home, as we napped and watched *The Wizard of Oz* for the fifth time, we were feeling grateful for Lake Champion. We saw the hope in the kid's sleepy eyes. We reviewed the camper survey cards they were asked to complete, and card after card said "Awesome," or "Cool," or "Best week of my life." Something they had done or someone they had met at Lake Champion would stay with them and make a difference in their lives back home. "Couldn't wait to get home and tell Mommy," Tiffany proudly offered. Each kid came to know himself or herself more completely, and we were anticipating that half the kids would soon be part of the Ontario Spirit Street Leaders program. Of the forty-three kids we had been working with for more than a year, all forty-three were returning to their homes changed in ways we could not fully understand.

Central Presbyterian Church in Norristown, the Mustard Seed Foundation, and Young Life made the impossible happen at the corner of H and Ontario Streets in Philadelphia. Though we arrived back late at night, tired, two suitcases lost, still we knew it had been well worth the effort. The following week we started a "Pizza Bible Study" we called Campaigners that met on Tuesday at 5:30 p.m. (eventually it would grow into a Street Leaders program). More than twenty-five kids attended regularly. Family worship, offered in Spanish as well as in English, was another outcome of our camp experience. The kid's parents stayed involved, with more and more neighbors joining us in the following months. More than one hundred kids participated on Saturdays as our outreach consistently grew way beyond the traditional Sunday worship service. Crabtree describes the transformational state in which a church struggling to rediscover a clear purpose and sense of wholeness in its life and ministry begins to demonstrate a capacity "to positively impact those within the church and the community it serves."[12] Older and younger Kensington

---

12. Crabtree, *Owl Sight*, 211.

neighbors were encouraged that their neighborhood was better, different, and began to believe again that it could be a place of wholeness and peace as hope was restored.

11

Community of Hope

Figure 39

For many years, the wall of a row home next to the church building had been the target of vandals whose graffiti was a symbol of anger and hopelessness (see fig. 40). Prior to our camp experience, the wall was a constant reminder to us of a neighborhood disparagingly called "the Badlands" and how those who called it home suffered from its associated stigma.

Figure 40

Like a church, a neighborhood can choose to remain a victim to its past. Or (also like a church) it can instead live into a better future. After camp, the newly energized and hope-filled young people formed a group called Campaigners. They met together for sharing and conversational Bible study. They came to realize that the wall next to the church (which was itself stigmatized, marked and abused) now had a different job to do as a witness to newfound hope.

During one Campaigners meeting, the kids wanted to take on a project to show the entire neighborhood the transformation they had experienced. Walking around the community provoked many good ideas, but as the group paused at the corner of the church, Renaldo pointed to the graffiti-filled wall and exclaimed, "Let's paint the wall!" Within a few moments, the kids agreed that transforming that wall would become their new project.

With the help of our Temple University intern, Ms. Pamela Stump, the kids were determined to create a neighborhood mural that reflected their joyful hope in the community. We made our proposal to the renowned Mural Arts Philadelphia, the nation's largest public arts program, and they agreed to contract their artist, Mr. Wade Williams, to assist with our project. In response to their summer adventure, the kids contributed ideas for making a statement about camp and how they felt about the neighborhood, our home. Over many weeks, dozens of children and youth submitted ideas and concept drawings of what they imagined the wall should look like. We reviewed several narratives and themes, and in the end, the children selected the story of Noah's Ark. Mr. Williams produced a prototype sketch that we showed to the homeowner, our neighbor next door. With their approval the painting began. Figure 41 captures the painting energy on the wall. Because this was a "kid wall," only a few adults actually assisted with the painting. Inclement weather, shortened daylight hours, and the incremental nature of the work challenged all our fortitude and tested our painting skills.

Figure 41

Eight weeks later, the story of God's hope and peace was made visible on that wall (see fig. 42). A vibrant rainbow arches over a blue sea as the bold brown ark makes port in Philadelphia, whose skyline includes City Center's skyscrapers and Kensington's row homes and neighborhoods. Those who pass the wall on busy Ontario Street see the rainbow of hope and doves of peace (center), the ark signifying God's protection (left), and recognize that the city is a place of transformation and, for those who live here, home.

Figure 42

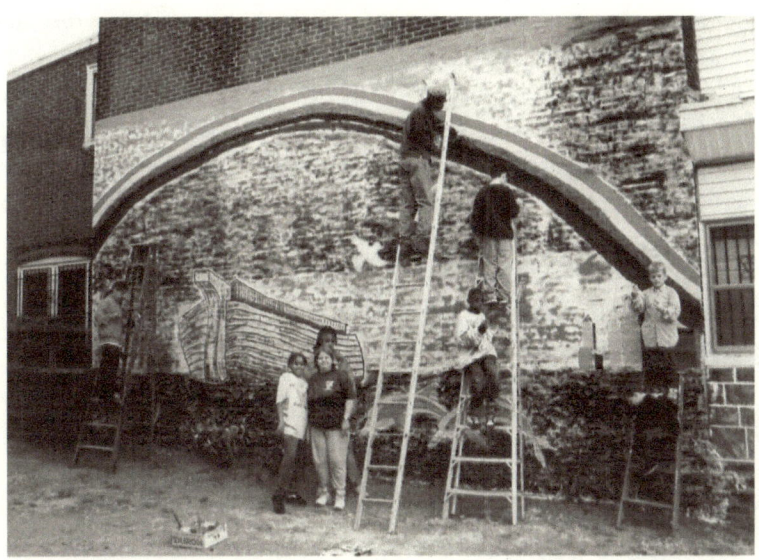

Remember Joe, the Stetson Middle School student I spoke to after the gunfire outside his school building? "It happens all the time," he said. I was pretty shook up that evening, the gunshots still ringing in my ears, as I mulled over Joe's words: "It happens all the time." Russian poet laureate Alexander Kushner, in his book *Apollo in the Snow*, has a poem called "Someone's Crying All Night," which echoes the sentiment expressed by Joe:

> Someone's crying all night.
> Just behind the wall someone's crying.
> If I could, I would go help,
> But the aggrieved won't invite me in . . .
> "Wake up! Listen!" you say. "Someone's crying."[1]

Wake up. That's what the church needs to do. Giving a child a voice and then listening to it is a sacred act. The pictures drawn by the children were intimate expressions of their inner world. A sensitive listener who

---

1. Kushner, *Apollo in the Snow*, 31.

has won the right to engage with children in "crayon conversations" can become the voice of hope. Truly transformational leaders must never stop listening.

Using the Goffman and Mead framework, we understand that the children create an extension of themselves with each drawing. The reception of this crayon gift builds trust. Moreover, it actually invites the child into a dialogue within himself or herself in reference to the topic, which builds esteems and even challenges the other Me's that are stigmatized. The drawing intervention creates a more accurate view of self to displace the stigmatized virtual one. Comparing the early drawings of the primary intervention group with the after-intervention mural demonstrates the degree to which the intervention enabled transformation.

As pastor, I functioned as a transformational agent for the congregation, for the children and their families, and for the neighborhood, in a number of ways I will elaborate below:

The Institutional Review Board and Congregation

Perhaps your role as a community leader or pastor of a worshipping community does not require you to develop and test a new intervention model, but if it does, you will want to consider the significant behavioral and ethical aspects to that level of work and convene an Institutional Review Board (IRB), also known as an institutional support group or ethical review board. This team of professionals provides necessary supervision, monitoring, and review of behavioral research that involves human intervention. The design of our intervention established a primary intervention group at Wilkey Church, with a secondary control group at Stetson Middle School. Empowering a group of leaders within the congregation to be the Institutional Review Board was a transformational act because it required their active engagement in the intervention design and monitoring of results. One elder, Eleanor Heinz, wrote a personal statement of her experience on the IRB. "Now I have a deeper sense of God's call; that if we don't give ourselves away to the neighborhood, we will cease to exist. I know we have a future now," she stated. Another elder, Linda Burns, wrote, "Our purpose in the neighborhood is to serve the neighborhood. We must stop serving ourselves." These leaders were certain the church would close unless the congregation engaged with one another and with the community. They were transformed as they monitored the intervention in their role as members of the IRB. It was as if the entire congregation had been called back to active duty, called to use their God-given gifts to love their neighborhood, and could be described by these words of the Apostle Paul:

> It was he who gave some to be apostles, some to be prophets, some to be evangelists, and some to be pastors and teachers, to prepare God's people for works of service, so that the body of Christ may be built up until we all reach unity in the faith and in the knowledge of the Son of God and become mature, attaining to the whole measure of the fullness of Christ. (Eph 4:11–13)

I invited the IRB into an incarnational model of leadership, Jesus becoming flesh, dwelling among us, walking where we walked, lingering with us, with the assurance that "we will be with the Lord forever" (1 Thess 4:17). This model fully affirmed the reality of community and the powerful results of taking community seriously. The incarnational model of moving into the community resonated within me, too. Nothing in my spiritual journey had meant so much to me as realizing that God is present where I am, present with us where we are.

The IRB caught the heart of the Gospel when it began to see itself as a representative of God's presence within the neighborhood. The congregation set aside its emotional trend toward retirement, and instead of accepting that the church would soon close, established the beginnings of a Centennial Planning Committee for a great celebration! I taught them about connecting with the neighborhood, walked with them through demographics and ethnographies, but it was when the congregation experienced it themselves that they began to connect, too. In our worship we often had as many persons from the neighborhood as members. We celebrated the ethnic and racial diversity in the neighborhood so that in a very short time, after our new members discovery class, our neighborhood represented up to 50 percent of our actual membership and worship attendance. From 5 percent to 50 percent is evidence of transformation.

Our congregation reneighbored after decades of detachment and neglect, a renewal of relationship visually depicted in our mural (fig. 42). By becoming reneighbored, a community stigma was lifted through authentic and persistent engagement and relationship building. A few years ago, if you had inquired at the house directly across from the church building, "Do you happen to know where Wilkey Church is?" the answer might have been no. Now you can travel blocks away from our site, ask the same question, and get a smile and confirming nod. Cheerleaders from our Ontario Spirit sports program even led a worship service with a Cheer for God, another sign of our transformation (see fig. 44).

Figure 43

Figure 44

The Children and Their Families

Jesus welcomed the praise of children. Jesus welcomed children when the disciples were intolerant of them. Jesus said children would understand his teaching, rather than the wise.

Inviting children to draw was a transformational act. I listened to their stories. I entered their world repeatedly, with every drawing they shared with me. Jesus' love for children enabled my own love. As a child of God, I am an object of love. As a child of God, I am a giver of love. As one who has been ordained to model my life after the life of the Master, I longed to see what Jesus saw, to hear what Jesus heard, to feel what Jesus felt. To offer the love that only he could give.

I often imagined Jesus' great descent from the Mount of Olives overlooking Jerusalem as his descent into Kensington. As his spirit touched my heart, I began to hear his tears hit the hard streets and hot asphalt roofs of the homes where the children lived. I came to know, feel, and see the child's hurt and pain, realizing that loving the child was the first step towards transformation. When I walked the streets of the neighborhood, God walked with me. First as a stranger, then as Wilkey's pastor, and finally, after earning the right to be heard, as the children's priest. Some of the kids even called me "Father Kevin," though most called me "Pastor Kev." I have come to embrace the function of priest, as I love the kids on Ontario Street. Bringing children and their families to see the marks (stigma) of Jesus and his image upon them is a sacred calling as I help free them from the bondage of stigma. The children and their families were being told who they really were, their actual identity. Jesus has given the children and their families a new name, a new name of hope.

Camper survey cards documented the transformation that many of the children experienced. Twenty-one spoke of their hope—saying, for example, "I committed my life to Jesus Christ this week." One handwritten card said, "I love Jesus and he is my savior." Others said they were "still thinking about what [was] heard and experienced this week." Two families began attending worship with their children after the camp experience. People who were strangers to us heard about camp and that Wilkey church was a safe place where kids had fun and learned about Jesus. They actively participated more than five times a month, and a new in-home Bible study formed. All of this occurred because some adults cared enough to love kids for Jesus' sake.

The Neighborhood

Inviting the children and adult leaders to Lake Champion was a transformational act. It was in a setting far removed from their city streets that they embraced the power to become agents of their neighborhood's rebirth. They saw their neighborhood for what it was and, in their own way, believed that God was just as present with them there as he was in the mountains by the lake.

The neighborhood noticed a change after the children returned from camp. One parent thoughtfully said, "The neighborhood felt empty while you were gone." Children who had often been blamed for violence and graffiti (sometimes rightly so, of course) were now seen in another light. The parents missed the children. On a lonely and dirty street in a neighborhood no one seemed to care about, the children were missed. Each home welcomed the kids back as precious gifts. When the camp kids put their mark on the wall in the form of a mural, a neighborhood knew that something was different.

Forty-three children had an opportunity to see themselves, their neighborhood, and their future differently; they drew the sanctified "graffiti" on the wall to reclaim space, to give abundant testimony that a stigmatized neighborhood was being transformed into a sign of hope.

The Pastor in Community

Pastoral intervention requires the transformational leader to be a tangible presence with people where they are and to do so over a long period. The role of urban pastor, a community pastor, is particularly challenging. I discovered that my personal transformation and self-awareness were critically important to the success of the mission. Without a sense of self-awareness, the sustainability of any transformation would be at risk. But aside from the ministry context, the other reality facing the inner-city pastor is pastoral residence. Often, the pastor's residence is immediately in the neighborhood of ministry. In earlier times, it was common for congregations to provide the pastor's residence in the form of a manse, parsonage, or rectory, typically one adjacent to the church building. The whole family's orbit was localized at the place of ministry. There are many obvious advantages to this time-tested arrangement. However, there are many variables to consider in any living arrangement, including the availability of suitable transportation, which minimizes the time and distance problems but does not address the class and affluence issues. Still, a pastor is generally considered more accessible and available when located close to the ministry context. In my case, the place of ministry was not my place of residence, which left me feeling conflicted. I lived outside the city but desired to relocate to the city because I believed I could be more effective. Testing this would be problematic.

How can I identify fully with my people if I do not live in the same neighborhood as they do? Residence is a primary assertion and a priori statement. The legal address for citizens is their residence, not a work address or alternate address. Citizens are registered to vote where they live. Residency establishes viability and validity of mission, personal and vocational. What does it say to the neighborhood when their community pastor, at the end of the day, gets into a car and drives up Interstate 95 about twenty-five miles? Regardless of my physical proximity, the realities of the streets of Kensington do not diminish. In fact, my heart and mind were continually with the kids and families I loved and sought to serve. Some of my advisors suggested that the personal resources I received when home with my family in a more affluent, suburban area actually benefited my efforts. That might have been true. Nevertheless, these words of Jesus kept ringing in my ears: "Where your treasure is..."

My call to the city can be seen as similar to Abram's call (Gen 12:1ff.), when the Lord told him to go to a specific place of ministry. In "Bible story" time, what happens in a few verses is amazing. In 12:1 Abram receives the call, and by 12:4 he has packed and is on the road. What actually happened between verses 1 and 4? What of his wife, Sarai? Did she want to go? How did Abram's call connect with her call? Even given the most patriarchal of contexts, how did the clan get up and embrace the same vision, including even Lot and his family?

My family enjoyed where we had been living for more than a decade. I liked it, too. Using Abram's call as a paradigm, I was somewhere between verse 1 and verse 4. My family represented a wonderful treasure that is localized in suburban Philadelphia. My ministry represents a wonderful treasure, too, localized in the inner city of Philadelphia. Now, I have seen the hand of God work in both contexts, each one often blessing the other. At other times, these two realms compete for attention and are in direct conflict, and I am not the only victim. I choose to live in the midst of this conflict and have found nourishment from the same source Abram did: "I will bless you," said the Lord (Gen 12:2).

In a profound, sublime way, my inner conflict about residency and ministry was a metaphor of the church of Jesus Christ. Needs are everywhere. Need does not dictate the call. Lack of accessible resources in dense urban centers creates a high risk of leaving severe needs unmet. Why is it that places of severe need are often matched with inadequate resources? The suburban church is intentionally localized in the suburbs to avoid confronting severe need. The effective urban church will intentionally locate itself in the inner city to meet the severe need. A partnership and collaboration of suburban and urban voices must come to understand the difference between Genesis 12:1 and Genesis 12:4. Internally, I understoond this dissonance. God's grace and persistence on the part of the suburban and urban church will result in a new paradigm of ministry in the new millennium. Until then, the church and I remain conflicted, but not ineffective, in the midst of compromise.

Epilogue

Lessons Learned by an Urban Pastor

Lesson 1—Mission Sustainability

We learned how to bring hope to and transform a neighborhood in Philadelphia by reneighboring a worshipping community. This success, however, was not sustainable, as we struggled to implement new funding models. After more than five years of transformational work, the leaders of Wilkey congregation grew tired. These dear saints were the prayer warriors and wise counselors who blessed us as leaders. Our multichurch collaboration Kensington Hope was fueled by the spiritual energy of the Mission Prayer Breakfasts and our ongoing partnership with the Youth Violence Reduction Project and neighborhood pastors. These pastors were some of the most talented leaders I have ever worked with. We developed a plan that we later proposed to the Presbytery of Philadelphia that would graciously dissolve Wilkey Memorial Presbyterian Church as a congregation and, at the same time, ensure that the building would be sold to our community partner, KenCrest, a social and educational services organization. Our request proposed that 100 percent of the proceeds be released by the presbytery to provide start-up funding for a new hybrid 501(c)(3) organization with an independent and community-centric board of directors and board of advisors. This organization intended to create a new worshipping community and other neighborhood-centric programs to continue the work we had done as Wilkey Memorial Presbyterian Church while grants were written. Unfortunately, while the presbytery agreed to dissolve the congregation, it decided to divert the proceeds from the sale of our building to the undesignated general fund instead of to the Kensington neighborhood we loved and served.

The last worship service weekend of Wilkey Memorial Presbyterian Church was a celebration of God's power, presence, and peace. One of the largest crowds ever gathered to give witness to the remarkable transformational work that the entire community achieved in five short years. It seemed like every one of our neighborhood kids was in attendance, and that sanctuary was in no way large enough to contain them all. Parents were there, too. So were police officers, members of the Youth Violence Reduction Project, and representatives from the school board, the mayor's office, and even several crossing guards. Neighborhood pastors who shared the vision of a new worshipping community simply called Ontario Spirit Community Church were there, too. As the kids sang and testimonies from parents were heard, we sang and prayed and even received an offering to go to a local ministry around the corner. Laughing, crying, and moments of quiet reflection combined for a truly therapeutic experience that in many ways seemed bittersweet.

The closing worship was not just a farewell to a worshipping community that had earned the right to be a reneighbored congregation and to become a strategic presence. That core ministry would now be incarnate in the lives touched by that transformation. But it was a farewell to something far more significant; it was a final letting go, at least for many of us in the sanctuary. Our reneighboring efforts had been like new wine in an old wineskin (Luke 5:37–39). The new wine cannot be long contained within old wineskins because inevitably it will burst through those old skins—and that we did!

We deeply understood the wineskin connection. Five years ago Wilkey was the incumbent, brittle and fragile, like an old wineskin. As with many other churches, its primary focus was on self-preservation. It had been transformed, however (unlike most other churches). We had said goodbye to an anachronistic church organization in an outdated building, with disconnected drive-in attendees, and said hello to a new community freed from the stigma that had been its curse. And with that recognition, we knew our efforts had been a success. But unfortunately, at least as far as we were concerned, the new model was not a sustainable one.

Though I knew that God was not abandoning the corner of H and Ontario Streets, I recognized that the structure of a traditional church was no longer a suitable container to achieve God's purposes. More work needed to be done. Community leaders and minister colleagues and I would continue to meet together and try to listen to the Spirit. We also had our eyes opened to the realities that incumbent denominational and regional church systems were clearly focused on their own survival. I made a vow during that last worship service: I told God that if I ever became a regional council leader responsible for the wellness and effectiveness of dozens of congregations, I would never forget the transforming spiritual power of a neighborhood to change the lives of thousands. (As it turned out, God heard my prayer, and I have kept my vow in my role as a denominational mid council regional leader.) Dr. Ray Bakke prods us to ask again and again what God is doing in the city. When you see God at work, Dr. Bakke urges, your mission is to get there as quickly as possible. God is always doing something great and inviting us to participate, but only when we have eyes to see and the courage to get there.

Lesson 2—Mission Connectivity: A Tale of Two Cities

I have found that God's work in Philadelphia is also continuing in other cities, and even in nonurban areas, too. At a national gathering, I was invited to present a seminar on how to build the capacity of urban regional councils, or presbyteries. One mid council leader and attendee approached me afterward and remarked, "You know, I think this reneighboring thing could work in our rural area, too." I smiled. Earning the right to be heard and being a good neighbor is everyone's job to do. While there are unique urban factors that must be addressed if you are called to transform a city through your urban ministry, being a good neighbor—demonstrating good neighborship, not only good discipleship—must be the objective of every regional council.

Do you believe that anything is possible? Pastors and church leaders in very diverse ministry contexts consistently tell me they want to make a difference in their community. Many do make a difference. But many others have retreated into their sanctuaries as they face unexpected obstacles and challenges. The Apostle Paul proclaimed in the Greek marketplace, "The God who made the world and everything in it is the Lord of heaven and earth and does not live in temples built by hands" (Acts 17:24 NIV). God's spiritual network is powered by Jesus Christ and must not terminate at your church. To improve our mission connectivity, we will learn how God's spiritual network is experienced in two different cities.[1] First, a story from Racine, Wisconsin, a Midwestern city of about

1. Yoho, "Connectivity," 20.

80,000 between Milwaukee and Chicago on the shore of Lake Michigan. Then, a story from Newark, New Jersey, an urban hub in the Northeast that is home to more than 280,000 people.

City Seeks Church Connections: Racine, Wisconsin

> Jesus asked, "Were not all ten cleansed? Where are the other nine? Was no one found to return and give praise to God except this foreigner?" Then he said to him, "Rise and go; your faith has made you well." (Luke 17:17–19 NIV)

The story of the ten lepers in Luke 17 helps us understand that grace and gratitude are core values of the good news of Jesus Christ. Though ten individuals received a healing touch, only one returned to give thanks. This is not a tithe that God delights in. In response to God's amazing grace, how does your church show its gratitude through community connectivity?

The mayor and council in Racine, Wisconsin, faced a dire budget deficit. Mayor John Dickert wanted to try one more thing. He sent letters to 182 local nonprofits asking for financial assistance. According to the *Journal Times*, tax-exempt organizations were asked if "they would consider paying a portion of the property tax the city would normally charge them if their properties were taxed."[2]

Mayor Dickert said his "Racine's Fair Share" program was based on similar initiatives in cities like Boston and Milwaukee. In the United States, property tax exemptions relieve churches from paying billions of dollars to their communities that businesses are obligated to pay. But churches enjoy all the same benefits, such as the services of police and fire departments, equal access to community places, and repairs to roads. Mayor Dickert reasoned that though churches did not owe property tax, they had a civic duty to do what they could to help solve a mutual crisis.

Mayor Dickert told me in a phone interview that he was grateful for the many churches that expressed authentic connectivity to the greater community, but the town needed a financial boost to serve all its citizens. Two months passed as the town's leadership anxiously awaited responses to their financial appeal. "City Administrator Tom Friedel

---

2. "Church Members Give $1,500 to City," *The Journal Times*, November 20, 2012, http://journaltimes.com/news/local/church-members-give-to-city-money-comes-after-mayor-s/article_17cc894a-330e-11e2-9008-0019bb2963f4.html.

told the aldermen that the city has yet to collect any money through the program," the *Journal Times* reported. But two weeks later, the mayor's office received a free-will gift from the parishioners at Olympia Brown Unitarian Universalist Church in the amount of $1,500. Of the 182 organizations asked to help, only one came forward to give thanks before the budget deadline. A few months later, Mayor Dickert expressed gratitude for two more contributions: $100 from Beth Israel Sinai and $500 from the Racine Education Association.

Church Seeks City Connections: Newark, New Jersey

> When they had all had enough to eat, he said to his disciples, "Gather the pieces that are left over. Let nothing be wasted." So they gathered them and filled twelve baskets with the pieces of the five barley loaves left over by those who had eaten. (John 6:12–13 NIV)

Other than the resurrection of Jesus Christ, the feeding of the multitudes is the only other story told in all four Gospels. A core value of the good news of Jesus Christ is that we do not have to be present to be blessed. God will reach us where we are. The basketfuls of leftovers made their way down the hill to bless those unable to attend the main event. How does your church distribute blessings through its community connectivity?

There are many reasons to walk, and many reasons to go to church, but I bet you have not considered walking to church for shoes. One church decided to pay attention to their community by applying a new model for mission connectivity.

Leaders at Emanuel First Hispanic Presbyterian Church told me they were not satisfied with their annual "Everybody Is Welcome" campaign. Hospitality, abundance, and generosity were slowly beginning to resonate within the congregation through Bible study and worship. Over the years they incrementally improved their methods, but simply "getting people into church" seemed misguided, if not too limited a goal. They began to ask themselves, "What jobs do our neighbors need to get done in their lives?" The church was ready for a change as they embraced a renewed community focus I call the Jobs To Be Done model for church connectivity.[3]

---

3. Yoho, "Walking to Church for Shoes," 12.

The church's earlier focus, "getting people into church," left many parishioners experiencing low ministry satisfaction and low energy, with correspondingly disappointing results. As they shifted from invitations to church to inquiries about what the church's neighbors needed the church to do, their ministry satisfaction and energy increased. Week by week, they shared stories and improved their community intelligence and their connectivity.

To the surprise of the church, the community identified the job to be done as meeting a pressing need for shoes. Kids needed shoes for school and play. Parents needed shoes for work. But shoes were expensive and they quickly wore out or were outgrown. Those with a shoe surplus needed to do more with them than fill up their closets or eventually throw them away.

Since the job to be done was that of acquiring good shoes, the church decided to be a kind of Shoe Depot. The "Walk to Church for Shoes" project offered shoes in good condition for free. People met around the tables as they shared shoes. Kids played, food was enjoyed, prayers were offered. Strangers and new immigrants, young and old came for the shoes they needed. Once that job had been accomplished, many found that other immediate or longer-range jobs could be accomplished. New people participated in new ways. A community was blessed!

Connectivity Is a Gospel Mandate—and a Mission Opportunity

> The Word became flesh and made his dwelling among us. We have seen his glory, the glory of the one and only Son, who came from the Father, full of grace and truth. (John 1:14 NIV)

From Racine to Newark, communities are looking to receive a blessing from this kind of tangible connectivity, a point of contact. Connectivity describes a reciprocal, beneficial relationship. As disciples of Jesus Christ, we are not strangers or exiles in a foreign land. Our communities consider us resident neighbors. Communites appreciate the potential value a church and its ministers provide.

The opportunity for every church in America is to understand that mission connectivity begins by cultivating a spirit of grace and gratitude for your community, then delivering tangible blessings in the name of Jesus Christ.

To get started on the connectivity path, consider two questions:

1. What unique mission will God send your congregation to achieve in the world? Cultivating connectivity in a spirit of grace and gratitude allows your congregation to focus on a few clear ministry outcomes. Remember the one out of ten who returned to give thanks!
2. How will you connect your neighbors to God's spiritual network? Discover and deliver what is important to the community. Remember the leftovers in the story of the feeding of the multitudes!

Track your results! Create a Church Connectivity Scale to measure and promote how involved your people are with one another. But also keep a Community Connectivity Scale that measures and promotes how involved your people are with community groups, programs, events, and issues. A church that demonstrates a high degree of inside and outside connectivity will likely have a higher involvement index (spiritual energy and ministry satisfaction) than congregations that score lower in these two key areas. I believe the most promising opportunity ahead is building new networks and collaborating with community assets. Remember that the impact of our ministries must be evaluated by the communities themselves.

Lesson 3—Are You a Mission Farmer or a Mission Miner?

Imagine you have just purchased a plot of land. Your story unfolds as you decide what you are going to do with the land—will you mine it or farm it? Your response to that question may say something about your priorities, your processes, and how you allocate resources. Your plot of land is your *mission* as a community nonprofit, congregation, or new worshipping community.

My grandkids, like millions of other gamers, enjoy playing *Minecraft*. The game presents challenges and provokes decisions, though the object is not to win or lose, or even to survive, but to grow and thrive. To gain ground, successful players must build alliances and invest resources as they enjoy the splendor of the created world. Everyone is different, but some enjoy the rewards of farming versus mining. To be successful, you need some resources at the outset. Farmers work with the ground, on the surface where people live, while miners go underground, extract what is sought and bring it to the surface.

After my dad retired from being an attorney in the city, he moved to the mountains of West Virginia and became a tree farmer. The softwood trees he tended on one hundred acres of West Virginia forestland were harvested for their pulp, which was used primarily for the packaging and publishing industries. Farming requires a lot of hard work, planning, and back-breaking labor. (On our farm the back-breaking labor was not always performed by my father; sometimes it was the back-breaking labor of those he hired to do the work!) When you farm, you have to purchase seed (or, in my dad's case, healthy seedlings) up front.

The forest around our house was initially used for our own recreation, fishing, and hunting. Signs declaring "Posted—No Trespassing—No Hunting" were placed along the access roads, and those signs (mostly) kept strangers away. Later in his life, my dad decided that the forestland would be farmed. Imagine my shock the first time I saw photos of the land after the trees had been harvested! Where before I had seen the beauty of the forest I now saw bare earth. During harvesttime, the tranquility of the forest's flora and fauna, the comforting sounds of birds overhead and water flowing into ponds gave way to the cacophony of heavy machines cutting and huge trucks hauling. The trees were taken and turned into the desired product: mulch. The three-year harvest cycle began with another round of seedlings being planted in the ground and new signs along the road: Tree Farm—Protected Land.

I learned that with nearly every harvest Dad plowed most of the profits back into the land. A farm requires attention, maintenance, and additional resources to cover the cost of seedlings and the harvesting operation. On a tree farm *planning* is just as important as *planting*. The price Dad negotiated for his mulch varied depending on the prevailing market. The buyers had to make sure that the mulch they paid for would meet the standards of the producers who would purchase it from them. Building productive and collaborative relationships with the buyers helped ensure a productive harvest. In a good year, Dad would sell at a small profit, and over time he generated a positive cash flow.

What is great about farming is that if you do it right, if you take care not to remove more nutrients from the soil than you replenish, the farm will be sustainable and will keep producing a harvest long after you are gone. Such was the case with my dad's tree farm. "What a person plants, a person will harvest" (Gal 6:7 MSG).

So You're a Miner?

Given a choice between farming and mining that imaginitive plot of land, perhaps you would prefer (unlike my dad) to work under the ground. Though there are abundant examples of farming in the Torah, the Christian Scriptures, and the Quran (written during primarily agricultural periods of civilization), mining examples are harder to come by. In fact, in the Bible the only direct reference to mining is found in the book of Job: "There is a mine for silver and a place where gold is refined. Iron is taken from the earth, and copper is smelted from ore" (28:1–2). Looking more carefully at the original text, we see that the word translated as *mine* is actually the Hebrew word for a source or place where a mineral, such as gold or silver, is found. Before heavy tools were developed, precious minerals could be acquired only near the surface of the ground, in broken rock and naturally occurring caves, where mineral veins were more easily accessible.

In later periods, under-the-ground mining operations required enormous start-up costs. If you are going to be a miner, the only way you will derive value is to have access to what is valued, the stored resource, the vein. You will need to lease mining equipment, and you will definitely need to hire skilled people to work the mine, to convert what is under the ground to useful capital above the ground. Then (maybe) you will derive a profit.

Not far from Wilkey Church, back in the mid-1800s, many of Philadelphia's widows and orphans seeking shelter amid the travails of the urban industrial revolution found a welcoming place with loving Presbyterians at Penn Home. I spoke to residents of Kensington who filled me in on the history of the place. Members of several congregations purchased a residence in the Kensington neighborhood and operated a ministry of hospitality. Though many of the widows attributed their plight to family illness, economic downturns, or war, more than a few were abandoned by their husbands who sought fame and fortune in California. The Gold Rush lured farmers from the East to become part of a group we know as the Forty-Niners.

Mining in the nineteenth century was not too different from mining today. In mountains not far from my dad's tree farm in West Virginia, mines owned by large glass-manufacturing companies continue to be costly and are dangerously operated, both in risking the lives of workers and in the lasting and devastating effects on the environment. A mine takes resources out of the ground that can never be replenished. An operating mine produces income by tearing a huge hole in the earth, and the process continues until every last ounce of value is depleted. In fact, the faster the resources are drained the better. There is nothing to preserve, nothing to maintain, no soil to build. There is no cyclical harvest since there is no replanting. The land is spent while the miners spend, leaving an unusable and unsightly crater.

Mission Farmer or Miner?

To achieve community impact, as we did at Wilkey Church, *healthy congregations must be in the farming business*. Wilkey Church transformed itself; it went from a mining church to a farming church, from consuming resources to producing them in abundance. Farming churches must give evidence of life-sustaining cycles of planting and harvesting. As Jesus explains in his parable about seed falling on various types of soil, "But the seed in the good earth—these are the good-hearts who seize the Word and hold on no matter what, sticking with it until there's a harvest" (Luke 8:15 MSG). The church is a gathered community of worship, witness, and mission that is deployed to have an impact in the world, just as seeds scattered by a farmer produce a crop that feeds and clothes people. God creates, Jesus disrupts, and the Spirit connects people to be planted in the soil of life. Not to survive but to grow and to change. The healthy church is a living community embracing the regular rhythms of worship, confession, repentance, forgiveness, and re-engagement with the world. From childhood to adolescence, to productive adulthood, to the maturity and wisdom of age, the faith community represents a cycle of life that is celebrated in birth and in death and has a generative impact in the world.

The Farmer Church plants individuals in communities as useful agents of reconciliation, as transformative leaders. You can understand, then, that it is not by accident that *farming* is based on a nurturing, living, and life-giving cycle of co-creating with God and collaborating with the world at large. Mining, on the other hand, takes from the ground what was produced eons ago.

Of course, mining has its place. Modern civilization depends on mining done well. But mining must be guided by resolute wisdom and a commitment to balance economic and ecologic priorities because once the mine is empty, nothing can replace what was taken.

Every new church starts as a "plant" not a mine. It is "planted" and established as a farm. Sadly, I know too many congregations that have become miners not farmers. Mining churches are characterized as systems of ministry that consume stored-up resources and do not produce anything new. The vein of their mine is "under the ground" in the form of endowments, investments, rental income, and proceeds from property sales. The priority of mining churches is to survive; their processes ensure that the incumbent group retains power while resources are consumed not replenished. It is difficult for a congregation that has devolved into a mining church to come up from underground and work the soil in the light of day again. But such a transformation is not impossible.

A mining church that is ready for a new future will come up from underground, out of their building, out of their traditional and archaic ways of survival; they will meet the new day in the real world. Surviving is individualistic. Thriving, in contrast, is a community effort. A mining church that is transformed into a farming church will embrace God's emerging future. It will reaffirm baptismal vows and invite the Spirit to reconnect them to the world of the living. Authentic collaboration becomes possible with the community at large. Honoring each contributor-member as a farmer will engage the real world of relationships, plant healthy seeds, and nurture the soil, so that abundant and useful resources are produced.

Farming or Mining Is Recognized by Its Impact

The impact of a mining church is hard to notice outside the mine itself. (Drive by a mine and you will know what I mean. Likewise, drive by a mining church. See any similarities?) What goes on in a mining church is out of view.

Farming churches, however, are visible and known by the product and content produced. Communities benefit from and welcome their produce, their fruits, which have a positive impact. Though the work is hard, a church committed to farming will begin to reduce their dependence on mining and instead reinvest resources by plowing them back into the soil. Remember, in this analogy the soil is not the congregation only but the intersection of the congregation and community. You reap what is sown.

How did your plot of land do in you imagined story? What did you choose to do—to farm or mine? For those in mid council and regional work, what resources and tools would be useful to farming churches? What can you do to make farmers out of miners? How can your staff resource this transition?

"So let's not allow ourselves to get fatigued doing good. At the right time we will harvest a good crop if we don't give up, or quit. Right now, therefore, every time we get the chance, let us work for the benefit of all, starting with the people closest to us in the community of faith" (Gal 6:9–10 MSG). Our communities need mission farmers. Every community has its unique context, challenges, and assets. Likewise, every worshipping, witnessing, and mission community has its unique mandate, challenges, and assets. You are the possibility that lives will be transformed as you apply insights gained from the stories of Philadelphia, Racine, and Newark. Every community deserves to experience spiritual health and wellness, justice and reconciliation, prosperity and peace in the name of Jesus Christ. The possibilities are limitless.

Lesson 4—Lessons from Baseball for Urban Ministry

John Sexton, the president of New York University, thinks baseball has the "power to teach, inspire, and transport us."[4] I found that baseball helped me develop a better understanding of leadership and how to build an urban pastor's competency in ministry.[5]

Consider an analogy between baseball and your ministry. As a pastoral leader, imagine for a moment that your congregation is like a baseball organization. You love baseball more than anything in the whole world. Your mission is to experience the fullness of baseball in all its glory and enjoy it forever. But even more, you want to be the very best baseball player you can be. Question: Who would you turn to improve your skills? There may be many good choices.

How about your *fans*? There is nothing like the passion and energy of fans. Fans correlate to the community in our baseball analogy. The community can become big fans of an effective and neighborhood-serving ministry, and that's really great when it happens. But your fans'

---

4. Sexton, Oliphant, and Schwartz, *Baseball as a Road to God*, 126.

5. This section is adapted from the author's previously published article in *Presbyterians Today* magazine titled "Presbyterian Baseball."

inspiration alone cannot improve your skills—they cannot transform you into the very best baseball player (pastoral leader) you can be. Fans are not a good choice to improve your game.

How about other *players*? Baseball players may look up to other players, but improvement requires more than admiration. In our analogy, peer learning and connections to other pastors, especially in the community, can be vitally important. But if they can teach at all, peers can only take you as far as they themselves have gone. Let's keep looking in your community for someone who really knows the game and can improve yours.

Perhaps the official *scorer* could help? While the official scorer records what baseball position you played in our imaginary game on a certain date and how many runs you earned, a scorer cannot provide essential performance-improving data like *how* you ran, or *why* you ran the way you did. Keep looking!

Would you go to the *umpire*, then? After all, the umpire knows baseball better than anyone. Consider the following advice for umpires found in the Major League Baseball rulebook: "When you enter a ballpark your sole duty is to umpire a ball game as the representative of baseball. Do not allow criticism to keep you from studying out bad situations that may lead to protested games. Carry your rulebook. It is better to consult the rules and hold up the game 10 minutes to decide a knotty problem than to have a game thrown out on protest and replayed."[6] (Try substituting the reference to the baseball "rulebook" above with the words found in your denomination's or church organization's Book of Order and reread the guidance. Sounds strangely familiar, doesn't it?)

While the umpire offers incredibly valuable experience, he or she cannot play baseball, at least not at the level you aspire to. Although the umpire calls a strike, the umpire cannot swing the bat or help with game strategy. An umpire may quickly tell if a play is out of order, however, because his or her job is to ensure that the game is played decently and in order.

To truly improve your game (that is, the competencies you need to fulfill your unique call from God), you need a *coach*—an independent practitioner you invite into your professional sphere of influence to resource your own deep thinking, intentionality, and honesty in evaluating

---

6. *Official Baseball Rules, 2015 Edition*, Rule 9.05.

your outcomes by your own metrics. A coach represents the possibility that you will improve your outcomes.

Baseball can help us consider our congregation and denominational connections as a functional not a divisional organization. Titles are secondary in importance. Role responsibilities, authority, and accountability should align with the clear mission of the organization. The essential and distinct functions of clerk and coach must be delivered effectively and in the right ratio if your church's mission is to be realized. In your church's life, which function, clerk or coach, do you call upon the most? Here are four questions to consider how this distinct functional alignment can work as an urban pastor in your community. Which role—fans, players, umpire, or coach—has added the most value to your ministry wellness and effectiveness as an urban pastoral leader?

- Which role has added the most to your overall effective, satisfying ministry experience?
- In times of conflict or anxiety, which role have you sought out most often? What were the outcomes?
- In the past year, which role improved your pastoral and ministry skills and competencies?
- In the next thirty days, which role will you access to increase your ministry energy and ministry satisfaction?

For example, if your church or denominational council depends on the role of the umpire-scorer/clerk to manage conflicts, you likely will focus on technical, ecclesiastical, or judicial fixes. While many leaders with the title of clerk are also gifted in pastoral and missional leadership, the umpire-scorer/clerk's primary function is to build the capacity of the organization by interpreting the rules, while the coach/denominational leader's primary role is to build the capacity of the organization through leadership coaching. Overfunctioning in either role requires a realignment or retuning to achieve the best balance of clerk and coach your urban ministry requires.

Our communities deserve the very best and most competent pastoral leaders. The coaching role is therefore vitally important. Seek out a capable and competent urban ministry coach. Its probably wise not to confuse coaching with the important but distinct functions of administration, accounting, or even clerking. John Sexton is right that baseball offers us important lessons. What kind of urban ministry baseball do you play? The answer will be found in who you choose to improve your skills and love for the game.

The heart of the matter for all good coaching is captured in Thich Nhat Hanh's wise counsel: "You cannot transmit wisdom and insight to another person. The seed is already there. A good teacher touches the seed, allowing it to wake up, to sprout, and to grow."[7]

In loving, I was loved. In transforming, I was transformed. Kensington will never be the same as a reneighbored congregation removed the stigma and restored hope. The restoration of Kensington's hope resulted from a reneighbored community of faith. Something good can come from Nazareth, after all. It is truly amazing what a few crayons can do. Just ask the kids at the corner of H and Ontario Streets.

> Through the blessing of the upright a city is exalted,
> but by the mouth of the wicked it is destroyed. (Prov 11:11)

---

7. Nhat Hanh, *Planting Seeds*, 15.

Afterword by W. Wilson Goode

When I first met Kevin Yoho I knew that he was not the normal seminarian. His words, his walk, and his relationship with us made many of us better in his presence. I knew that we were of a kindred spirit. This book is further evidence that Pastor Kevin stands in a space with few others. Dedicated to livable communities and with a firm belief that churches can play a key role in rebuilding neighborhoods, he knows that first they must reneighbor themselves.

His leadership shows us a way forward for congregations and communities.

Let me connect this work to my journey of hope. In 1950, when I was twelve years old and living in the rural South, a white hobo came to our farm shack about a mile from the road. My mother, without regard to his race, fed him. Later, as he was leaving, I ran after him and gave him all the money I had—a single dollar. That was a turning point in my life. For sixty-five years years now I have embraced the poor, the homeless, the hungry, the marginalized, the mistreated, the disregarded and the disrespected.

Led by my passion for this population, after graduating from college and serving in the army I intentionally moved back to the neighborhood I had migrated to in 1954, where I became a block captain and later president of the civic association in the Paschall community in southwest Philadelphia. At that time, Kensington was off limits to African Americans. What Kevin has done through his book is to show us how to transform and humanize a community that for decades was disrespected by many and avoided altogether by others.

As mayor of Philadelphia, I instituted the first homeless program of any city in the country. Likewise, I instituted the first literacy program and the first drug coordinating office. I had a cabinet meeting on a drug corner to show my staff the danger of living in certain neighborhoods in the city.

While in graduate school with Kevin, my dissertation centered on how to transform congregations from clubhouses to lighthouses in their neighborhoods. To me it was all too evident that, as D. G. Miller writes in *The Nature and Mission of the Church*, "To [some] others, the church is like a club or a lodge, or a fraternity. It is a group of like-minded people who enjoy each other's company. They chose to band together in a human organization for mutual benefit or enjoyment. They give money to keep the building in repair . . . and to support the various activities they engage in." We believed that congregations could become vehicles for community transformation, but to do so they needed leadership, exposure, and demonstrated success.

One of the findings in my research was that congregants modify their attitudes and behaviors if they are exposed to the successful work of other congregations. In *Crayons for the City* Pastor Kevin paints a revealing portrait of how a church can succeed at reneighboring itself and impacting an entire neighborhood. He demonstrates how a clubhouse with a steeple can become a lighthouse that gives light not only to the city but eventually to the nation and the world.

Carlyle Fielding Stewart, in *African American Church Growth*, writes that "the church . . . engages in the development of programs to meet the needs of both the outer and inner community." Pastor Kevin would certainly agree with Stewart's emphasis on meeting the needs of those within the church and those without. Robert O. Carle and Louis A. DeCaro, in *Signs of Hope in the City*, write, "Churches are making neighborhoods more livable by building houses, rehabilitating vacant buildings, opening charter schools, and applying pressure on public officials to improve police responses." Pastor Kevin and those who followed his leadership brought these words to life in practical and replicable ways on the streets of Kensington.

This book presents a practical tool for community organizers, preachers, congregation leaders, political leaders, seminary professors, and those who seek to improve the quality of life for communities across the nation and around the globe. Allan Aubrey Boesak, in his book *Dare We Speak of Hope*, says, "The servant . . . will not consider anyone worthless, or not worth the effort, useless trash, or as disposable, dispensable, forgettable . . . as if their lives did not matter because they are poor, or defenseless, or different." Kevin's model makes the point that every life is valued—a view I have held for sixty-five years. That is why, once again, I intentionally moved back to my old neighborhood where I grew up after leaving the South—a neighborhood that had all the challenges of Kensington. There I went from a block captain on the 6900 block of Greenway Avenue to mayor of the City of Philadelphia in thirty years.

Crayons for the City gives us a needed way forward, a practical model for transforming neighborhoods from places of despair to places of hope. We should follow Kevin's Road to Hope by reneighboring our churches to help transform our communities.

Max Lucado, in his book *God Came Near*, writes, "Grant us eyes to see, a heart to feel, tears to weep and courage to go. As you have given us, let us now give to others." When I consider these words, this simple but challenging prayer, I think of Kevin Yoho.

Appendix

Vision Statement of Wilkey Memorial Presbyterian Church

We envision a future when Christian values undergird the attitudes and actions of not only our congregation, but of Kensington residents; when faith-based ministry is rooted in the neighborhood as salt and light; when existing community people are empowered to live in harmony and security; when vacant lots and abandoned buildings are converted into new, affordable homes; when most homes and businesses are owner occupied; when high school and college graduation are accepted expectations; when job skills and employment opportunities abound; when all people have quality affordable health care; when families want to move into not out of our neighborhoods; when Kensington is known as a great place for kids; and when Jesus Christ is Lord.

Mission Statement of Wilkey Memorial Presbyterian Church

In order to achieve our Vision, Wilkey Church commits to the following Mission:

Our mission is to rebuild the Kensington community in the name of Jesus Christ in the power of the Holy Spirit to the glory of God. We will invite people to hope and faith in Jesus Christ as Savior and Lord. We will work with others to bring Christian holistic transformation to the people and environment of Kensington through Christian worship, evangelism, discipleship, stewardship, and acts of kindness and love. We will reach out in relevant ways to all our neighbors, committing ourselves to leadership development, personal and economic empowerment, housing improvement, educational enrichment, and Christian discipleship for the second millennium.

Core Values of Wilkey Memorial Presbyterian Church

We affirm and believe that God is our creator, redeemer, and sustainer and that the Bible is the inerrant and infallible written word of God which became incarnate in Jesus Christ.

We believe the redeemed are saved by the grace of God through faith in Jesus Christ for the forgiveness of sins and have assurance of eternal life.

We accept our call by Jesus Christ, Lord of the universe, to be both a sign and an agent of God's kingdom in the world as a congregation of the connectional Presbyterian Church (U.S.A.).

We believe all of us in community as Christ's church are the true ministers of the church—ordained by God and gifted by the Holy Spirit for all the ministries required in the retrieval of our neighborhoods and culture.

We believe the church and all things belong to God, not to us, and we commitment his kingdom, together with our sisters and brothers in Christ and ourselves in loving, enthusiastic sacrificial service to Jesus.

We will balance the mind, body, and spirit dimensions of our personal, corporate, and global life and seek to affirm the wholeness of life.

We believe God's people in the world, whether in business, institution, media, health care, or government, must once again be change agents in the neighborhood they are located in.

We must preach the true gospel of sin, repentance, and forgiveness to the hurting, the poor, and the lost, even while we try to understand the real physical, social, political, relational context we are in and attempt to make a positive difference in measurable ways.

We will reach out in whatever language or form necessary to build bridges of friendship and care, and in the church, enhance worship, evangelism, discipleship, stewardship, fellowship, and service.

We will not impose our own models or expectations across racial, ethnic, class, age, gender, linguistic, physiological or physical lines, but rather seek to be servants of the Servant in *every* way.

Bibliography

Agosto, Efrain. *Servant Leadership: Jesus & Paul*. St. Louis: Chalice, 2005.
Anderson, Elijah. *Street Wise: Race, Class, and Change in an Urban Community*. Chicago: University of Chicago Press, 1990.
Anniversary Committee. *Wilkey Memorial United Presbyterian Church Golden Anniversary*. Philadelphia: Wilkey Memorial United Presbyterian Church, 1960.
Anonymous. *Relocating to Kensington*. 1998.
Associated Press. "Newsletter's Humor Spicing Up Faith." *The Pantagraph* (Bloomington, IL), November 11, 1993, second ed., 21.
Bakke, Raymond J. *A Theology as Big as the City*. Downers Grove, IL: Intervarsity, 1997.
———, ed. *The Word in Life Study Bible*. Nashville: Thomas Nelson, 1996.
Bakke, Raymond J., and Samuel K. Roberts. *The Expanded Mission of "Old First" Churches*. Valley Forge, PA: Judson, 1986.
Barker, Joel Arthur. *Paradigms: The Business of Discovering the Future*. New York: HarperCollins, 1993.
Barna, George. *Evangelism That Works: How to Reach Changing Generations with the Unchanging Gospel*. Ventura, CA: Regal, 1995.
———. *The Frog in the Kettle: What Christians Need to Know about Life in the 21st Century*. Ventura, CA: Regal, 1990.
———. *Generation Next: What You Need to Know about Today's Youth*. Ventura, CA: Regal, 1995.
———. *The Index of Leading Spiritual Indicators: A Statistical Report on the State of Religion in America; Trends in Morality, Beliefs, Lifestyles, Religious and Spiritual Thought, Behavior, and Church Involvement*. Dallas: Word, 1996.
———. *Ministry and Change*. Cassette tape. Colorado Springs: Focus on the Family, 1996.
———. *The Second Coming of the Church: A Blueprint for Survival*. Orange, CA: Word, 1998.
Bartholomew, Craig G. *Where Mortals Dwell: A Christian View of Place for Today*. Grand Rapids: Baker Academic, 2011.
Binzen, Peter. *Whitetown USA: A First-Hand Study of How the "Silent Majority" Lives, Learns, Works, and Thinks*. New York: Random House, 1970.
Bissinger, Buzz. *A Prayer for the City*. New York: Random House, 1997.
Block, Peter. *Community: The Structure of Belonging*. San Francisco: Berrett-Koehler, 2008.
Boesak, Allan Aubrey. *Dare We Speak of Hope? Searching for a Language of Life in Faith and Politics*. Grand Rapids: Eerdmans, 2014.

Borgman, Dean. *When Kumbaya Is Not Enough: A Practical Theology for Youth Ministry.* Peabody, MA: Hendrickson, 1997.

Bosch, David Jacobus. *Transforming Mission: Paradigm Shifts in Theology of Mission.* Maryknoll, NY: Orbis, 1991.

Brinckerhoff, Peter C. *Mission-Based Marketing: How Your Not-for-Profit Can Succeed in a More Competitive World.* Dillon, CO: Alpine Guild, 1997.

Brueggemann, Walter. *Finally Comes the Poet: Daring Speech for Proclamation.* Minneapolis: Fortress, 1989.

Canino, Ian A., and Jeanne Spurlock. *Culturally Diverse Children and Adolescents.* New York: Guilford, 1994.

Carle, Robert D., and Louis A. DeCaro Jr., eds. *Signs of Hope in the City: Ministries of Community Renewal.* Rev. ed. Valley Forge, PA: Judson, 1999.

Carter, Michelle, and Michael J. Christensen. *Children of Chernobyl: Raising Hope from the Ashes.* Minneapolis: Augsburg Fortress, 1993.

Casey, Edward S. *The Fate of Place: A Philosophical History.* Berkeley: University of California Press, 1997.

Catrambone, Jamie, and Harry C. Silcox, eds. *Kensington History: Stories and Memories.* Philadelphia: Brighton, 1996.

Chalmers, Thomas. *The Christian and Civic Economy of Large Towns.* Glasgow: Chalmers & Collins, 1821.

Christensen, Clayton M., James Allworth, and Karen Dillon. *How Will You Measure Your Life?* New York: HarperBusiness, 2012.

Christensen, Clayton M., Scott D. Anthony, and Erik A. Roth. *Seeing What's Next: Using the Theories of Innovation to Predict Industry Change.* Boston: Harvard Business School Press, 2004.

Christensen, Michael J. *City Streets, City People: A Call for Compassion.* Nashville: Abingdon, 1988.

Cohen, Aryeh. *Justice in the City.* Brighton, MA: Academic Studies, 2012.

Conn, Harvey M., ed. *Planting and Growing Urban Churches: From Dream to Reality.* Grand Rapids: Baker, 1997.

Covey, Stephen R. *The 7 Habits of Highly Effective People: Powerful Lessons in Personal Change.* 25th anniversary ed. New York: Simon and Schuster, 2004.

Crabtree, J. Russell. *Owl Sight: Evidence-Based Discernment and the Promise of Organizational Intelligence for Ministry.* Columbus: Holy Cow! Consulting, 2012.

Denzin, Norman, and Yvonna Lincoln, eds. *Handbook of Qualitative Research.* Thousand Oaks, CA: Sage, 1994.

Dilulio, John, Jr. "Jeremiah's Call." *Prism*, March/April 1998, 19–23, 31–34.

Dulles, Avery. *Models of the Church.* Garden City, NY: Doubleday, 1974.

Ellis, Susan J. *The Volunteer Recruitment (and Membership Development) Book.* Philadelphia: Energize, 1996.

Erickson, Victoria Lee. *Where Silence Speaks: Feminism, Social Theory, and Religion.* Minneapolis: Fortress, 1993.

Fenn, Richard K. *The End of Time.* Cleveland: Pilgrim, 1997.

Finkelman, Sol. "Why a Stigma." http://geniepub.com/hypmail/poem-of-the-day/0200.html.

Freedman, Samuel G. *Upon This Rock: The Miracles of a Black Church.* New York: HarperCollins, 1993.

"Gentlemen, This Is a Football." *Packerville, U.S.A.* (blog). May 30, 2010. http://packerville.blogspot.com/2010/05/gentlemen-this-is-football.html.

George, Carl. *Ministry and Change.* Cassette tape. Colorado Springs: Focus on the Family, 1996.

Goffman, Erving. *Stigma: Notes on the Management of Spoiled Identity.* New York: Simon & Schuster, 1986.

Goode, Judith, and Jo Anne Schneider. *Reshaping Ethnic and Racial Relations in Philadelphia: Immigrants in a Divided City.* Philadelphia: Temple University Press, 1994.

Gordon, Wayne L., and Randall Frame. *Real Hope in Chicago: The Incredible Story of How the Gospel Is Transforming a Chicago Neighborhood.* Grand Rapids: Zondervan, 1995.

Gozdz, Kazimierz, ed. *Community Building: Renewing Spirit & Learning in Business.* San Francisco: New Leaders, 1995.

Green, Clifford J., ed. *Churches, Cities, and Human Community: Urban Ministry in the United States, 1945–1985.* Grand Rapids: Eerdmans, 1996.

Hankins, Katherine, and Andy Walter. "Gentrification with Justice: An Urban Ministry Collective and the Practice of Place-Making in Atlanta's Inner-City Neighbourhoods." *Urban Studies* 49 (2012) 1507–26.

Haroutunian, Joseph. *God With Us: A Theology of Transpersonal Life.* Philadelphia: Westminster, 1965.

Howarth, Caroline, Cathy Nicholson, and Teresa Whitney. "Stigma." In *Encyclopedia of Race and Racism*, edited by Patrick L. Mason. Detroit: Macmillan Reference USA, 2013.

Igoa, Cristina. *The Inner World of the Immigrant Child.* New York: St. Martin's, 1995.

Job, Rueben P., and Norman Shawchuck. *A Guide to Prayer for Ministers and Other Servants.* Nashville: Upper Room, 1983.

Jones, Richard, and Craig R. McCoy. "District Gives Itself Failing Grade." *Philadelphia Inquirer*, January 17, 1997, A1.

Kaduson, Heidi Gerard, and Charles E. Schaefer, eds. *101 Favorite Play Therapy Techniques.* Vol. 1. Northvale, NJ: Jason Aronson, 1997.

Kasdan, Lawrence. *The Empire Strikes Back: Shooting Script Fourth Draft.* 1978. http://www.starwars-union.de/diefilme/episode4/30jahrekds/THE%20EMPIRE%20STRIKES%20BACK%20-%20Fourth%20Draft%20-%20Shooting%20Script%20-%20Oktober%201978.pdf.

Kawulich, Barbara B. "Participant Observation as a Data Collection Method." *Forum: Qualitative Social Research* 6.2 (2005). http://www.qualitative-research.net/index.php/fqs/article/view/466/996.

Kimel, Martin. "Slackers, Stigma, and Depression: Americans' Disdain for the 'Psychological.'" *Perspectives* 2.2 (1997). https://www.seabhs.org/poc/view_doc.php?type=doc&id=325.

Kissane, Rebecca Joyce. "'We Call It the Badlands': How Social-Spatial Geographies Influence Social Service Use." *Social Service Review* 84 (2010) 3–28.

Kramer, Edith. *Art as Therapy with Children.* New York: Schocken, 1971.

Kretzmann, John P., and John L. McKnight. *Building Communities from the Inside Out: A Path Toward Finding and Mobilizing a Community's Assets.* Evanston, IL: Center for Urban Affairs and Policy Research, 1993.

Kushner, Aleksandr. *Apollo in the Snow: Selected Poems*. Translated by Paul Graves and Carol Ueland. New York: Farrar, Straus and Giroux, 1991.

Ladwig, Tim. *Psalm Twenty-Three*. 2nd ed. Los Angeles: Eerdmans Books for Young Readers, 1996.

Laidlaw, Walter. "The Church and the City Community." *American Journal of Sociology* 16 (1911) 794–804.

Lee, Morgan. "6 Uncomfortable Takeaways from Urban Church Leader Ray Bakke: The Oldest Churches in Christendom Are the Newest Churches in America." *Christian Post*, October 14, 2013. http://www.christianpost.com/news/6-uncomfortable-takeaways-from-urban-church-leader-ray-bakke-the-oldest-churches-in-christendom-are-the-newest-churches-in-america-106490.

Lemert, Charles, ed. *Social Theory: The Multicultural and Classic Readings*. Boulder, CO: Westview, 1993.

Linthicum, Robert C. *City of God, City of Satan: A Biblical Theology of the Urban Church*. Grand Rapids: Zondervan, 1991.

Lovelace, Richard. *Dynamics of Spiritual Life: An Evangelical Theology of Renewal*. Downers Grove, IL: InterVarsity, 1979.

Lowe, Leslie Hartley. "Scribble Art." In *101 Favorite Play Therapy Techniques*, edited by Heidi G. Kaduson and Charles E. Schaefer, 121–24. Northvale, NJ: Jason Aronson, 1997.

Lucado, Max. *God Came Near: Chronicles of the Christ*. Portland, OR: Multnomah, 1987.

Lupton, Robert. "gen-tri-fi-ca-tion (jen´tre-fi-ka´shen) noun." *Urban Perspectives • FCS Ministries* (blog), February 1, 1997. http://www.fcsministries.org/fcs-ministries/urban-perspectives/gen-tri-fi-ca-tion-jen´tre-fi-kashen-noun?rq=gentrification.

———. *Renewing the City: Reflections on Community Development and Urban Renewal*. Downers Grove, IL: InterVarsity, 2005.

———. *Return Flight: Community Redevelopment through Reneighboring Our Cities*. Atlanta: FCS Urban Ministries, 1993.

———. *Theirs Is the Kingdom: Celebrating the Gospel in Urban America*. Edited by Barbara R. Thompson. San Francisco: Harper & Row, 1989.

———. *Toxic Charity: How Churches and Charities Hurt Those They Help (and How to Reverse It)*. New York: HarperOne, 2011.

May, Gerald G. *Care of Mind, Care of Spirit: A Psychiatrist Explores Spiritual Direction*. San Francisco: HarperSanFrancisco, 1992.

McClanahan, Wendy S. *Alive at 25: Reducing Youth Violence through Monitoring and Support*. Field Report Series. Philadelphia: Public/Private Ventures, 2004. http://ppv.issuelab.org/resource/alive_at_25_reducing_youth_violence_through_monitoring_and_support.

Mead, George Herbert. *Mind, Self, and Society: From the Standpoint of a Social Behaviorist*. Edited by Charles W. Morris. Chicago: University of Chicago Press, 1962.

———. "The Social Self." *Journal of Philosophy, Psychology and Scientific Methods* 10 (1913) 374–80.

Meyers, Eleanor Scott, ed. *Envisioning the New City: A Reader on Urban Ministry*. Louisville: Westminster John Knox, 1992.

Miller, Donald G. *The Nature and Mission of the Church*. Richmond: John Knox, 1957.

Nhat Hanh, Thich. *Planting Seeds: Practicing Mindfulness with Children.* Berkeley: Parallax, 2011.

North, Tim. "The Internet and Usenet Global Computer Networks: An Investigation of Their Culutre and Its Effects on New Users." Unpublished master's thesis, Curtin University of Technology, 1994.

O'Brien, Anne Sibley. "Diversity in Action Is . . ." *Coloring Between the Lines: Reflections on Race, Culture and Children's Books* (blog), December 1, 2008. http://coloringbetween.blogspot.com/2008/12/diversity-in-action-is.html.

Official Baseball Rules, 2015 Edition. Edited by Tom Lepperd. http://mlb.mlb.com/mlb/official_info/official_rules/official_rules.jsp.

Olson, Stan, et al. *National Guide to Funding in Religion.* Washington, DC: Foundation Center, 1991.

Ontario Presbyterian Church Anniversary Committee. *Silver Anniversary Review.* Philadelphia: 1935.

Paul, Annie Murphy. "Your Brain on Fiction." *New York Times*, March 17, 2012. http://www.nytimes.com/2012/03/18/opinion/sunday/the-neuroscience-of-your-brain-on-fiction.html?_r=0.

Peck, M. Scott. *The Different Drum: Community-Making and Peace.* New York: Simon & Schuster, 1987.

Perkins, John, ed. *Restoring At-Risk Communities.* Grand Rapids: Baker, 1993.

Peterson, Eugene H. *The Pastor: A Memoir.* New York: HarperOne, 2011.

Peters, Tim. "10 Real Reasons Pastors Quit Too Soon." *ChurchLeaders.com.* http://www.churchleaders.com/pastors/pastor-articles/161343-tim_peters_10_common_reasons_pastors_quit_too_soon.html.

Philadelphia City Planning Commission. *Vacant Land in Philadelphia: A Report on Vacant Land Management and Neighborhood Restructuring.* Philadelphia: City of Philadelphia, 1995.

Philadelphia Public Schools. *Philadelphia Public Schools Two-Year Summary.* Office of Information Technology, 1998.

Prior, David. *Creating Community: An Every-Member Approach to Ministry in the Local Church.* Colorado Springs: NavPress, 1992.

Putnam, Robert D. *Our Kids: The American Dream in Crisis.* New York: Simon & Schuster, 2015.

Robson, Colin. *Real World Research: A Resource for Social Scientists and Practitioner-Researchers.* Malden, MA: Blackwell, 1993.

Sanders, J. Oswald. *Spiritual Leadership.* Chicago: Moody, 1967.

Seder, Jean. *Voices of Kensington: Vanishing Mills, Vanishing Neighborhoods.* 2nd ed. McLean, VA: EPM Publications, 1990.

Sexton, John, Thomas Oliphant, and Peter J. Schwartz. *Baseball as a Road to God: Seeing beyond the Game.* New York: Gotham, 2013.

Shenk, Wilbert R. *Write the Vision: The Church Renewed.* Valley Forge, PA: Trinity Press International, 1995.

Sider, Ronald J. *Genuine Christianity.* Grand Rapids: Zondervan, 1996.

———. *One-Sided Christianity? Uniting the Church to Heal a Lost and Broken World.* Grand Rapids: Zondervan, 1993.

Slaughter, Michael. *Spiritual Entrepreneurs: 6 Principles for Risking Renewal.* Edited by Herb Miller. Nashville: Abingdon, 1995.

Snyder, Howard. *The Community of the King.* Downers Grove, IL: InterVarsity, 1996.

———. *Liberating the Church: The Ecology of Church & Kingdom*. Downers Grove, IL: InterVarsity, 1983.

———. *Signs of the Spirit*. Grand Rapids: Zondervan, 1989.

"General Characteristics of Persons: 1990." Census.gov. http://www.census.gov/prod/1/90dec/cph4/tables/cph4tb40/table-01.pdf.

Spradley, James P., and David W. McCurdy, eds. *The Cultural Experience: Ethnography in Complex Society*. Chicago: Science Research Associates, 1972.

Stewart, Carlyle Fielding. *African American Church Growth: 12 Principles of Prophetic Ministry*. Nashville: Abingdon, 1994.

Sweet, Leonard. *11 Genetic Gateways to Spiritual Awakening*. Nashville: Abingdon, 1998.

Teringo, J. Robert. *The Land & People Jesus Knew: A Comprehensive Handbook on Life in First-Century Palestine*. Minneapolis: Bethany House, 1985.

Villafañe, Eldin. *Seek the Peace of the City: Reflections on Urban Ministry*. Grand Rapids: Eerdmans, 1995.

Von Oech, Roger. *A Kick in the Seat of the Pants: Using Your Explorer, Artist, Judge, & Warrior to Be More Creative*. New York: Harper and Row, 1986.

Wailoo, Keith. "Stigma, Race, and Disease in 20th Century America." *The Lancet* 367 (2006) 531–33.

———. "Stigma, Race, and Disease in 20th Century America: An Historical Overview." Paper presented at Stigma and Global Health: Developing a Research Agenda, September 5–7, 2001, Bethesda, Maryland.

Warren, Rick. *The Purpose Driven Church: Growth without Compromising Your Message & Mission*. Grand Rapids: Zondervan, 1995.

Weiss, Robert S. *Learning from Strangers: The Art and Method of Qualitative Interview Studies*. New York: Free Press, 1994.

White, Randy. *Journey to the Center of the City: Making a Difference in an Urban Neighborhood*. Downers Grove, IL: InterVarsity, 1996.

Wink, Walter. *The Powers That Be: Theology for a New Millennium*. New York: Doubleday, 1998.

Wüstenbecker, Michael. "Welfare Stigma." Arbeitspapiere des Fachbereichs Wirtschaftswissenschaften 45. Universität-Gesamthochschule Paderborn, 1996.

Yoho, Kevin R. "Building a Durable Mission." *The Living Pulpit*, August 1, 2014, 20–21.

———. "Mission Connectivity: A Tale of Two Cities." *The Living Pulpit*, November 1, 2015, 10–12.

———. "Presbyterian Baseball: Looking to Improve Your Game? Consider Turning to Your mid Council." *Presbyterians Today*, March 15, 2015, 64–65.

———. "Walking to Church for Shoes: The Jobs-to-Be-Done Model for Mission Innovation." *Presbyterian Outlook*, September 30, 2013, 12.

Young, A. F., and E. T. Ashton. *British Social Work in the Nineteenth Century*. London: Routledge and Kegan Paul, 1956.

Index

Abel, 32
Abram, 187
activities
    at Camp Lake Champion, 173–74
    realigning, 93
acts of grace, extending towards strangers, 132
aerial photograph, of the Kensington neighborhood, 27–28, 59
affirmations, about community-directed ministry, 112–13
affordable housing, need for, 74
African American Church Growth (Stewart), 206
African Americans, moved into Kensington, 19, 124
African-American leadership, lagging behind, 29
after-action reports, following each drawing session, 148
Aging Cautious Retirees, demographic category, 29
aliens, in an alien land, 106
"alive at 25," strong partnership for kids, 88
alliances, building and investing resources, 195
American Red Cross, racial segregation of blood plasma during World War II, 41
Andrew, description of Jesus to Simon, 33
anger, by the children about their neighborhood, 163
animal branding, classical root word for, 32
Apartment Complex Initiative, 81
Apollo in the Snow (Kushner), 181
Apostle John. *See also* Gospel of John; James and John
    on the Word becoming flesh, 62
Apostle Paul. *See also* Saul
    on attaining to the fullness of Christ, 183
    on being Christ's ambassadors, 164
    cautioned believers to get back to their ordinary work, 5
    on faith, 66
    on the image of a stigma, 32
    Lord of heaven and earth not living in temples built by hands, 191
    on marriage and the church, 72
    on the pattern of sound teaching, 117
    on the road to Damascus, 137
    shared leadership in the life of, 65n22
    on the struggle against the forces of evil, 85
    use of the phrase "flesh and blood" in Ephesians, 86
    vision of grand processions of people, 138
apostles, as a mighty team, 99
appreciation, as mission-critical, 148
ark, signifying God's protection, 181
Arons, Bernard, 35
art, 131, 132

Art as Therapy with Children (Kramer), 143n17
art therapy, 131
artful expression, of a child, 132
Ascension Roman Catholic Church, 133
asset-based community development, 46, 47
asset-based possibilities, shifting from problems to, 29
asset-based spiritual development, 47
"at home" feelings, in a church, 81
Atlanta, Georgia, neighborhoods similar to Kensington in, 43, 45–47
attribution, of stigma as a root of discrimination, 38
Augustine, 70
authentic connections, 71, 117, 160
authentic identity, of Kensington, 38–39
authentic leaders, 133. *See also* leaders
Azariah, 31–32

Babylon's well-being, praying for, 74
back to basics, as the credo of transformation, 55
back-to-work initiatives, 49
"the Badlands," Kensington called, 43, 178
Bakke, Ray, 13, 72–73, 79, 191
Baron of Kensington, 44
baseball, lessons from for urban ministry, 200–203
battlefield, neighborhood as, 59
becoming present for others, 77
being present in a place, resulting in deeper connections, 82
Beth Israel Sinai, in Racine, Wisconsin, 193
biases
 about Nazareth, 33
 left unaddressed, 103
biblical salvation, creating a new Christian community, 56

bilingual community worship service, connecting Kensington churches, 29
Binzen, Peter, 19
Bissinger, Buzz, 44
Block, Peter, on community, 28, 63–64, 101
body of Christ, 56, 65
Boesak, Allan Aubrey, 206
Book of Order, 201
Borgman, Dean, 169
Bosch, David J., 39
Bowen, Bill, 142, 146–47, 160, 163
boys, doing the "hoop thing," 135
brain-storming sessions, of focus group participants,' 121
"branding," Stigma synonymous with, 34
brokenness, members sharing, 104
Bruse, James, 34
building, church as a, 57
Burns, Linda, 182
bus ride home, from camp, 176
business world, realities of sales and market share, 66

Cain, 32
"called-out ones," church as, 70
Calvinist confidence, in God's providence, 60
camp experience, life-changing, 8
camp funding goal, 171
camp intervention, intended to restore hope, 172
Camp Lake Champion, arriving at, 173
camp promotion sheet, in the online Appendix companion, 173n11
Campaigners, group formed by young people, 179
camper survey cards, 176, 185
camping, with the Damascus Project, 165–70
camping methodology, not just intense activity, 175
capacity assessments, interactive, 69

capacity building, 48
capacity change, source for, 99
career day, at Stetson, 161
caring adults
    committed to going to camp with the children, 169
    contributing to the self-esteem and wellbeing of children, 160
Carle, Robert O., 206
Casey, Edward S., 5–6
Catholic children, reading the King James Bible, 19
"CB," organizing leader known for public ridicule of drug dealers, 16
Census Bureau, demographic data from, 58
Centennial Planning Committee, 183
Chalmers, Thomas, 60–61
change agent, Christian church as, 117
chaos
    ebbing and flowing, 103
    in Nehemiah, 105–7
character stigma, 38
Cheer for God, 184
cheerleaders, led a worship service, 183–84
cheerleading teams, for the girls, 135
Chernobyl nuclear power plant disaster, serving victims of, 132
Child J, neighborhood of, 148–49
Child K, drawing of his famiy, 149–51
Child L
    drawing on the topic of Me and My Neighborhood, 151–52
    uncle had taken his gun with him, 152n25
Child M, colored a blue sky and a big tree with a trash overturned, 152
Child N, drawing of a large trash can, 154
children. *See also* kids
    actively participated multiple times a week, 166
    all interested in Christopher's condition, 158
    bound by the stigma of hopelessness and despair, 130
    building experiences of importance, 164
    creating extensions of themselves with each drawing, 182
    deserving better, 44
    discovering something about themselves, 163
    drawings by, received as sacred offerings, 163
    drew pictures for Christopher as a community project, 158
    earning money for camp, 170
    expressed ideas of who was at fault for the fire, 156
    gaining a clearer self-perception, 131
    getting safely to church activities, 24
    giving a voice, 181
    internalizing their Chernobyl "me," 132
    inviting to draw as a transformational act, 185
    of Kensington, 42
    learning early to abhor their neighborhood, 3
    needing a new view, 130
    not having to cross Kensington Avenue to go to Sunday school, 69
    number codes assigned to, 145
    participating with families in conversational Bible studies, 168
    providing each with his or her own box of crayons, 146n22
    seen in another light after camp, 186

children (*continued*)
    at Stetson meeting on their turf, 163
    suffering stigma rooted in their location, 41
    understanding the teaching of Jesus, 185
    wanting to draw on every topic every week, 144n19
    who had never been to a summer camp, 169n5
children of Chernobyl, desire to connect with, 144n18
Christ. *See* Jesus
Christensen, Clay, 91
Christensen, Michael J., 25, 132, 143
Christian and Civic Economy of Large Towns (Chalmers), 60
Christian and Missionary Alliance team, youth video produced by, 4
Christian church, emphasis on spiritual things, 5
Christian community, life and work of, 39
Christian Community Development Association, 75
Christian Community Development Corporation (CCDC), 46
"Christian kid" tag, 166
Christopher
    needed connections, 156
    seriously injured in a row house fire, 9–10
    suffered from a lack of oxygen during the fire, 155
    treated in the burn unit at St. Christopher's Medical Center for Children, 10, 155
Christopher's mom, feared for his safety prior to the fire, 155
Christopher's vacant, ash-ridden, burned-out home, 157
Christ's body, church as, 64
church(es)
    belonging to the neighborhood, 97
    changing the name of, 122–23
    choosing to invest in the neighborhood, 86
    in the city, not having parking lots, 78
    connecting to the realities in the neighborhood, 59
    credibility of, 140
    deployed to have an impact in the world, 198
    detached from communities, 12
    detached itself from the community, 55
    developing a theology of location, 26
    established "so children did not need to cross the busy avenues to go to Sunday school," 120
    expressing itself as a local organization, 56
    feedback from people already attending, 92
    few doing urban ministry, 25
    forgetting its core mission to reach the neighborhood, 86
    as healthy as the neighborhood, 49
    intended as a neighborhood church, 120
    as invisible, 119
    looking like medieval fortresses, 76, 80
    motivation for self-preservation, 12
    as no longer a neighbor but a stranger, 126
    not a building, 78
    offering products, 91
    opportunity on how to "give yourself away," 91
    point of naming, 24
    questions to consider, 94
    reinforcing church identity and beliefs, 95
    representing the possibility of making the world different, 138

requiring a tangible presence in the neighborhood, 57
from Rochester, New York, sent to a goup to MissionWorks, 84–85
seeking city connections, 193
seeming least equipped to add value, 89
sent to engage the world to transform the world, 57
views of in the neighborhood, 107
as a worshipping and witnessing community, 117
church building, as the setting for ministry, 58
church community, embedded in the greater community, 70
Church Connectivity Scale, creating, 195
church documents, capturing events, 123
church experience, all not wanting to share, 115
church governance, not created in a vacuum, 65
church growth, great days of, 55
"church kids," 166
church leaders. *See also* leaders; pastoral leader
ethnography of, 116–19
fostering deep connections with the community, 58
church ministries, in the inner city, 78
church model, choosing, 109
Church Model Evaluation Chart, 107, 111
Church Models exercise, 107
Church Models Grid, 107, 109–10
church office, renamed "Mission Control," 67
"Church" sheet, 122, 124
church systems, cost structure of, 90
church-centered people, 69, 70
church-neighborhood distance, increased, 126

circle of love, for the neighborhood, 98
citizens, failing to train good, 96
city
exalted through the blessing of the upright, 203
as a place of possibilities, 10
seeking church connections, 192–93
civil rights movement, "not significant" to the focus group, 126
class distinctions, English Poor Laws and, 61
clerk, essential and distinct functions of, 202
Clock Tower of London, inscription on, 56
clockmaker, repairing a Swiss town's clock, 53–54
closing worship, as a final letting go, 190
"Club Ontario Spirit" T-shirts, 173
coach
essential and distinct functions of, 202
needed to truly improve your game, 201
coaching role, vitally important for pastoral leaders, 202
Cohen, Aryeh, rabbinic story about the gatehouse in ancient times, 73–74
collaborations of faith, reneighboring through, 87–89
collaborative partnerships, with other community organizations, 133
color interpretations, helpful in art therapy and clinical settings, 146n22
commitments, for change and renewal, 113
community
achieving authentic, 107
attempting to purchase cheaply, 102

community (*continued*)
  being an agent of transformation defined by, 70
  as big fans of an effective and neighborhood-serving ministry, 200
  building a sense of, 103
  building through social encounters, 40-41
  flipping the focus from the church to, 93
  as the focus, 99-100
  jobs to be done in, 92
  looking to get jobs done, 91
  looking to receive a blessing of tangible connectivity, 194
  modeling the behaviors of loving, 95
  needing an authentic relationship with, 90
  needing mission farmers, 200
  of Nehemiah, tithed themselves back into the urban center, 107
  as neighbors, not others, 114
  offering feedback to the entire, 51
  as an organic and living experience, 101
  pastor in, 186-88
  pattern of abandonment, 61
  reconnecting, 129-64
  reconnecting to, 61
  shifting focus to help save, 96
  taking shape, 106
  transformation of, 69
  understanding through social encounters, 36-40
community assets, collecting lists of, 81-82
community building
  fostering through neighborhood churches, 46
  as the point of mission, 100
community chaplain, pastor acting as, 73
community church, as a model in Asia, 117
community collaboration, developed with the assistance of Charles Harris, 168
community connections
  churches distributing blessings through, 193
  making, 97-98
community development
  Lupton's three *R*'s of, 75-76
  process of, 46-47
community efforts, secondary to fraternal ones, 20
community formation process, 103
community health, developing a barometer of, 50-51
community impact, achieving as a strategic neighbor, 117
community intervention project, crayon drawings produced by, 8
community issues, church failing to address, 27
community leaders, panel of, 51
community life, absence from, undermining the mission of our congregation, 119
community of faith
  bridging the gap with the community at large, 112
  chose to embrace God's preferred and emerging future, 12
  as an effective ambassador of the loving Creator God, 164
community of hope, 178-88
"community of obligation," creating, 74
community participation, correlating with new behaviors of the worshipping community, 130
community pastor, role of, 13
community receivables, focusing on, 90
community services, important to the laborer and blue-collar majority, 18

"Community" sheet, 122, 123, 125
community stigma
   lifting, 183
   visualizing, 37
community-wide collaboration, 75
commuter church, 25
companies, finding success, 91
"compartmentalized life" mentality, 85
Compassion Clinics, 81
Compassion Connect, partnering to build neighborhood health and wellness, 80–81
congregation(s). *See also* Wilkey congregation
   addressing neighborhood problems, 27
   called to live with Jesus Christ in the streets, 60
   closing ineffective, unable-to-be-reneighbored, 89
   connecting to original charters, 77
   credibility of, 140
   disengaged from the community's life, 126
   empathy of, 139
   empowering, 65
   growing distant from the neighborhood, 23
   languishing in the untreated trauma of decline, 89
   like baseball organizations, 200
   logic of, 141
   mission of, 60
   names as vehicles for mission, 24
   needing more connecting with the neighborhood, 26
   needing to live in the neighborhood, 79
   not remaining a stranger, 25
   obsessed with "self-preservation," 63
   percent from the neighborhood, 125
   reconnecting to its neighborhood, 96
   reneighboring, 72–77, 116–28, 183
   represented by its resources, values, and priorities, 64
   three "rushed to get the Wilkey money," 124
   too many have become miners not farmers, 199
   of trusting relationships, 134
   as vehicles for community transformation, 206
congregation and denominational connections, as a functional not a divisional organization, 202
connected congregation, thinking twice before closing, 89
connected people, calling the church back to being, 66
connectivity, as a gospel mandate and a mission opportunity, 194–95
consolidated mission, compared to isolated ministry, 66
contact work, 119
cooperative neighborhood ministry, developing, 57
core business, of the church, 66
core mission, of a church, 91
core values, of Wilkey Memorial Presbyterian Church, 209
corner market, assistance from, 77
corporate transformation, 63–69
council of churches, 65
counselors, at camp, 172, 174–75
Cousins, Tom, 45
Covey, Stephen R., 69
Crabtree, Russell, 63
   on effective leadership, 118
   founder of HolyCow! Consulting, 138
   on low-satisfaction, high-energy churches as chaotic, 103
   on the transformational state for a church, 176
   on a vital and healthy church, 90
Crayola crayons, boxes of, 145, 147

crayon drawings, available from the book's online companion, 154n27–155n27
crayon-drawing exercises, by two groups of children, 7
crayons
 gift of building trust, 182
 power to remove stigma, 132
credibility (Greek: *ethos*), 139, 140
cross or a crucifix, drawings of by children, 163
crossing guard, visited Christopher, 155–56
Cultural/Academic/Psychological (CAP) approach, of Igoa, 132
culture, post-Christian, post-church, 88

Damascus Project intervention
 camping with, 165–70
 different from most traditional camps, 169
 mission rationale for, 167
 objective of, 166
Daniel 3, story of Shadrach, Meshach, and Abednego, 158n28
Dare We Speak of Hope (Boesak), 206
deacons, in Acts 7, 19
deacons' board, 24–25
DeCaro, Louis A., 206
defeat, accepting, 104
demographic realities, studying, 27–29
denominational mid council regional leader, role of, 191
depictions, of Christopher drawn by the children, 156
deplacialization, of native peoples, 6
destination, domain of, 58–59
Dickert, John, 192, 193
Different Drum (Peck), 103
digital gaming, as completely immersive, 137
DiIulio, John J., Jr., 88

disciples, alone on the lake during a storm, 159
discipleship
 as a behavior not originating with Jesus, 95
 being effective in, 170
 leading to good neighborship, 126
discreditable, being, 37
discredited
 being, 37
 interacting with, 38
discrimination
 behaviors of, 41
 stigma as a root of, 38
disengagement, reversing decades of, 7
displacement
 of churches from neighborhoods, 88
 tragic consequence of, 79
disruption, technical, 11–14
disruptive innovation, inviting conflict, 12
dissertation, of Goode, 206
diversity
 being together in with a common mission, 99
 representing amazing opportunities, 114
divine space, continuum of, 168
domains
 of destination, 58–59
 of location, 56–57
 of process, 59–63
 restoring health in, 56–63
doves of peace, 181
"downward mobility," life of, 75
drawing(s)
 by the children of Chernobyl, 132
 coded to ensure security and protect privacy, 145
 displaying, 145n21
 giving voice, 129–32
 helpful in educational settings and in clinical settings, 131

led to a merger of the two
separate groups of children,
8
not a requirement during
sessions, 163
at Stetson captured a range of
expressions, 161
topics for, 143
type as irrelevant, 146n22
drawing intervention, 142–44
creating a more accurate view of
self, 182
developed with several
additional classes at Stetson
Middle School, 161n32
enabling the children to express
themselves, 42
invited children to articulate
their vision of the world, 164
process of, 147–48
technique, 145–47
drawing intervention model, 7
drawing sessions, routines for each,
147–48
drawing skill level, higher at Stetson,
159
drive-in attendees, 74
drug community, preventing from
preparing, 17
drug coordinating office, first, 205
drug crime, in Kensington, 2
drug dealers
considered to be model tenants,
48
creating a living hell, 16
drug walk, around McPherson
Library in Kensington,
15–16
drugs
organizing against the dangers
of, 43
vacuum created by getting rid
of, 49
Dulles, Avery, 27
dysfunction, keeping from
metastasizing, 118

early church

aversion to place, 5
practices of, recorded in Acts, 55
East Lake neighborhood near
Atlanta, suffering from
stigma, 45–47
ecclesiastical disruption, 11
ecclesiastical engineers, need for, 12
economic development, doing, 74
educational and community-
building, implementing, 28
ego strength, interfering with
expressive drawing, 143n17
Emanuel First Hispanic Presbyterian
Church, renewed
community focus, 193
empathy (Greek: *pathos*), 139
emptiness stage, of community
formation, 103–4
Empty Nesters, 29
emptying, as a sense of repentance,
106
engagement
blessing neighborhoods, 75
criteria for the focus group
team, 121
designed for the camping
intervention, 173–76
engaging
in action at Camp Lake
Champion, 173–74
in relationships at Camp Lake
Champion, 174–75
in transformation at Camp Lake
Champion, 175–76
English Poor Laws, Chalmers
familiar with, 61
English Quakers, purchasing land
from the Indians, 17
environment, children expressing
messages of judgment
concerning, 161, 162
Erickson, Victoria Lee, 132, 143, 167
Esther, motivation of, 13
ethical review board. *See*
Institutional Review Board
(IRB)
ethnic fighting, in the early 1800s,
18

ethnic groups, segregated into convenient neighborhoods, 19
ethnographic discoveries, in the focus-group setting, 120
ethnographic process, capturing an entirely different storyline, 123
ethnographic tools, providing the learning stimulus, 7
ethnography
    as the basis for social change, 119
    benefitting from an optimal, open, conversational space, 120
    of church leaders, 116–19
    as an effective instrument, 117–18
    ensuring that participants control the story, 122
    as a self-discovery experience, 123
ethnography/documentary video, Kensington through the eyes of five Kensington high school kids, 4
European-Americans, vacating urban neighborhoods, 126
event-focused turnarounds, having little lasting value, 55
events, defining the Christian church experience, 55
"Everybody Is Welcome" campaign, 193
evidence
    of hope restored, 176–77
    of a reneighbored congregation, 128
    of stigma removed, 148–59
evidence-based discernment, 63
external collaboration, essential to success, 46
external force, releasing stigma's debilitating grasp, 46

face, our feelings "become attached to it," 36
face born, male and female, 39
"face" concept, 37
face died, with Jesus' broken body, 40
face established, 39
face lifting up again, with the ascension, 40
face loved, as Jesus, 40
Face Loved, in our Transformation Paradigm, 137
face restored, 40
face stained, with sin like a mark, 39
facelessness, as sin's consequence, 39
failure, becoming accustomed to, 68
faith
    conversations about, 163
    described, 164
    reneighboring through collaborations of, 87–89
    reported all over the world, 66
    to see God in the midst of a fire, 157
faith communities
    dynamic stories of many tribes within, 138
    learning and growing, 7
    representing a cycle of life, 198
    same framework for more than one hundred years, 90
faith statements, children offering, 161, 162
faith-based community, engagement by, 49–50
faith-based ministries, silent on the street, 4
faith-based organizations (FBOs), 11n1
    building sustainable community wellness, 80
    not consulted in regard to Operation Sunrise, 43
    sustainability dependent on the neighborhood, 76
faith-based systems, inability to adapt to urbanization of American life, 11

families
    asked to contribute for camp, 170
    Kevin Yoho's located in suburban Philadelphia, 187
    low-income in Kensington, 2
family conflict, stick figures of, 150
family fragmentation, stemming, 28
"family model" congregation, 101
family system, affirming the value of, 170
family worship, resulting from the camp experience, 176
fans, correlating to the community, 200–201
farming
    based on nurturing, living, and life-giving cycle, 198
    rewards of versus mining, 195
    in the Torah, the Christian Scriptures, and the Quran, 197
farming churches, 198, 199
farms, 196
Father, Son, and Holy Spirit, 53
feeding of the multitudes, told in all four Gospels, 193
Finkelman, Sol, 35–36
fire, traumatized the neighborhood, 155
firsthand knowledge, importance of, 118n3
first-time profession of faith in Jesus Christ, made by seventeen kids at camp, 175
FloorTalk
    affirmations of, 137–38
    including the biblical story of Daniel's three friends, 157–58
    messages, content of progressed developmentally, 142
    sessions, not all the children attended every, 144n19
    shared stories in, 141
    twenty-minute period of, 135–36
    welcomed youthful participants, 137
focus group
    as a data collecting process, 121
    pain in, 125–27
    rationale of, 119–21
    reflection by, 127–28
    selecting individuals for, 119, 121
    as a self-contained entity, 127n13
forgiveness, setting the (once stained) face free, 40
fortress, church as, 109–10
fortresslike churches, becoming accessible, 6
Four Reneighboring Steps, developed at Wilkey, 96–98
Saint Francis of Assisi, 34, 77
fraternal lodges and orders, designed to bar certain ethnic groups, 19–20
Friedel, Tom, 192–93
"fully alive," for children, 130n2–131n2
funding, for camp, 170–73
future, power of claiming and envisioning, 58
future focus group, exploring reneighboring, 127

Gardner, John W., 100
gatehouse, rabbinic story about, 73–74
generative change, 98
gentrification, 61
Gethsemane prayer, of Jesus, 57
"getting people into church," focusing on as disappointing, 194
get-well card, for Christopher, 158
giving voice
    affirming the children and their worldview, 146
    to children through intervention, 142
    removing stigma, 132

giving voice (*continued*)
   through drawing, 129–32
   to whole world experience, 143
God
   as always present, 159
   assured Cain that no one would harm him, 32
   became fully human in Jesus, 81
   cared about the children, 136
   created the heavens and the earth, 53
   drawing a picture of, 1
   expressed as a Trinity of community, communion, and relationship, 70
   here in the good times and the bad, 136
   inviting to confront principalities and powers, 60
   loving us exactly where we are, 87
   as the model maker, 98–99
   "moved into the neighborhood," 81
   in the news business, 67
   as not absent and not silent, 159
   reconciliation to, 164
   in the redemption business, 65
   releasing power in reconciliation and transformation, 54
   story of life and purpose, 137
   as an ultimate validation of acceptance, forgiveness, and hope, 164
God Came Near (Lucado), 207
God with us, as core motivation for the church's mission, 11
God With Us (Haroutunian), 56
Godhead, agency and facility of, 53
God's angel, with Daniel's friends even in the fire, 158
God's life, realigning with, 164
God's love, experiencing together at camp, 172
God's mission, building in Kensington, 99
God's people, preparing for works of service, 183

God's story
   resonating using three components of persuasive storytelling, 139
   telling, 137
God's work in Philadelphia, continuing in other cities, 191
Goffman, Erving, 36–40
"going to church," 92
Gold Rush, 197
good citizenship, necessary for good discipleship, 96
good informant, "knowing the culture well," 127n13
good intentions, proverb about, 114
good neighboring, as a powerful and transformative force, 158
Good Samaritan (Luke 10:25-37), 51
Goode, W. Wilson, afterword by, 205–7
Gospel
   as the basis for societal reform, 60
   has not changed, 117
Gospel of John. *See also* Apostle John
   beginning with "In the beginning was the Word...," 140
   first chapter of, 33
Gospel of the kingdom, preached in all the world, 60
graffiti
   drawing sanctified, to reclaim space, 186
   painting over, 179
   on the wall of the row home behind the church, 153n26
gratitude, showing through community connectivity, 192
grave clothes, representing the stigma to be lifted, 168
Great Commission, encompassed all of life, 72
Great Depression, hit Kensington hard, 22

Green Bay Packers, coach of, 55
group photograph, for camp, 172, 173
groups, forming, 57
guilds, forming, 19
gym, acoustically challenging, 147–48

handguns, in drawings by the children, 151–52
Haroutunian, Joseph, 56, 57
Harris, Charles, 168, 171n9
Hartley, Lloyd, 23
healthy church, as a living community, 198
healthy systems, self-correcting, 46
Heinz, Eleanor, 182
Hellenist and Jewish widows, perceived unequal treatment of, 19
Herald church, Ontario Church began as, 27
high-crime neighborhoods, repeating YVRP in, 88
Hispanic leadership, lagging behind, 29
historic dynamic changes, understanding, 120
historic vision, recovery of, 73
historical community relationship, credibility from, 140
historical stigmatizing, 40
history, stigma through the lens of, 31–32
Holy Cow! Consulting, 63
Holy Spirit
    building a community, 108
    connecting people to be planted in the soil of life, 198
    connecting us to what is working, 85
    determined heeding of, 82
    gifted individuals guided by, 65
    indwelling at Pentecost ensured empowered storytellers, 137
    revealing God's love story in the biblical record, 117

homeowners, decreasing around the church, 28–29
homework, for becoming present in your community, 81–82
hope
    cannot be enforced, 44
    community of, 178–88
    at the hoops in the gym, 134
    providing the infrastructure of, 47–48
    restoring, 165–77
hopelessness, 47, 50
houses, vacated by the drug dealers, 48
housing statistics, in Kensington, 28
human beings
    created in the image of God, 87
    as partners and producers with God, 64–65
human experience, as fully integrated, 54
humanity, created in God's image, 39

I and Me
    produced through engagement, 40
    theologically narcissistic emphasis of, 57
"I Can Do That!" mission theme, 84
I without Me, equaling slavery, 41
identity formation and deformation, understanding of, 41
Igoa, Cristina, 130–31, 143
illicit economic base, alternatives to, 49
immigrant students, serving the needs of, 130–31
immigrants, arrival of more and more, 19
improvement, requiring more than admiration, 201
incarnation, 81, 137, 141
incarnational ministry, 60, 62
incarnational model, of moving into the community, 183

230 Index

inclusion, ensuring for every child's contribution, 147
incumbent group, retaining power, 199
indicators for success, as the elimination of drug dealing and prostitution, 48
"indigenizing," proactive, 62
indigenous congregation, reflecting the neighborhood, 60
individualism, traditional Christianity and its theologies dominated by, 57
individuals, as products of several systems, 169
infectious disease, social isolation and, 31
in-flesh, in-person ministry, 62
inner life, of balance, 70
inner spirit, of members resonating around personal safety, 76
The Inner World of the Immigrant Child (Igoa), 130
insiders, presuming that outsiders want to be churched, 114
Institution church, focused primarily on self-preservation, 27
institutional concerns, taking priority over consideration of mission, 5–6
Institutional Review Board (IRB), 8, 27, 182, 183
Institutional Support Group, 70. *See also* Institutional Review Board (IRB)
integrated life, comprehensive view of, 54
interns, from Temple University's school of social work administration, 134
intervention
 designed utilizing a control group, 143
 giving voice to the children, 142
 in Kensington in three parts, 7

led by those prepared to think critically and theologically, 170n7
needing community leaders and safe places, 88
provided opportunities for self-expression, trust building, and discovery, 145
resourcing a new I for the children, 42
involvement, created love of neighbor, 75
involvement index, 195
IRB. *See* Institutional Review Board (IRB)
Ireland (Roman Catholic), immigrants from, 123
Irish immigrants, not welcome in most neighborhoods, 18
Irish Roman Catholic, 87
Israel, cyclical pattern during the time of the judges, 66

J. B. Stetson Junior High School. *See* Stetson Middle School
James and John, mighty thunder in, 99
Jerusalem
 men volunteered to live in, 79
 seeing as Nehemiah saw it, 106
 in shambles with walls torn down, 105
Jesus
 appointed twelve disciples as apostles, 99
 came back to life again to build a new community, 70
 coming from Nazareth (a place like Kensington), 141
 descent from the Mount of Olives like his descent into Kensington, 185
 displayed a face loved, 40
 disruption by, 85, 113
 efforts to reach the poor, the outcast, widows, orphans and women, and stigmatized groups, 87

extended love in identifying his
    betrayer, 100n2
on having faith in him, 93
healed on the Sabbath, 70
healing the blind and those with
    leprosy, 141
as the image of the invisible
    God, 117
inviting believers to give up the
    sacred, 167
knowing what it is like to live in
    the neighborhood, 136
as the light of the world, 96
love for children, 185
in a manger, 163
marks of, 32
method of ministry in a group
    context, 57
moved into our neighborhood,
    117
Nathanael encountering, 33
from Nazareth, 33, 34
not excluding anyone, 113
parable about seed falling on
    various types of soil, 198
pointing to God for the
    oppressed, 167
powering God's spiritual
    network, 191
redefinition of "neighbor," 72
set aside the privileges of deity
    and took on the status of a
    slave, 104
short vignettes about the life of,
    at camp, 175
as someone who could be
    known, 163–64
speaking to Thomas, 33n5
stigma and, 33–34
on the truth, 130
twelve disciples of, 95
weeping as he looked into
    Jerusalem, 82
weeping over Lazarus, 159
welcomed children, 185
on where your treasure is, 82,
    187
"Jesus and Me" theme, 57

Jesus Christ. *See* Jesus
Jesus' story, as a story of power, 137
Jewish neighbors, 123, 124
Jewish people, lived in a foreign
    country for many years, 106
Job (book of), on mining, 197
job classifications, for residents of
    Kensington, 42
"Job To Be Done" (JTBD)
    framework, 91, 93
jobs, formulating a list of possible,
    92
Jobs To Be Done model, for church
    connectivity, 193
Joe (Stetson Middle School student),
    words about gunfire, 181
Jonathan (Kevin Yoho's son), 172
Jordan, Michael, switched his
    athletic shoe endorsement
    from Reebok to Nike, 24
journey, with the children, 144
Judas Iscariot, 99–100, 100n2
judgmental message, of detachment
    and isolation, 76
Justice in the City (Cohen), 73

Kawulich, Barbara, 118
KenCrest, 189
Kensington
    children of, 42
    as a dangerous neighborhood, 3
    as a favored neighborhood in
        London, 44, 45
    as a forgotten place, 44
    history of, 17
    industrial dollars to in the early
        1900s, 19
    needing transformation, 53
    neighborhood of Philadelphia, 2
    number of widowed or divorced
        persons in, 28
    as own city, independent of
        Philadelphia, 122
    as a place to escape from, 44
    population of, 5
    provided motivated volunteers
        for the Revolutionary War,
        18

Kensington (*continued*)
   restoration of hope, 203
   social interaction data points, 37
   in steep decline, 45
   street economy in, 48
   suffering from a tribal stigma, 38
   true identity of, 38
   as a type of Nazareth, 42–45
Kensington and Allegheny Avenues, intersection of, 21
"Kensington Artillery," 18
Kensington High School, "Coat of Arms of the Baron of Kensington," 44
Kensington Hope, 189
Kensington Ministry Partnership, 97, 112–13
Kensington Riots, in 1844, 18
Kensington Through Our Eyes (video), 4
"kid wall," mural as, 180
kids. *See also* children
   asking to draw pictures, 142
   belonging to a system of relationships, 169
   connecting to their Creator, 174
   explored areas of interest, 174
   invited to go with us, 169
   learned that God had not abandoned them, 159
   listening because adult leaders cared, 141
   loved what became their project, 145
   moving out with their families to a better neighborhood, 3
   offered their works of art for display, 145
   positive camp experience, 175
   responded in faith to Jesus Christ, 176
   updated on Christopher's condition, 156
Kramer, Edith, 131, 143
Kushner, Alexander, 181

Ladwig, Tim, 131
land, after trees had been harvested, 196
language and behaviors, considering the impact of, 114
Lateau, Louise, 34
law code, sin getting written into, 13
law enforcement models, requiring additional reflection, 49
law enforcement officers, understanding that illicit activities are symptoms, 50
laws, not lifting Kensington's stigma, 44
lawsuit, brought by the heirs of the Wilkey sisters, 125
Lazarus, words heard from Jesus, 168
leaders. *See also* authentic leaders; church leaders; leadership; pastoral leader
   role of, 12
   in Wilkey Church, 98, 118
leadership. *See also* leaders
   capacity in a community, 100
   fragmentation of in our cities, 100
   incarnational model of, 183
   for a new community, 166
   paradigm for building for the new millennium, 61
   as the shared work of spiritually graced men and women, 65
   transformative, 133, 182
leadership team, reintroducing to your community, 59
learners, Jesus' disciples as, 95
learning community, 94, 100–105
learning community transformation, resource manual and tools for, 108–13
learning styles, different, 102
Learning Styles Inventory (LSI), 102, 102n7
learning team, establishing, 7
learning together, resulting in a sense of accomplishment, 127

leftovers, blessing those unable to attend, 193
legal address, for citizens as their residence, 187
Lenni Lenape Indians' summer camping grounds, 17
lepers, story of 10 in Luke 17, 192
leprosy
　person with marked as "unclean," 31
　stigma endured after death, 32
Levitical cleansing protocol, 31
life-giving change, making evolutionary leaps, 98
"Lifting the Stigma of Mental Illness," 35
light of Christ, reaching all of life, 68–69
lighthouse, church as, 110
Linthicum, Robert, 82
literacy program, first, 205
Little Vietnam, East Lake known as, 45
local churches, investing in the lives of neighbors, 81
local congregations, importance of, 65
local organization, as the body of Christ, 56
location, domain of, 56–57
logic (Greek: *logos*), 139, 140–42
logo, for MissionWorks, 83
Lombardi, Vince, 55
long-range planning, downside of, 97
Lonsinger, Jesse
　moved to Westmoreland Street, 21–22
　opposed to the name change, 22, 125
　resigned in April 1941, 23
"looking for a church" category, fewer people in, 92
losing face, 37
Louis (neighbor), living next to a drug house, 16
love, making visible, 97

love of God and other persons, becoming absorbed in, 53
love of neighbor, 75
love-in-action changes, making in your neighborhood, 81
Lovelace, Richard, 53
Lucado, Max, 207
Luke 15, cascading set of parables, 96
Luke Skywalker, Yoda and, 138
Lupton, Robert, 12, 43, 61, 72, 75–76
Lutheran Settlement House, 20

market share, in the business world, 66
marriage relationship, church's loving relationship with its neighborhood analogous to, 72
Martha, to Jesus in John 11:21, 159n31
Matthew, as a future story-teller of the promised King, 99
mayor of Philadelphia, instituted the first homeless program in the US, 205
Me, wearing the stigma, as does the I, 41
Me and My Church (Mosque, Synagogue, God, or Religious Life) domain, 143
Me and My Family domain, 143
Me and My Friends domain, 143
Me and My Future domain, 143, 144
Me and My Neighborhood domain, 143
Me and My School domain, 143
Me and My World domain, 143
Mead, George H., 40–41, 42
media, stigma through the lens of, 34–36
meeting the needs, of those within the church and those without, 206

members
  began moving out of the immediate neighborhood in the 1950s, 25
  buying homes in close proximity to the church building, 79–80
  detached from effective ministry in their live-in neighborhood, 79
membership
  consequences of flight of, 79
  not measuring the effectiveness of a congregation, 66
  percentage of living in the neighborhood, 119, 125
  stasis in, 25
mental illness professionals, disassociating illness from stigma, 35
mental map, shifting from stigma to hope, 12
mentoring relationships, with community and business leaders, 46
Miller, D. G., 206
Minecraft (game), 195
mining, 197, 198
mining churches, 199
ministry
  evidence-based discernment for, 63
  needing to build many conections, 83
Ministry Learning Community (MLC)
  affirmed the importance of the neighborhood, 111
  to be a ministry, 99
  bridging to the neighborhood, 101
  developed the following affirmations, 112–13
  ensuring shared ownership of, 108
  establishing as an exercise in problem-solving, 98
  evaluated the developing model and provided needed accountability and assistance, 100
  exploring and discussing the Church Models Grid, 109
  invited church leaders to form as a learning group, 95
  as a kind of mission experiment, 102
  members connected with this emptying stage of Nehemiah, 106
  retreat mornings, 105
  stages of, 103
  task was to listen to the voice of God, 100
  traveled the first three stages of community building, 104
ministry models
  designing sustainable, 8
  not producing energy, 90
  notion of, 99
ministry of hospitality, operating, 197
Miriam, removed from the general population for seven days, 31
mission
  challenging the status quo, 27
  evaluating your, 90
  like a plot of land, 195
mission arrogance and paternalism, deconstructing, 85
mission connectivity, 191–95
mission deliverables, focusing on, 90
mission disconnect, tipping point to a severe, 74
mission endurance, not the same as mission longevity, 57
mission engagement, new methodology of, 14
mission farmer, versus mission miner, 195–200
mission miner, working as, 197
Mission Prayer Breakfasts, 189
mission statement
  developing, 67–68

of Wilkey Memorial
    Presbyterian Church, 208–9
mission storytelling, 136–38
missional health, walking for, 93–94
MissionInsite, 28, 58
MissionWorks
    created to promote our
        open invitation to other
        organizations, 133
    crew from Gwynedd Square
        Presbyterian Church, 134
    crew of, 84–85
    direct-ministry effort, 83
    logo, 83
    urban plunge, 78
mixed income, housing residents
    of, 46
model, as a symbol, 99
model maker, God as, 98–99
modeling, reneighboring through,
    78–80
Models Grid, 109
Models of the Church (Dulles),
    congregational identities
    in, 27
monetizing models, for
    congregational ministry, 76
money, raising for camp, 170n8
monthly prayer breakfasts, 97
Moody, Dwight L., 20
Mordecai, on remaining silent, 13
Moses, taking so long on the
    mountain, 159, 159n29
mosques (Muslim), 11n1
Multi-church Consultation, 111–12
Mural Arts Philadelphia, 179
Mustard Seed Foundation, in
    Virginia, 171
Mystical Communion, Church as,
    27

Naaman, cured of leprosy, 31
"nail-pierced hands," became a sign
    of the resurrection, 33
name change
    as a death knell to neighborhood
        ministry, 23

mentioned again, 124
as significant, 123
suggesting a hypothesis, 120
symbolic of a lack of
    congregational interest in
    the neighborhood, 26
names, empowering or enslaving,
    167
Nathanael, 33
native peoples, domination of, 6
*The Nature and Mission of the
    Church* (Miller), 206
nature of the church, as a living
    thing in relation to Christ,
    56
Nazareth
    as a bad place to come from, 33
    Kensington as a type of, 42–45
needs, trying to meet as a slippery
    slope, 92
Nehemiah
    book of, beginning and ending
        with remembering, 107
    carefully planned his strategy, 68
    chaos in, 105–7
    demonstrating the importance
        of a transformed
        community, 85–86
    exhorted families to take
        responsibility for their
        section, 100
    knowing his community was
        inauthentic, 105
    metaphor of taking a walk with,
        102
    offering a much-needed new
        paradigm, 68
    providing the primary biblical
        frame for Bible studies, 105
    pseudocommunity in, 105
    solution to the dilemma of
        displaced disciple, 79
    on subjecting sons and
        daughters to slavery, 86
Nehemiah Project housing business,
    74
"neighbor" laws, in the Torah, 72

Index

"neighbored" church, disengaged from the community, 7
neighborhood(s)
   affected by stigma, 37
   as a battlefield, 59
   becoming stigmatized, 37
   building relationships with adjacent, 29
   celebrating ethnic and racial diversity in, 183
   choosing to remain a victim to or live into a better future, 179
   deteriorating without a strong economy, 25
   drawing, 148
   embracing, 86
   fleeing from, 61
   focus on serving, 84
   loving, 73, 96
   as a place of possibilities, 10
   reconnecting with, 63
   seeing as a place of value, 129
   transformation in, 186
   walks through, 2
neighborhood chaplain, 134, 136
neighborhood church, serving the neighborhood, 78
neighborhood crossing guard, visited Christopher, 155–56
neighborhood diversity, as an enormous challenge and opportunity, 29
neighborhood economy, realities of an unstable, 25
neighborhood image, of the church, 110
neighborhood kids, 166
neighborhood leaders, building a core group of, 166
neighborhood mural, kids determined to create, 179
neighborhood walks, with interns and visiting leaders, 59
neighborhood youth, prioritized neighborhood projects for the MissionWorks crew, 85
neighborhood-based name, changed to a personality-based name, 24
neighborhood-directed initiatives, evaluating, 50
neighbors
   asking God to direct you to, 93
   attending activities, 130
   listening to, 92
   looking at the church from the perspective of, 93
   most not wanting to be churched in the first place, 115
   wants and needs of, 80
   willing to make the neighborhood their own, 13
neighborship, 168, 170
new church, starting as a "plant," 199
new members discovery class, 183
New Year's convocation, of Kevin Yoho's graduate school, 98
Newark, New Jersey, church seeking city conections, 193
newsprint sheets
   captured real-time connections, 123
   stories taking shape on, 122
Nhat Hanh, Thich, 203
Nicene Creed, one Lord Jesus Christ, 62n16
Nixon, Bo, 175
"No minute lost comes back again," 56
Noah's Ark, story of, selected for the mural, 180
"non-Christian kid" tags, 166
non-European-American ministry, capacity for intentional, 29
noninfectious "unclean" designations, period of outcast status, 31n1
nonprofit and charitable organizations, motives of, 11
Northern Ireland (Protestant), immigrants from, 123

Northern Liberties section of Philadelphia, city tax not collected there, 122n11
nostalgia, powerless to evoke change, 60
"not yet dead," of Chernobyl, 132
nurturing relationships, in the community, 160

Oatley, Keith, 137
official scorer, not providing performance-improving data, 201
Olympia Brown Unitarian Universalist Church, free-will gift from, 193
101 Favorite Play Therapy Techniques (Kaduson and Schaefer), 146n22
One Segment Leaders, 100
online Appendix companion, for this book, 173n11
online companion, at Kevin Yoho's website, 8
Ontario Community Church, chartered to be a transformational presence, 26
Ontario Presbyterian Church, 22
 applied for the Wilkey money, 124–25
 charter of, 69
 membership of, 24
 offering special Sunday school classes for the kids, 24
 photo from 1925, 21
 pre-1940, 20
 renamed Wilkey Memorial Presbyterian Church, 52, 62, 120, 125
 return of as a neighborhood community church, 134
Ontario Spirit, new, emerging, 77
Ontario Spirit basketball program, 134
Ontario Spirit Community Church, 190

Ontario Spirit sports program, 102, 133
 start-up of, 85
 at Wilkey Church and at Stetson Middle School, 50
Ontario Spirit Street Leaders, 168
openness, in the conversations of the focus group, 120
Operation Liberty Bell mission project, 4
Operation Sunrise, 16–17
 beginning of, 43
 as a deficit model, 48
 did not live up to its promise, 44
 objectives of, 17, 43, 47
Orangemen (Protestant Irish), 87
Origen, on Jesus and the poor, 32
outcomes, paying attention to, 90
out-of-community experience, 167
outsiders
 excluding neighbors as, 80
 transforming into insiders, 114
outward mobility, replacing with inward mobility, 80

Padre Pio, Italian stigmatic, 34
painting energy, on the wall, 180
"papal school," 123
parables
 about seed falling on various types of soil, 198
 cascading set of, 96
paradigm, of forgiveness and transformation, 67
paradigm shift, of Nehemiah, 105
parental permissions, securing, 143
parents, missed their children, 186
parish, ethnography of, 73
parking lot, representing a missed opportunity, 78
"Participant Observation as a Data Collection Method" (Kawulich), 118n3
partnership and collaboration, as a mutual process, 64
Paschall community, in southwest Philadelphia, 205

past
  enabling a mighty power for transformation, 72
  giving permission to the present, 73
  leveraging, 97
pastor(s)
  in community, 186–88
  embracing the role of ethnographer, 127
  leaving the ministry every month, 90
  as observer-participant, 120
  with postgraduate degrees, 95
The Pastor (Peterson), 63
pastoral intervention, 131, 186
pastoral leader. *See also* church leaders; leaders
  investing resource into the neighborhood mix, 62
  not allowing dysfunctional behaviors to be normalized, 118
  responsibility to call a congregation to its history, 60
  serving the community at large, 134
  at Wilkey and the Kensington Parish, 82
pastoral residence, 186–87
pastoral staff, perceived and actual roles of, 73
Paul. *See* Apostle Paul
Peck, M. Scott
  on letting groups struggle toward community, 107
  on "pseudocommunity," 102
  on stage of chaos, 103
  on true community, 101
peers, taking one only as far as they have gone, 201
Penn, William, 17
Penn Home, 197
"Pennsauken, New Jersey: A Nice Place to Grow," 44
Pennsauken community, as safer, 35

performing arts, engaging the audience, 137
Perkins, John, 75, 87
permission, to display the children's pictures in public places, 145
permission slips, return rate, 144n20
"perpetually poor," 49
personal interaction, reneighboring through, 82–86
personal mind share, affirmed by Paul, 67
personal transformation, 53–56
Peter, as a rock, 99
Peterson, Eugene, 63
Pew Research Center, demographic data from, 58
Philadelphia Board of Education, 23
Philadelphia Presbytery, 20, 22, 82, 124, 189
Philadelphia Safe and Sounds, 88
Philadelphia Young Life, 168
Philip, description of Jesus to Nathanael, 33
physical location, affecting perception of self-worth, 130
physical space, as decisive in creating community, 120
physical stigma, 38
pictures, drawn by the children, 181
piety, leading to political practice outside the building, 74
"Pizza Bible Study," called Campaigners, 176
place, recovering a sense of, 130
places, where need is greatest receiving the fewest resources, 89
planning
  long-range, downside of, 97
  on a tree farm, 196
police commissioner Timoney. *See* Timoney, John F.
police force, as a key community asset, 47
poor
  becoming dependent on society, 61
  being able to hear the cries of, 73

positive reneighboring, 62
post-Christian, post-church culture, 88
power, giving to communal possibility, 101
prayer breakfast, monthly all-Kensington, 112
preconceived attitudes, left unaddressed, 103
Presbyterian Church (U.S.A.)
  connecting to clear biblical foundations, 65
  media campaign entitled "Lifting the Stigma of Mental Illness," 35
Presbyterian churches, three requesting to became "Wilkey Church," 23
Presbyterians
  impact on the world, 138
  neglecting this spiritual dimension, 59
  organized outreach efforts as the Summer Evangelistic Committee (SEC), 20
presbyteries, building the capacity of, 191
Presbytery of Philadelphia, 20, 22, 82, 124, 189
present, obscuring redeeming history and potential, 72
previously stigmatized, as another discredited group, 38
priest, embracing the function of, 185
primary and secondary intervention groups, displayed same theme of the trash can many times, 154–55
primary historical information, putting isolated facts in context, 120
Primary Intervention Group (a.k.a. the "Kids in the Gym")
  comparing the early drawings of with the after-intervention mural, 182
  composition of, 146
  participated in the Saturday sports program, 142–43
  at Wilkey Church, 182
printed words, children expressing themselves with, 147
problem-solving, deficit model, of policing, 47
process, domain of, 59–63
profane and the sacred, relationship between, 167
program staff, acted out a creative story at camp, 173
promise, of transformation, 69–70
property tax exemptions, of churches, 192
prostitution, in Kensington, 3
Protestant Christian faith, predominant in Kensington in the late eighteenth century, 18
Protestant denominations, considered the Catholics as outsiders, 19
protocol, for the intervention, 144–45
proximity, importance of, 80–82
Psalm Twenty-Three, setting in an urban landscape, 131
pseudocommunity
  as conflict-avoiding, 102
  MLC's experience of, 103
  in Nehemiah, 105
psychosomatic, stigmata as, 34
Public/Private Ventures (P/PV), start-up of, 88

qualitative assessments, on children expressing themselves, 148

racial conflict, church at large silent to, 126
racial groups
  intense energy of, 19
  preoccupying people, 18
racial mix, changing in Kensington, 87

Racine, Wisconsin, city seeking church connections, 192–93
Racine Education Association, 193
"Racine's Fair Share" program, 192
railroad riots, pitted class and ethnic groups against each other, 18
rainbow, of hope, 180–81
real estate, ministry of, 46
real service, providing to people, 74
rebuilding, in Lupton's three *R*'s of community development, 76
reciprocity, social expectation of, 73
recollection, process of by the focus group, 120
reconciliation
   to God, 164
   ministry of, 75
redeemed gentrification, 62
redeemed relationship, with God, 67
redemption business, God in, 65
redevelopment, in the East Lake neighborhood, 46
redistribution, goal of, 75
reflection, by the focus group, 127–28
Reformation leaders, Gutenberg's printing press and, 138
refreshments, at each drawing session, 148
regional council leader, role of, 191
regional councils, listening to their largest membership churches, 90
re-harnessing market forces, in Lupton's three *R*'s of community development, 76
relationships with the children
   at Camp Lake Champion, 174–75
   existing before the camp, 169
religious faith, conversations about, 163
religious imagery, in the drawings, 163
religious traditions, in Igoa's triangular model, 132
religious zoning, neighborhood challenge of, 123
relocated members, removed from the primary neighborhood mission, 78
relocation, considering the sacrifice of, 75
remembrance, restoring vision, 105, 106
Rendell, Mayor, 44
reneighbored church, as an accessible church, 133
reneighbored congregation, evidence of, 128
reneighboring
   applying to other cities, 8
   the church, 26, 75, 126
   concept of, 7
   the congregation, 72–77, 116–28
   described, 63
   journey to, 13
   like new wine in an old wineskin, 190
   in Lupton's three *R*'s of community development, 76
   producing tears of joyful relief, 130
   of the prophet Nehemiah, 133
   through collaborations of faith, 87–89
   through modeling, 78–80
   through personal interaction, 82–86
Reneighboring Steps, developed at Wilkey, 96–98
Reneighboring Steps, Step 1, loving your neighborhood, 96
Reneighboring Steps, Step 2, making love visible, 97
Reneighboring Steps, Step 3, leveraging the past, 97
Reneighboring Steps, Step 4, making community connections, 97–98
renewal
   in terms of reconciliation, 54
   towards transformation, 67
representatives from the community, recruited to serve on the MLC, 101

"reputation for service," 133
residency
    establishing viability and validity
        of mission, 187
    Kevin Yoho's inner conflict
        about, 188
residency model, of Jesus, 81
Resource 1, Church Models Grid,
    109–10
Resource 2, Church Model
    Evaluation Chart, 111
Resource 3, Multi-church
    Consultation, 111–12
Resource 4, Kensington Ministry
    Partnership, 112–13
resourced persons, welcoming
    intentional relocation of, 62
resources
available, 141
reinvesting, 199
respect systems, commitment to,
    171
resurrection, good news of Jesus,' 40
Resurrection Church in Brooklyn,
    New York, 59–60
Rodriguez, Lucy, principal of
    Stetson Middle School,
    160–61
Roman Catholic Douay Bible, 18
Roman Catholic neighbors,
    frustration with, 87
Romanists, common dislike of, 20
Ross, Judith Joy, 8
Rotary Club, assistance from, 77
row home next to the church
    building, graffiti on, 178
row homes, near the church, 152–54
Rozanne, a member of ISG and an
    elder in the church, 172
rules, building the capacity of the
    organization by interpreting,
    202

Sabbath talk, informing our
    weekday walk, 70
Sacrament, Church as, 27
sales, in the business world, 66

Salvation Army, began its work in
    America in Kensington in
    1880, 20
salvation of the world, inextricably
    bound in community, 70
Samaritan, as the outsider, 51
Sanders, J. Oswald, 68
Saul. See also Apostle Paul
    on the road to Damascus, 34, 167
saving face, 37
scholarship fund, informal for camp,
    170
School of Discipleship, Church as,
    27
"Scribble Art" (Lowe), 146n22
sea glass, given to Christopher, 10
Secondary Intervention Group
    (a.k.a. the "Stetson Kids")
    composition of, 143, 146
    functioning as a control group,
        142
    responded to caring adults, 163
    at Stetson Middle School, 182
self
    as always a Me, 40
    deeper, shown and known as
        our face, 36
    needing objectivity, 41
self package, in the context of social
    experience, 41
self reimagining, 40
self-expression, through art as good
    for people, 131
self-referential storytelling, rarely
    interesting or effective, 139
seminaries, equipping pastors with
    anachronistic tools, 89
SEPTA (Southeastern Pennsylvania
    Transit Authority), 173n10
Servant, Church as, 27
servant leadership, based on
    the prophet Nehemiah's
    ministry, 84
service, in the name of Jesus Christ,
    91
Sexton, John, 200, 202
shalom, ministry of, 70
Shoe Depot, church as, 194

shooting incidents
  drawing of, 149
  resulted in the death of a young
    person, 49
short-term thinking, consumed with
  fighting, 68
Sider, Ron, 56, 58, 82
Signs of Hope in the City (Carle and
  DeCaro), 206
Signs of the Spirit (Snyder), 56
silo mentality, transforming a
  congregation with, 64
"silo" spirituality, substituting for
  true renewal, 66
silos, communities separated into,
  63
Simmel, Georg, 25
Simon the Stone, became Peter the
  Rock, 167
small group interactions, increased
  during the week, 175
Snyder, Howard, 56, 66
social and family systems,
  connecting, 169
social capital, 77, 88
social consequences, of infectious
  diseases, 31
social encounters
  building community through,
    40–41
  defining our world, 36
social entrepreneurs, need for, 12
social media, as completely
  immersive, 137
social power, getting rid of a
  problem, 16
social systems, dislocating a child
  from, 169
social work, father of modern, 60
sociology, stigma through the lens
  of, 36–41
"Someone's Crying All Night"
  (Kushner), 181
soup kitchens, organized in 1780, 18
sovereignty of God, utter
  dependence on, 60
Spirit. *See* Holy Spirit
"Spirit," as team name, 135

Spirit of Transformation, placement
  within the believer, 56
spiritual clock, at times in need of
  repair, 54
spiritual energy, alignment of, 69
spiritual forces, affecting ministry in
  the neighborhood, 59
spiritual formation training, being
  effective in, 170
spiritual giftedness, affirming
  everyone's, 69
spiritual life force, 56
spiritual location, as children of
  God, 130
spiritual networks, constructing, 12
spiritual realities, as reality, 85
spirituality, goal of authentic, 53
sports, as a vehicle for mission, 133
Spradley, James P., 118, 127n13
St. Paul Community Baptist Church
  Brooklyn, 74
*Star Wars Episode V: The Empire
  Strikes Back* (movie), 139
Stetson Hat Company, 124
Stetson kids, took pride in their
  artwork, 161
Stetson Middle School
  erected on the Wilkey farm
    property, 124
  secondary intervention group at,
    159–64
Stew, a colleague's college-aged son,
  172
Stewart, Carlyle Fielding, 206
stigma
  affecting many different Me's, 42
  as both real and painful, 35
  bound and market the children
    of Kensington, 130
  cannot be lifted alone, 35
  as clearly negative, 35
  closely correlated to behaviors of
    discrimination, 41
  community, 37, 183
  diagnosis of Kensington as face
    sees, 40
  domains of, 38

effect on people who endure
    it, 35
evidence of removal of, 148–59
freeing children and their
    families from, 185
imposed by social processes, 37
Jesus and, 33–34
localized contextually, 37
profound power of, 34
as redemptive, 32
referring to a singular mark, 34
referring to bodily signs, 32
removing by giving voice, 132
removing requiring an
    alternative observation, 42
stifling openness, 151
those living without as normal,
    38
through the lens of history,
    31–32
through the lens of sociology,
    36–41
through the lens of the media,
    34–36
as undesirable differentness, 38
Stigma Italian marketing company,
    34
stigma paradigm, beginning and
    ending with God, 39
stigmata
    mention of in the Greek New
        Testament, 32
    referring to multiple marks, 34
stigmatic reports, as hoaxes, 34
stigmatized identity, informing
    broader discriminatory
    social policies, 41
stigmatized neighborhood, 38, 44
store owners, reinvesting earned
    income outside the
    neighborhood, 3
stories, sharing with children, 137
storytelling
    of the children, 163
    components of persuasive, 139
    as a core experience, 136
    engaging people completely, 137
    as old as language, 136–37
    as the task of the church, 138
    in three acts, 138–39
    transforming lives through
        empathy, 139
"strategic neighbors," 12–13
strategic partnerships, 43
street conflict, throughout the entire
    history of Kensington, 18
street economics, 48–49
Street Leaders, from young
    Damascus Project
    participants, 168
street milieu, becoming connected
    with, 134
street violence, stigma associated
    with diminished for Child
    J, 149
structure of belonging, creating, 101
student engagement, in drawing
    interventions, 161n32
Stump, Pamela, 145n21, 179
suburban and urban collaboration,
    of suburban and urban kids,
    85
suburban churches, 82, 188
suburban development, federal
    government policies
    favoring, 62
suburban isolationism, 85
suburban kids, inviting to the city,
    84
suburban planning, not engendering
    a holistic view of life, 83
suburbs
    flight to, 126
    spirit of disconnect and
        confusion in, 83
    traveling by personal car as
        commonplace, 78
Suhard, Cardinal, 62
summer camp, restoring hope, 164
Summer Evangelistic Committee
    (SEC), 20, 21, 24
"supermarket" model of church
    ministry, 78
supplies, distributing for drawing
    sessions, 147
surviving, as individualistic, 199

Surviving Multi-Ethnic Urbanites, within a half-mile radius of Wilkey, 29
symbolic permission, given to members to take flight, 62
symptoms
    compared to causes, 50
    sustaining by trying to solve, 28
synagogues (Jewish), 11n1
systems of meaning, between the church and the community, 118

tax-exempt organizations, asked to consider paying a portion of property tax, 192
"Teacher Bill." *See* Bowen, Bill
technical, ecclesiastical, or judicial fixes, focusing on, 202
technical disruption, met with effective innovation, 11
technique, for the drawing intervention, 145–47
Temple University, social work department, 134
temples (Hindu), 11n1
ten lepers, story of in Luke 17, 192
tension management, suggested, 38
theology of location, 46, 56
theology of place, 6
therapeutic milieu, 133–36
Thomas, Jesus speaking to, 33n5
"Thomas of faith," instead of doubting Thomas, 99
thriving, as a community effort, 199
"Through a Child's Eyes," newspaper article, 3
Timoney, John F., 3, 16–17, 43, 47–48, 49
Tom (neighbor), 2–3
Top 10 Challenges Facing the Neighborhood, 111
topics
    for the drawing sessions, 147
    drawn in regular sessions over a seven-week period, during FloorTalk time, 144
    order of as intentional, 143
trade unions, forming, 19
traditional church, structure no longer suitable, 190
Tran, Ms. Hoa, 4
transformation
    any faith community experiencing, 6
    beginning with God, 53
    call to requiring a big God, 67
    at Camp Lake Champion, 175–76
    clearly occurring, 148
    as connected, 54
    critical path for, 69
    focusing on the goal of, 52
    model of, 98
    not individualistic, 65
    paradigm of tracking renewal in Kensington, 39
    personal, 53–56
    process of, 52–53
    promise of, 69–70
Transformation Paradigm for Intervention, 39
transformational agent, 182
transformational journey, designed to restore the children's hope, 167
transformational models, building successful and sustainable, 89
transformational self-understanding, moments of, 40
transformative leadership, 133, 182. *See also* leadership
transformed community, sharing the vision of with other churches, 133
trash cans
    as disproportionately large, 152, 154
    as an intrinsic part of the children's mental landscape, 155
treasure, hearts of people with, 82

tree farmer, Kevin Yoho's dad as, 195–96
tribal stigma, 38
Triune God, expressed as Father, Son, and Holy Spirit, 57
Tron parish of Glasgow, visiting every family in, 61
Trulear, Dean, 143
trust
    disproportionate for their group, 20
    relationships of, between caring adults and the children, 8
truth
    knowing, 42
    as powerful motivation, 60
    will set you free, 130
turnaround, compared to a "transformation," 54

umpires, consulting the rules, 201
umpire-scorer/clerk, role of, 202
unchanging church, ill-prepared for the rapidly changing world, 5
unchurched, as shorthand describing outsiders, 114
under the ground, working as a miner, 197
unhealthy system, lacking the capacity to remediate its deficiencies, 46
unique individuals, story of, 138
United Nations, expressed the power of broad-based community connections, 46–47
unity, complete, 57
urban church
    connecting with the city, 10
    intentionally locating itself in the inner city, 188
urban environments, precluding us from seeing God in, 5
urban hopelessness, stories of hope in the midst of, 4
urban ministry
    lessons from baseball for, 200–203
    most people today ignoring, 84
urban neighborhoods, complex and interconnected systems at work, 48
urban pastor
    lessons learned by, 189–203
    role of, 186
urban plunge experience, 85
urban regional councils, 191
urban settings, including God in, 5
"urban workers," compared to "strategic neighbors," 12
us-and-them language, 115
Uzziah, 31

values, reflecting the life-giving actions of Jesus Christ, 113
Veltrop, Bill, 98
venue, selected for the focus group, 122
victimization, cycle of, 38
virtual identity, of Kensington, 38
"visible in the community," 133
vision, to reclaim and restore, 59
vision statement, of Wilkey Memorial Presbyterian Church, 208
visionary people, keeping in the neighborhood, 80
vision-based cooperation, building in the community at large, 97
vision-building, remaining focused on, 108
visual arts, as completely immersive, 137
visual workspace, capturing the focus group stories, 121
voice to youth, removing stigma by giving, 169
voice-giving program, for the children of Kensington, 132
volunteers, entering the classroom having an incredible impact, 161

Wailoo, Keith, 41

"Walk to Church for Shoes" project, 194
walking
    around the neighborhood, 74, 119
    to better understand a neighborhood, 2
    for missional health, 92, 93–94
    physically and "digitally," 58
walls of Jerusalem
    commitment to rebuild, 106
    reduced to rubble, 114
Wanamaker, John, 20
water, turning into wine, 141
"the Way," leaders of convened in groups, 65
welcoming committee, of Work Crew and college-aged Summer Staff, 173
welfare stigma, 35
Welfare Stigma (Wüstenbecker), 35n7
Wendy, cheerleading coach, 135
White, Randy, 75
white paper, piece of, 145
"White Town," nickname for Kensington, 123
"Whitetown," Kensington as, 19
whole world experience, giving voice to, 143
wholeness, Jewish, biblical sense of, 54
"Why a Stigma" (poem), 35–36
Wilberforce, William, 61
Wilkey congregation. *See also* congregation(s)
    began experiencing reneighbored connections, 134
    leaders of grew tired, 189
    needing transformation from the inside out, 67
Wilkey Memorial Presbyterian Church
    capacity for ministry, 26–27
    core values of, 209
    cut off from its own neighborhood, 25
    in a cycle of decline, 82
    dissolving as a congregation, 189
    establishing connections essential, 83
    kids found a safe, nurturing place at, 166
    last worship service weekend, 190
    like an old wineskin with focus on self-preservation, 190
    located at the corner of H and Ontario Streets in the Kensington neighborhood, 27
    mission statement, 208–9
    neighbors indictment of, 119
    Ontario Presbyterian Church rebranded as, 52
    recognizing the transformation of, 98
    selected to participate in a national model for youth violence reduction, 87–88
    transformed from a mining church to a farming church, 198
    vision statement, 208
Wilkey Memorial United Presbyterian Church, changing the church's name to, 22
Wilkey sisters, 23, 124
William Penn Foundation, 4n9
Williams, Wade, 179, 180
wineskin, metaphor of, 54
without a Me, I am I-less, 41
the Word, as the essence of God's identity, 140
Word became flesh, and "moved into our neighborhood," 126
words, effects of, 31
working, for the benefit of all, 200
Working Urban Singles, within a half-mile radius of Wilkey, 29
world, loved by God, 93
world events, in the 1960s, 126
"World" sheet, 122, 123

worship attendance, not measuring
    the effectiveness of a
    congregation, 66
worshipping community
  becoming strategic neighbors,
    12
  building the capacity of, 166
  connecting with the broader
    community, 130
  reneighboring, 189
  responsibility to change the
    structure of, 13
  visible and accessible in tangible
    ways, 130
worthlessness, stigma of, 42
Wray, Tom, 171
"WWII" (World War II), effects of,
    122–23

Yoho, Kevin, 8, 98, 172, 187, 188,
    205, 206
Young Life, 171, 173
Young Life's Lake Champion, in
    southern New York, 167
young people, beginning to
    understand worship as a
    verb, 166
Youngblood, Johnny Ray, 74
youth, 29, 49
youth ministers, as "adult role
    models, 170n7
youth outreach effort, 133
Youth Violence Reduction Project
    (YVRP), 88, 189

www.ingramcontent.com/pod-product-compliance
Lightning Source LLC
Chambersburg PA
CBHW030614230426
43661CB00053B/1979